INNER HEALTH

INNER HEALTH

THE HEALTH BENEFITS OF
RELAXATION, MEDITATION & VISUALISATION

Edited by
NEVILL DRURY

PRISM PRESS
Bridport, Dorset. San Leandro, California

Published in Great Britain by
Prism Press, Bridport, Dorset
and in the USA by
Prism Press USA, PO Box 778, San Leandro, CA 94577
Distributed by:
USA — Interbook Inc., 14895 E. 14th Street, Suite 370, San Leandro, CA 94577
Canada — Raincoast Book Distribution Ltd., 15 West 6th Avenue, Vancouver, BC V5Y 1K2

ISBN 0 907061 73 7

Designed by Judy Hungerford
Cover photograph by Kate Wimble
Printed in Singapore by Kyodo

CONTENTS

FOREWORD

Health authorities may vary in their assessment of how much modern disease is stress-related but there is no doubt that an important realisation has dawned: to stay truly healthy we should heed the inner self.

At first glance the idea of 'inner health' might seem faddish, perhaps even trendy. After all, the dominant image we have of health — an image reinforced by the popular media and commercial advertising — is of gleaming suntanned skin, luxuriant hair, firm and well-proportioned bodies and a salad or a bowl of muesli on the table. Not that these should be decried, but they are, quite simply, the more obvious aspects of health, and most people fall short of the glamorous ideal.

More significantly, in focusing on the more accessible aspects of health — what we eat, how we look, and how much we exercise — an important factor is ignored. There is no point in being aerobically fit if our mental attitude to life and those around us is selfish, vain or hostile. Similarly, there is little value in projecting a well-honed facade through our musculature and assertive smile if the inner person shrinks in upon itself with pettiness or despair. Indeed, in so many ways we *are* our thoughts and attitudes. The sense of purpose we share with those around us, our beliefs, values and self-image — each of these things owes its source in large degree to the concept we call 'self'. And it is the role of the 'self' — of the true inner person — that is at the core of this book.

Inner Health focuses on the way we conceptualise, form images and belief systems, respond intuitively and creatively — and tap into the life-force that sustains each of us. For many of us, the way to do that involves overcoming stress. Some degree of stress can, of course, stimulate and excite, but most of us recognise the need to reduce the impact of negative stress on our lives — whether in the work or home environment, among people or in circumstances that inflict it upon us, or in situations where we bring it upon ourselves. Reduce the destructive aspects of stress in modern society and we could not only substantially reduce the incidence of hypertension, and fatigue, but quite possibly eliminate what Dr Hans Selye called the 'diseases of adaptation' — hardening of the arteries, peptic ulcers, and some arthritic complaints and kidney disorders. There is also substantial evidence that many forms of cancer might also be stress-induced. As holistic health authority Dr Kenneth Pelletier puts it,

Stress-induced disorders have long since replaced epidemics of infectious disease as the major medical problem of the post-industrial nations.

The topic of stress is a predictable starting point for this anthology because, no doubt, it is the most obvious factor of inner health that should concern us. However there are many approaches to inner balance which can have enormous impact on our health. We can learn to form images of positive outcomes for our lives, broaden our vision, and expand our creativity. We can pass through barriers of pain by controlling them in our thoughts through will, and we can enrich and purify ourselves by imagining life-giving light coursing through our bodies. And perhaps, most importantly, we can tap a deep peace within ourselves.

This deep and unencumbered peace — which characterises the harmonised inner self — reveals one's individual wholeness: a condition of being where dis-ease simply does not arise. For this reason, many systems of meditation and guided imagery have come to the fore in recent times as treatments for psychosomatic conditions — including cancer.

Finally, in this anthology, we add a metaphysical and speculative component. Perhaps the concept of 'who we are' extends beyond the identity we link to an ego, and what we are calling disease encompasses the experiences of more than one lifetime.

There are, indeed, many facets to consider and, in relation to inner health, many apparently subjective approaches with new-found validity. From the holistic health viewpoint — which posits health for the whole person — we are not only body, but mind and spirit as well. If this book is able to help the reader tap that potentiality in some degree it will have achieved its purpose.

Nevill Drury

CHAPTER 1

MANAGING STRESS

David Gorovic

INTRODUCTION

The problem of stress has been receiving wide publicity in the media in recent years. We have heard about the many different ways in which stress can damage or even kill you. We have also heard the cliché that it is the epidemic of the '80s. Consequently the word 'stress' has become another buzzword and it has acquired a highly negative connotation — almost as bad as cancer (in which it is also implicated). We have also received plenty of advice over the last few years, from all sorts of sources, about the many different approaches to controlling stress, and all the alarmist and negative publicity has created anxiety and concern in many people's minds — a fear, which in itself can lead to further stress. Having become aware of it, everyone now wants to manage their stress and catering to this growing market is a rapidly-multiplying mixed bag of experts, consultants and therapists. We are offered everything from allergy therapy and vitamins, to fitness programmes, to expensive personal development courses, all in the name of stress management. All sorts of experts, both qualified and self-appointed, want to manage your stress for you and are trying to convince you that their particular product or service will banish your stress for good. Making sense of all that is enough to distress anybody.

However, despite all the promises, the fact remains that there are no magic cures. Stress is basically a result of interaction between a harmful environment, unhealthy lifestyle and self-defeating attitudes and beliefs. Hence no one particular technique, method, programme or a course of vitamins can reduce our long-term stress. We may be stuck in our polluted environment, but we can do much about the other two factors. Unless we are prepared to review our lifestyle and our attitudes and alter those aspects which generate stress, we are simply left with short-term palliatives.

STRESS

Before going any further we need to define what we mean by stress. Most people think of stress as the outside pressures and problems which impinge on them, including such things as deadlines, excessive work load, noise, city traffic, problems with spouse or children, excessive demands made on our time by others etc. This view is analogous to the engineering concept of a physical force exerting pressure on an object which produces strain in that object (for example, in building a bridge an engineer has to consider how much weight the bridge can support before it collapses). A different view of stress has been offered by Dr Hans Selye, the 'father' of modern stress research. He has defined stress as 'the non-specific response of the organism to any demands that are placed upon it.' This implies that stress is not 'those things out there' but rather it is what happens inside us as we react to those things (or people). Normally, we experience some degree of stress in everything we do and everything that happens to us. In fact we need some stress to motivate us and keep us going. It provides energy which enables us to do the things we want to do. Selye named a moderate, productive level of stress *'eustress'* and he described it as 'the spice of life'.

Stress becomes a problem when it reaches excessive levels, when the demands exceed our ability to respond or to cope effectively. When we are under excessive, prolonged stress, when we can't adjust or cope with it and can see no way out of it, then it becomes *'distress'*. This means that we begin to develop symptoms which can lead to stress-induced illnesses, and in extreme cases even death. We can say that our body 'engine' is 'revving' at high speed, but there is no movement or progress and eventually the wear-and-tear begins to take its toll.

As we are all aware, different individuals respond differently to stress. We all know people who can remain cool, calm and collected under the most trying circumstances, and we know others who are unable to cope when faced with even minor difficulties. The differences are due partly to our genetic make up (ie. our body's ability to cope with pressure), but mostly to our upbringing, experiences, coping skills acquired over the years, our attitudes, beliefs, values and perceptions. Furthermore, when different individuals experience distress, the symptoms they develop differ. This results from the fact that different people seem to channel their excessive stress into, and express it through, different parts of the body. Thus some people get indigestion (we say: 'he churns my stomach'); others a muscular ache or pain (he is a 'pain in the neck'); others still respond to high stress with increase in blood pressure ('she makes my blood boil'). The long-term effects of such different responses include such physical illnesses as stomach ulcers, headaches and chronic backaches, and high blood pressure which can result in heart disease and strokes.

However we can learn to control our responses to stress and to make them more appropriate and constructive. That is what stress management is all about. However, before we can manage our stress, we will need to acquaint ourselves with the agents of stress, known as 'stressors', that is those 'things out there' that give rise to or trigger our stress.

STRESSORS

One type of stressor which we all experience regularly is change. 'Life wasn't meant to be easy', said former Australian Prime Minister, and he was right. If by 'easy' we mean life free of cares and worries, hardships, disappointments, tragedy, personal loss, sorrow and pain, then indeed there is no such thing as an easy life, even for the rich and famous. We all face and often experience problems, challenges, frustration, conflicting demands and occasional loss, grief and suffering. These 'life events' which everyone experiences at some time require us to adapt to the new situation. If we don't adapt we suffer and may even die as a result. Adaptation to change involves stress. When changes take place in our environment, circumstances, personal relationships or even inside ourselves, we have to learn how to behave, think and feel differently to cope with a new situation effectively. This requires work and any work (whether physical, mental or emotional) involves stress.

We are all continuously adjusting to changing conditions, rather like an air-conditioner that is controlled by the thermostat. As the weather outside changes the

Stress — a response to the pace of modern life

thermostat turns on the air-conditioning unit which begins to work to bring the interior temperature back to a specified normal level. The greater the changes outside, the harder the machine has to work to keep up with them (we might say it goes into a higher gear). If the external temperature moves into the extreme ranges, the machine will be pushed to the limit and if goes over its specified limit it will eventually break down (burn out the motor or whatever).

So it is with the human machine. Our bodies continuously react to whatever is happening around us or inside of us. We respond physically, mentally and emotionally to even the most minute changes and it happens all the time, even if we are not consciously aware of this. Even when we are asleep we are never completely free of stress; our digestive system is processing the previous night's dinner, our heart and lungs continue to work, and as we dream we experience mental and emotional arousal (a nightmare can cause us to wake up in cold sweat).

By definition, stress is our physiological and emotional response to demands placed upon us and stressors are those things that trigger that response. Change demands adaptation on our part and hence change is an ubiquitous stressor. Therefore, in terms of the above definition, stress is life, for life involves change, growth and evolution. (The only constant in life is change.) Total lack of stress means death. On the other hand, if the stress is extreme and exceeds our ability to cope, then this can also lead to disease and death.

Change is one type of stressor, but there are many others.

First there are the physical stressors. These are fairly clear-cut and include such things as extremes of temperature, humidity and barometric pressure, radiation exposure (ultra-violet, x-rays, etc.), motion (especially rapid acceleration and/or extreme speed), dust suspended in the air we breathe, physical exertion (hard work) and physical injury.

More subtle and thus more insidious are chemical and biological stressors. Chemical stressors, including air and water pollution, pesticides, additives in our food and water and environmental contaminants are all by-products of our modern way of life, and are potential hazards to our health. Generally, we are not consciously aware of these stressors directly but experience their long-term adverse effects.

Then there are biological stressors. These include hunger and thirst, poor or inadequate diet, the effects of various drugs, alcohol and nicotine, being out of phase with our natural body rhythms (biorhythms) through hectic or chaotic lifestyle, bacterial or viral infections and allergens of various sorts.

Scanning this far from complete list of physical, chemical and biological stressors, which constantly threaten our health and well-being, it is surprising that we survive for any length of time at all. However, thanks to our body's resilience and its marvellous defence mechanisms, most of us do manage to survive and live and grow.

And yet it is in this process of growth and development and change that much of our stress is generated. As we move through various stages of our lives from birth through childhood, adolescence and maturity to old age and death, we continuously face new challenges and demands that are peculiar to each life stage. It is in this process of living that we encounter psychological and social pressures which create much of our daily stress.

Whereas physical, chemical and biological, stressors affect most people in pretty much the same way, social and psychological stressors tend to trigger highly individual, idiosyncratic and varied emotional and behavioural responses in different people. The same situation can generate fear in one person, pleasant excitement in another, and indifference in the third. (Horse-riding and public speaking are just two examples.)

And yet, in the course of our lives, we all go through certain stages in our development which are common sources of stress. Even before we are born we can be affected by stress. Recent studies have shown that if a mother experiences high levels of stress (i.e. trauma, severe anxiety, excessive demands, etc.) during pregnancy, this can have adverse effects on the foetus, ranging from reduced size and weight at birth to birth defects, mental retardation and obstetric complications which can harm the baby. Stress triggers a series of complex hormonal changes in the body and it is the change in mother's hormonal levels that seems to affect the foetus.

The birth itself is a stressful and traumatic process for the baby. In the process of birth the baby is expelled from the security and comfort of its mother's womb by violent forces, pushing, pulling and forcing it out into the cold, 'cruel' world outside. If forceps or other instruments are used in delivery, or if there are birth complications (for example, if the umbilical cord wraps around the baby's neck), this adds to the baby's pain and suffering. Contrary to the popular opinion, the recent work of Dr Stanislav Grof and other researchers has shown that traumas of birth remain locked in our subconscious memory and can be a source of long-term personality and emotional problems for the individual. The current move towards 'gentle birth', first advocated by Frederick Leboyer, recognises the trauma that birth can generate and aims at reducing that stress for both the mother and the baby.

As the baby grows, its carefree existence is interrupted when toilet training begins (usually in the second year). The parental pressure and demands that the child control its natural biological functions of bladder and bowels can be a source of extreme stress for the baby, especially when parents expect too much too soon. Psychologist Jerome Kagan has described a number of long-term emotional and behavioural problems resulting from severe toilet training. These include: anger at and fear of the trainer (usually the mother); anxiety about genital organs which may contribute to later sexual problems; feelings of insecurity and inadequacy; and a lack of curiosity and spontaneity in behaviour.

Toilet training is but the first of the major stressors of childhood. Next comes the stress involved in learning to speak and walk. This can be an enjoyable, exciting time for the child, but it can also be very stressful if the parents pressure and demand the child to perform beyond its ability.

Going to kindergarten involves the first significant separation of the child from its mother and can be another source of extreme stress and trauma. Learning to get along with other children, accepting the authority of the teacher and learning the discipline of the classroom are all new and potentially stressful experiences, especially for the only (and hence usually pampered) child.

Then comes school. Learning to read is generally the first stressful educational task that the child is faced with. Again, excessive pressure and demands to perform and achieve from parents and teachers, as well as competition from other children, can create much stress. Acting out and aggression, school phobia, learning difficulties, depression and other behavioural and emotional problems can be symptoms of the child's distress at this stage. As the child progresses through the school system, pressure and competition (both academic and athletic) increase. Older children faced with important examinations often suffer from stress-related complaints such as sleep problems, headaches, tension, anxiety and depression. The extreme example of educational stress can be seen in Japanese children. There, the competition for places in select

schools, leading eventually to prestigious universities and an assured desirable career, is so great that many children suffer emotional breakdowns and some are driven to suicide.

Change involved in transition from kindergarten to primary school, to high school and finally to university also produces high levels of stress. (As we saw earlier, any change is a stressor.) And children can be faced with other stressful changes as well. In modern Western society there exists a high degree of mobility, especially for executives, business and professional people and their families. Each such move involves a whole series of readjustments for all the members of the family, but it can be particularly traumatic for children, who have to leave behind their friends and familiar environment and start all over again elsewhere.

Changing a job — one of many potential stressors

And then there is the current high incidence of marital breakdown and divorce which can be a major trauma to children and can leave severe psychological scars for life. Add to this other possible sources of severe childhood stress such as family violence, child abuse and/or neglect, alcoholism and drug abuse by the parents, as well as such traumatic events as long-term illness or death in the family, serious accidents, poverty and deprivation and many others, and it becomes obvious that indeed life wasn't meant to be easy for many children (even though we tend to think of childhood nostalgically as a carefree and stressless time).

But, of course, stress is not limited to children, by any means. However, the reason I have dwelt on childhood stress is that it plays an important role in shaping our personality and character. As children, we learn to respond to stress in certain individual habitual ways. Some people learn to face stressors directly, see them as challenges or problems to solve and strive to overcome them (that is, they learn to face and fight adversity). This occurs when we receive support and encouragement from our parents, friends and other significant people in our lives. We also learn to adopt this approach when we see that our actions culminate in success (at least some of the time) and thus our efforts are rewarded. However, if we are ridiculed or criticised or punished for our mistakes or failures, or if we are over-protected, or we are constantly told that 'it's no use', we feel discouraged and eventually give up the struggle and withdraw (that is, we 'flee' the adversity).

Despite the fact that we develop habitual patterns of behaviour (or response) when faced with stressors, these behavioural patterns are not finite. If, as adults, we can recognise that we respond to stressful situations in habitually self-defeating, self-limiting ways, we can then decide to change and to learn new ways of behaving and handling stressors. As adults, we face many and varied types of stressors. There are stressors associated with our work: choosing a career, finding a job, changing jobs, promotions, demotions, retrenchment, dismissal and retirement, competition and conflicts with people at work, work overload, inadequate pay, frustrating, boring, repetitive work and many others. For many women an additional stressor is a role conflict between pursuing a career and being a wife and mother.

Then there are stressors involved in our relationships, marriage and family life. Meeting potential partners, falling in love, marriage and having children are all stressful events. (Yes, that's right, even the desirable or positive events like marriage and birth of a child carry with it a certain amount of stress.) Loss of partners through death or divorce, children leaving home, ageing (with its accompanied decline in our physical capacities) and possibly institutionalisation (that is, nursing or retirement home) all generate stress.

Two American researchers, Thomas Holmes and Richard Rahe, have developed a questionnaire, called the Social Readjustment Rating Scale, designed to measure the impact of various common 'life events' on our health and well-being. There are 43 specific life events listed and each one carries a certain weighting expressed in 'Life Change Units' (LCUs). At the top of the scale is 'Death of a Spouse', worth 100 LCUs. In the middle is 'Marriage' (a positive event) worth 50 LCUs, and at the bottom of the list is 'Minor Violations of the Law' worth 11 LCUs. Holmes and Rahe have found that the more life events are experienced by an individual during the past twelve months, and therefore the higher their LCU score, the higher were the chances of that individual suffering a major health problem within the following two years.

Scoring Guidelines:

–150 = one chance in three of a major health problem in the next two years.
150–300 = 50/50 chance of a major health problem in the next two years.
300+ = 90 per cent chance of a major health problem in the next two years.

THE SOCIAL READJUSTMENT RATING SCALE

Life Event	Mean Value
1 Death of spouse*	100
2 Divorce	73
3 Marital separation	65
4 Detention in jail or other institution	63
5 Death of a close family member	63
6 Major personal injury or illness	53
7 Marriage	50
8 Being fired at work	47
9 Marital reconciliation	45
10 Retirement from work	45
11 Major change in the health or behaviour of a family member	44
12 Pregnancy	40
13 Sexual difficulties	39
14 Gaining a new family member (e.g., through birth, adoption, oldster moving in, etc.)	39
15 Major business readjustment (e.g., merger, reorganisation, bankruptcy, etc.)	39

Life Event	Mean Value
16 Major change in financial state (e.g., a lot worse off or a lot better off than usual)	38
17 Death of a close friend	37
18 Changing to a different line of work	36
19 Major change in the number of arguments with spouse (e.g., either a lot more or a lot less than usual regarding child rearing, personal habits, etc.)	35
20 Taking on a mortgage greater than $10,000 (e.g., purchasing a home, business, etc.)**	31
21 Foreclosure on a mortgage or loan	30
22 Major change in responsibilities at work (e.g., promotion, demotion, lateral transfer)	29
23 Son or daughter leaving home (e.g., marriage, attending college, etc.)	29
24 In-law troubles	29
25 Outstanding personal achievement	28
26 Wife beginning or ceasing work outside the home	26
27 Beginning or ceasing formal schooling	26
28 Major change in living conditions (e.g., building a new home, remodelling, deterioration of home or neighbourhood)	25
29 Revision of personal habits (dress, manners, associations, etc.)	24
30 Troubles with the boss	23
31 Major change in working hours or conditions	20
32 Change in residence	20
33 Change to a new school	20
34 Major change in usual type and/or amount of recreation	19
35 Major change in church activities (e.g., a lot more or a lot less than usual)	19
36 Major change in social activities (e.g., clubs, dancing, movies, visiting, etc.)	18
37 Taking on a mortgage or loan of less than $10,000 (e.g., purchasing a car, TV, freezer, etc.)**	17
38 Major change in sleeping habits (a lot more or a lot less sleep, or change in part of day when asleep)	16
39 Major change in number of family get-togethers (e.g., a lot more or a lot less than usual)	15
40 Major change in eating habits (a lot more or a lot less food intake, or very different meal hours or surroundings)	15
41 Vacation	13
42 Christmas	12
43 Minor violations of the law (e.g., traffic tickets, jaywalking, disturbing the peace, etc.)	11

*Although not included in the original research, the death of a child may be at least as, if not more, traumatic than the death of a spouse.
**Original scale does not take account of inflationary changes in our economy. Make your own definition of 'large' or 'small' loan or mortgage. [From T. H. Holmes and R. H. Rahe: 'The Social Readjustment Rating Scale'. *Journal of Psychosomatic Research* 11:213–218, 1967. Reprinted with permission of Pergamon Press, Inc.]

STRESS AWARENESS

The above comments notwithstanding, other research has shown that not everyone is affected by the same life events in the same way. We have all heard stories of individuals who have experienced immense personal tragedy, hardship and suffering (for example, in wartime, natural disasters, severe personal handicaps, etc.) who have 'bounced back', found new strength, meaning and purpose in their lives, devoted themselves selflessly to a task, an ideal or to helping others, and hence continued to live a meaningful, fulfilling, satisfying life. (To quote a psychiatrist Viktor Frankl: 'He who has a ''why'' to live can put up with almost any ''how'' '.) We can learn from their example. Stressors lead to stress only when we perceive them as threats and see ourselves as incapable or helpless to deal with them.

However if we deliberately, consciously develop a habit of thinking of stressors as challenges or problems to be solved (rather than threats), commit ourselves to tackle the challenge (give it 'everything we've got), and accept that we usually have some degree of control over the situation, then we can use stress and adversity to grow, discover and develop our inner resources, acquire new coping skills and as a result increase our strength, confidence, and self-esteem. Therefore, stress is not all bad. Stress prods us into action. Without any stress at all life would be dull and meaningless. We can use the analogy of a rubber band. It is useless until it is stretched, but it mustn't be stretched too far or it will break. So it is with us. We need stress to motivate us, excite us, keep us going, give us energy. We deliberately seek out stress when life is too quiet.

The trick is to find and maintain just the right level of stress to keep us motivated and make our life exciting and fulfilling, but not too much stress, which can harm and in the long term kill us. This 'optimum' stress level is different for each individual (some people prefer more excitement, some less; some like a faster lifestyle, some a slower one) and it's up to each one of us to discover our optimum stress level. To do this we need to develop an awareness of those stressors that are harmful to us and those that are beneficial. We will then need to learn to control, modify, eliminate or avoid the harmful stressors. We also need to develop an awareness of our capabilities and resources and our coping skills. And this brings us to the subject of awareness.

Being aware of stressors in our lives and our individual responses to them is the first step in any stress management programme. Before we can deal with and control any situation or problem, including excessive stress (or distress), we must first realise that the problem exists and recognise the signs and symptoms which indicate that the problem is currently present. This means that first of all we need to know what these symptoms are and, secondly, be sensitive to their presence as they occur. And this is easier said than done.

Of course we are all aware of sudden stress, such as occurs in *alarm reaction* (also known as the 'fight-or-flight' response; for example, when we jump out of the path of a speeding car). We can certainly feel our heart racing, tension in our muscles, cold sweat on our skin, perhaps trembling all over, heavy breathing and other physical signs. On the emotional level we would also be aware of the resulting feeling of fear. Usually we will need some time to recover from such a stressful experience, to relax and calm down.

Much of our stress occurs at a fairly low level, however, and involves small frustrations, conflicts, hassles and annoyances rather than the sudden obvious high level of stress described in the example above. Since these little 'bits of stress' do not result

We can use stress and adversity to grow . . .

in the dramatic and highly-pronounced physical and emotional reactions, we tend to be less conscious of them and are often not aware of them at all. This is especially true when we are regularly confronted with the same stressor which triggers low or moderate levels of stress (for example, the daily struggle through peak hour traffic, or having to work with a person we don't like or get on with).

Although initially we may have consciously registered increased tension resulting from confronting such moderate stressors, after a while we become used to them and, as we do, we become less conscious of the signs of stress until eventually we take the unpleasant situation for granted and stop paying attention to our symptoms altogether. This process is known as habituation and is a well-known phenomenon in both the neurophysiology and the psychology of learning. Simply stated it means that when we are repeatedly exposed to a stimulus or a stressor which may be unpleasant but not in itself dangerous, after some time we stop reacting or paying conscious attention, and then psychologically adjust or adapt to it. For example, you may be trying to read a book while your neighbour starts playing loud music on his stereo. You may be initially annoyed, but if you can become absorbed in the book you will soon stop noticing the music. Habituation also occurs on neurological level. For example, if the electrical activity of your brain is monitored while you are watching a flashing light, you will find that your brain will react sharply when the light first begins to flash, but as you keep watching the electrical responses of the brain will gradually decrease until it doesn't seem to register the light at all.

Since it is impossible to pay conscious attention to everything that is perceived, habituation is a safety mechanism which prevents our brain from becoming overloaded with information or overstimulated with sensory input. As a result we tend to react only to novel stimuli, that is, new, sudden, unexpected events (which in the past indicated food or danger to our primitive ancestors). This means that we tend to get used to, tolerate and eventually ignore all sorts of stimulation, whether pleasant or unpleasant (for example, not being aware of the taste of the food we eat while we are busy talking during a business lunch, or being able to tolerate the constant noise of a jackhammer outside while concentrating on our work). Therefore, we can learn to live with our stressors.

But although we can ignore and be consciously unaware of our stressors, they nevertheless do affect us physically, emotionally and mentally. For example, studies have shown that people who live in a permanently noisy environment (such as near a busy highway) experience more stress (as indicated by higher levels of stress hormones in their blood and urine and a higher incidence of stress-related disorders which they suffer) than people who live in quiet areas. However, when interviewed, these people often state that they are used to the noise and it does not bother them.

In other words, we can learn to ignore our symptoms. There are many cases of athletes who have suffered a physical injury during an exciting game but were not aware of it, or the resultant pain, until the game ended (at which point they collapsed in agony). Similarly, people who suffer from excessive muscle tension often tend to ignore or not be aware of it while they are busy working or doing other things, until it becomes extreme and manifests itself as headache, backache or sore shoulders or jaw. Weekend migraine is another example of ignored tension. During the week the sufferers tend to push themselves to the limit, absorbed in their activity, skipping meals, working late, getting little sleep and worrying a lot. They are unaware of the accumulating tension, since all their attention is focused on their work. However, come weekend and the job is not there to occupy them, the accumulated tension comes to the fore and turns into migraine. So, despite the saying that 'ignorance is bliss', in the long run such ignorance can be harmful and even deadly.

Although development of awareness is a worthwhile goal, there are a number of obstacles to its accomplishment. For one thing there are our own attitudes and beliefs resulting from our upbringing. Many of us have been trained not to be preoccupied with ourselves, not to be a sissy, not to talk about our problems, and to keep a stiff upper lip when in pain. To do otherwise meant that we were self-centred, selfish or whingers. We have also been told that what really counts is achievement and its material symbols. And to achieve we need to be vigilant and alert, constantly monitoring our environment and people around us. While we are busy thinking, planning, analysing, calculating and scheming we stop paying attention to our bodies. Preoccupied with these mental activities we tend to live in our minds and forget our bodies.

And then there is the constant overstimulation characteristic of our modern, urban environment: crowds of people, noise, pollution, the dazzle of the neon signs and shop windows. All draw our attention 'out there' and we are so absorbed in the kaleidoscope of sensations arriving from the outside world that we hardly notice what is happening

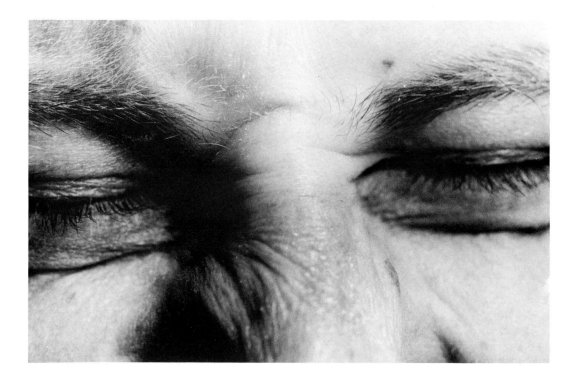

inside us. The glitter and din of the external world drown out the world within. Becoming acquainted or re-acquainted with that inner world is the aim of awareness training.

The word awareness is derived from the Old English, and originally meant watch-fulness. In awareness training we learn to become watchful and observant of our inner experiences, including physical sensations, emotions and thoughts as well as our behaviour in relation to various outside stressors or events. You observe yourself as if you were a scientist studying someone else, with the attitude of dispassionate, detached curiosity. The objects of your study are your physical sensations, emotions, thoughts and behaviour patterns, as they relate to the events around you.

Since we tend to react in habitual ways, without being aware of what we are doing, we need to learn to pay conscious attention to, or monitor, what happens inside us, especially in times of stress. In this way we can learn about our reactions as well as identify specific situations or events which trigger these reactions. Once we have observed certain patterns or relationships between our stress reactions and individual stressors, we can then take steps to deal with or handle these stressors in a more constructive way and thus prevent or reduce undue stress.

The easiest and most productive way to start self-observation process is to focus on our physical sensations. As I said before, our bodies continuously react to absolutely everything that happens to us (whether outside events like conflicts with other people or internal events like the strong emotions that result from our inner conflicts). By paying attention we can learn to become aware of the changes in tension in our muscles, breathing patterns, heart and pulse rate, and skin temperature as indicators of stress. Since most of our muscles are under our voluntary control, the sensations of tensions in them are also easiest to observe. Most people tend to have a 'favourite' part of the body in which they tend to store their tensions. Of course we do this unconsciously and that's why self-observation is so important. Because we are not aware of this storing process we need to discover where we accumulate our tension and under what external or internal conditions. Certain groups of muscles — buttocks, back, stomach, shoulders, neck, jaw and forehead — seem to be particularly common storage spots for accumulated tension. The muscles in the upper part of the body (shoulder, neck and face) seem to be especially sensitive to stress. A very common stress habit (or disorder) is jaw clenching and teeth grinding, and in people who have that problem muscles stand out and are constantly moving (some people do it to the point where they actually wear out their teeth). A permanent frown (which results from tense forehead muscles) is another indicator of stress and can lead to tension headaches.

So one thing we can do in developing stress awareness is to regularly check the state of our muscles in the shoulders, back of the neck, jaw and forehead. Simply become aware of these muscles and, when you notice tension build-up, let your shoulders hang loose, unlock your jaw and allow it to 'drop', relax and smooth out your forehead and straighten out your spine and neck. Practise this as frequently as you can — it takes only a few seconds to switch your attention from the external environment inward, and then let go. If you do these 'spot checks' and the quick relaxation regularly you will find that after a few weeks you have become more sensitive to the state of these muscles at any one time. You will also become more aware of smaller amounts of tension present in these muscles (that is, you will become more sensitive to stress and tension). This means that you will be able to relax your muscles just as soon as you notice tension increasing. This prevents the tension building up to the point of pain and at the same time it makes you aware of those situations or events which tend to trigger that rise in tension. Once you become aware of these stressors, you are then in a better position to deal with these sources of stress directly and if possible to eliminate them from your life.

Apart from focusing our attention on tense muscles, we can also practise consciously registering other physical symptoms of stress. These include: excessive sweating (especially on the palms of the hands), blushing, cold hands (or 'cold shivers' generally), palpitations (that is, racing heart), difficulty in breathing, giddiness, dry mouth and throat, shaking fingers and hands, facial twitches, upset stomach and many others. All of these are usually signs of stress. When you become aware of any of these symptoms (or a number of them together), instead of ignoring them and hoping that they go away, stop what you're doing for a few moments, and 'tune in' to your body. Your body is trying to tell you something so stop and listen. You will find that often simply by focusing your attention on your symptoms, and observing them, their intensity will begin to decrease. At the same time ask yourself: 'What was it that triggered these symptoms, what brought them on?' And when you find the same recurring stressors that trigger your stress reaction and its symptoms, ask: 'What can I do to control or eliminate these stressors?'

Apart from physical symptoms, we need to begin paying closer attention to our ongoing emotional and mental states. We often tend to hang on to strong negative emotions like anger, fear and guilt, long after the initial event, which gave rise to them, has gone. These high emotions will maintain our physical symptoms. Here again, once you become aware of the emotions that you experience, try to trace them back to their source. If the situation is still current, take practical steps to resolve it; if it's gone and there is nothing you can do about it, then accept it and focus your energies on something more worthwhile, satisfying and enjoyable.

Finally, since the source of much of our stress is our own negative, irrational, self-defeating patterns of thinking, we need to learn to become aware of our own thoughts. Our thinking process has been described as a 'stream of consciousness'. However in our modern, hectic way of life the stream has turned into a raging torrent carrying with it much foam, debris and refuse. We need to become conscious of our mental garbage, before we can take steps to control it.

MANAGING STRESS

When we talk about controlling or preventing stress, we need to look at a variety of strategies. Because our reaction or response to stress is highly individual, we need to tailor any stress management programme to our particular set of circumstances, needs and personality. This is known as a 'holistic approach' to stress management, which implies that stress is a complex phenomenon and hence must be dealt with on a number of different levels, using a variety of different approaches and techniques. Specifically, we can deal with stress on three different levels. I refer to this approach as the ABC of Stress Management, where: A stands for Agent (or stressor in your environment); B stands for Behaviour (or our reactions to stressors); and C stands for Cognitions (or our thoughts about our stressors).

This means that we can manage our stress by controlling stressors in our environment, by changing our habitual self-defeating behavioural responses to stress to a more productive behaviour, and finally by examining our negative thinking patterns that tend to trigger stress, and changing these to positive and constructive cognitions. As discussed previously, we need to develop awareness for each of these stages. That is, we need to be aware of what types of stressors trigger our stress and how we maintain or increase our stress through counter-productive or destructive behavioural and thinking habits. Although I have described these three levels as distinctive stages, they do, in fact, tend to overlap.

1 Controlling the Agents of Stress This means we can add, subtract from, rearrange or avoid or get out of the situation. For example if you can't do your work properly because of inadequate lighting or excessive heat, you can add extra lighting or install an air-conditioning unit. If you are upset by loud music you might turn off the stereo (subtracting). Often it is possible to reorganise your environment (for example, rearranging your study to make your surroundings more conducive to concentration and efficient work) and sometimes the situation may be so intolerable that you may have to get out of it altogether (for example, unsatisfactory job, bad marriage, moving from city to the country to escape noise, pollution and overcrowding, etc.).

The four strategies of adding, subtracting, rearranging and avoiding — as applied to physical environment — can also be applied to our social environment. That is, we may need to take stock of our current relationships with family, relatives, friends, colleagues at work and other significant people in our lives.

Often we tend to persist with maintaining unsatisfying or even destructive relationships due to a force of habit, false sense of obligation, or simply because we are afraid to let go in line with the saying: 'Better the devil you know than the devil you don't know'. However, we must remember that we are all free agents and we can choose whom we spend our time with. We *don't have to* keep inviting Aunt Mabel or Cousin Fred to our Christmas dinner, year after year, just because they are relatives, if they cause havoc (arguments, fights, disagreements) each time they come. This might go against the saying 'We can choose our friends but we are stuck with our relatives', but we don't have to be stuck with anybody that we don't want to be. We get on with some people and we don't get on with others and we can choose our social circle accordingly, without exceptions for relatives or other 'obligatory' but undesirable relationships. We all change as we grow older and may outgrow some relationships, whether friends, relatives, or lovers. We can add new people into our circle of friends, avoid others, reduce contact with others, and withdraw from those relationships which are no longer satisfying. More constructively, we need to concentrate on developing further those relationships which have the potential of bringing greater meaning, satisfaction and fulfilment into our lives.

2 Changing our Behavioural Responses Taking responsibility for and looking after your own health, and maintaining your body in good condition, help to make you more resistant to stress. This requires changing your behaviour and lifestyle accordingly, maintaining good nutritious diet, avoiding harmful substances (such as tobacco, alcohol, drugs, etc.), having adequate exercise, getting sufficient sleep and knowing and working to your individual biological rhythms. It also involves sufficient rest, satisfying recreational activities and creative hobbies and interests. Learning and practising effective interpersonal communication skills will enable you to develop positive and meaningful relationships with other people and these relationships, in turn, can help to buffer the harmful effects of stress.

Behavioural change also requires learning relaxation techniques which would help you to unwind and reduce your physical, emotional, and mental tension. Relaxation techniques (including progressive muscle relaxation, meditation or autogenic technique) practised regularly can be a powerful way of reducing and controlling your stress. Relaxation is an acquired skill. Hence you need to learn it from a competent teacher. And once you have learnt it, you need to practise it regularly, for maximum effect.

To sum up, behavioural change means reducing and eliminating harmful bad habits from our lives and cultivating new healthy habits instead.

3 Cognitive Change/Restructing (or changing your mind about your distress) A major determining factor in our stress reaction is our individual perception of the situation. In other words, our stress response is determined, to a large extent, by the way we view, perceive, think or feel about a given stressor. We can learn to change our minds about our stressors and this can alter our stress level. Whenever we take a negative view of any situation, we feel distressed. Strong negative emotions (such as anger, fear, hate, guilt, etc.) produce physical symptoms (for example, tension, palpitations, breathing difficulties), and in the long term this can produce physical disorders and disease. If you think that something is bad and threatening to you then you will feel threatened and hence stressed. However, if we can learn to think differently about stressors (for example, think of setbacks as opportunities for learning, or think of problems as challenges to achieve and succeed), then we can begin to feel better and hence reduce and control our stress response.

In short we can say that thoughts produce emotions, or feelings, and emotions produce a physical reaction in the body (that is, stress). But we can learn to control our thoughts and thus control our emotions and consequently our stress. This view was proposed by an American psychologist Albert Ellis in the 1950s and it has since been validated by research and practical application. Ellis has developed a systematic way of helping people with emotional problems to change their negative, self-defeating perceptions, attitudes, thinking, ideas and beliefs (known as 'irrational beliefs') which cause or contribute to individual distress. He named this system 'Rational-Emotive Therapy' (or RET for short). People who use this system have found that they can learn

Learn to think differently

to control or eliminate a wide range of psychosomatic symptoms and emotional disorders including tension, high blood pressure, headaches, insomnia, sexual difficulties, anxiety, depression, aggression and many others. This approach, which involves teaching people to *change their mind about their distress*, is known as 'cognitive restructuring', and constitutes a crucial part of any effective stress management programme.

In order to think we need language, and the language that we use determines, to a large extent, our thoughts and hence our emotions. Therefore, we can change our mind (or our thoughts) by changing our language. The way we use our language to describe events, and even individual words that we use, can alter our beliefs, values, attitudes and ideas. Albert Ellis suggests that many of our emotional problems (and hence stress) are caused or at least influenced by irrational beliefs that we hold, or the negative 'self-talk' that we engage in regularly (for example, 'I mustn't make mistakes or fail'). When our behaviour, or the situation we find ourselves in, conflicts with our beliefs about how things, people, the world or ourselves should be, we worry and become upset, blood pressure goes up, tension rises . . . and this produces stress. Ellis says that our beliefs are not inherited but are learnt, and are maintained by certain phrases or words which we repeat to ourselves and which reinforce the irrational beliefs in our minds. However, whenever something is learnt, it can also be unlearnt, and this applies to beliefs. In essence, Ellis says that we cause our own stress by habitually reinforcing our own irrational beliefs. So how do we change our mind?

A A common way of producing irrational beliefs is to exaggerate the significance of our problems. When you use words like: 'terrible', 'horrible', 'awful', 'catastrophic', 'disastrous', 'unbearable' or 'impossible' to describe your experience of being stuck in traffic (and consequently running late), you are using inappropriate words. (This process is known as 'awfulising' or 'catastrophising'.) The consequences of running late are usually nowhere near 'disastrous'. The more appropriate words to describe the situation more accurately would be: 'unfortunate', 'inconvenient', 'annoying', 'unpleasant', 'uncomfortable', 'a nuisance' or simply, 'I don't like it.' Try changing the language and words you use to describe your world and your world will begin to look and feel much better.

B Another linguistic source of stress involves words which indicate demands. These words include: 'should', 'must', 'have to', 'ought to', 'supposed to' and others. We frequently apply these demands to ourselves, to people around us and to the world in general. As we have already seen, stress is produced by demands which are placed on us.

In this case we place our own, emotion-backed demands on ourselves and after a while this becomes a heavy burden. When we demand that the world delivers exactly what we want whenever we want it, and we don't get it, we feel frustrated, angry, upset and Bingo!: we are under stress again. If you avoid demanding things of yourself and others and think in terms of your own preferences you will find that your life will become a lot easier and more relaxed and enjoyable. Any time you catch yourself saying 'I must . . .', 'You must . . .', 'They must . . .' or 'It must . . .' — people who keep using that word frequently are known as 'musterbators' — change that to: 'I would rather . . .', 'I would prefer . . .', 'I want . . .', 'I'd like to . . .', 'It would be nice if that were the case . . .' and notice the difference.

C Labelling things or people 'good' and 'bad' implies absolutes which are unrealistic and therefore irrational and harmful. Nothing is ever black and white — everything is a shade of grey. When we judge, criticise or moralise then we generate within ourselves resentment, frustration and self-righteous anger — emotions which all produce stress. If you can't change things or people, then accept them. Remember the old prayer: 'God, give me the strength to change what I can change, the serenity to accept what I cannot and the wisdom to know the difference'.

CONCLUSION

To sum up, stress management is basically about learning skills — skills to change our thinking, emotions, behaviour and lifestyle. Stress management is not about vitamins and fitness (both of which can be part of a stress management programme but which can also become obsessions leading to further stress), but about learning to recognise and control pressures and demands from within and without as well as becoming proficient in controlling our mental, emotional and behavioural responses to these demands. This leads to awareness, self-confidence and self-control, and hence personal growth.

Stress is an evolutionary legacy which we have inherited from our ancestors and which enabled them and us to survive. Stress generates and is a source of energy. We need to learn to manage and use this energy wisely (just like we manage our money). Managed effectively, this energy can be channelled into worthwhile goals and projects, giving motivation, excitement, enjoyment, meaning and purpose to our lives. But if misused it can kill us. It is our choice.

CHAPTER 2
IMAGERY & SELF-HEALING
Janna Fineberg

You are in a rush. You have two more errands to do. You enter the bank. You find an extremely long line, and service is slow. You have a choice. You can become more and more irritated, and as stress builds in your system, do yourself emotional and physical harm. Instead you use this opportunity for self-healing. You suggest to yourself that with every exhale you are becoming more and more relaxed. After several cycles of breathing you begin to imagine that just above your head there is a ball of white light, like a little white sun. With each inhale you draw in some of this white light, in through the top of your head, into every cell in your body. You feel the light nourishing, cleansing, and healing every cell of your body. Every cell is energised and revitalised by this white light. And with each exhale, you send the light and anything your cells no longer need down through your body, out of the bottom of your feet, and way into the core of the earth. You continue to circulate white light in this way with each cycle of breath. You become relaxed and energised. It is suddenly your turn at the teller, and you know you have used this time to add to your health and well-being.

Imagery is a powerful tool that can be used for self-healing and self-understanding. As with many age-old techniques, we are simply now re-discovering it. The power of imagery comes from its ability to communicate with parts of us other than our conscious mind. It appears that imagery has the ability to 'speak' directly to our involuntary nervous system. This has been proven by biofeedback research, where ordinary individuals with minimal training have mastered the ability to purposefully effect changes in processes such as heart rate, blood pressure, and skin temperature, which were previously thought to be outside of voluntary control. When questioned, the individuals who were most successful in this control reported that what they were doing was using imagery. For example, the way they succeeded in lowering the skin temperature of a hand was by *imagining* that the hand was immersed in a bucket of ice water. Enough research has now been conducted to prove the efficacy of imagery at stimulating desired changes in the involuntary nervous system.

Imagery is also the language with which we can communicate with the deeper-than-conscious aspects of our mind. This is obvious when we consider the dream state, which communicates with us mainly in images. This communicative quality of imagery is very important, since so many of our feelings and behaviours are motivated by subconscious and unconscious aspects of ourselves. It certainly is an advantage to discover a language by which we can converse with the part of us that is primarily controlling us!

Communication with the unconscious has been the domain of hypnosis, which basically is comprised of two components: first, the use of a technique to induce a state of consciousness where there is a freer access to the deeper part of the mind; and second, a method of communicating with the deeper part of the mind. Often this communication will involve making suggestions to the depths of the mind; suggesting things that the individual desires for her/his betterment. Several different techniques are used to induce the necessary state of consciousness, some of them quite similar to more commonly known relaxation techniques, and to meditation techniques. Many of the recent hypnotic techniques use imagery as the method of communicating with the deeper part of the mind. They recognise the power of imagery for this purpose.

More and more attention is currently being paid to the ability of individuals to use these principles for their own healing and growth. Through meditation or repeated practice of an effective deep relaxation technique, individuals can bring themselves to a state of consciousness where they have increased access to deeper parts of their minds. Then, using imagery, they can 'programme in' what they wish. (It is advised that individuals receive expert instruction and guidance in the use of imagery for self-healing and self-suggestion at first, as there are definitely some tricks to this process, and one wouldn't want to programme in the wrong thing!) Many tapes are currently available to lead one through these 'self-programming' sessions. In many ways, this process is akin to self-hypnosis. A clinical hypnotherapist or a psychologist experienced in the use of imagery are excellent people from whom one can initially learn the necessary techniques and get assistance in developing appropriate and personalised suggestions. Then the individual can work on his/her own.

An important point might be made here about the term 'visualisation', which is often used when referring to imagery. Visualisation is an important, but limited aspect of imagery. All the relevant research has shown that the imagery which most powerfully speaks to the deeper levels of our mind involves *all* of the sense modalities. If we are suggesting something to ourselves, in addition to 'visualising' it, or 'seeing' it, we must attempt to also feel it, taste it, smell it, and hear it. We aim at involving as many of the sense modalities as possible, making it a total sensory experience. Similarly, when we receive messages from these deeper levels, they may come through in any one or combination of the sense modalities. Most of us have one or two of our senses more highly developed than the others. Although the largest percentage of us have our visual sense most developed, this is not true for all of us. By imaging in all senses, we are sure to make use of our strongest modality, while we add to the image with the others. We also gradually begin to develop our other senses, and thus become more aware of, and receptive to, our world; more alive.

Imagery work can be self-directed, where no second person is needed for the session, or other-directed, when an experienced person helps guide the session. It can be used in several ways to benefit oneself: for health maintenance, for self-healing, or for self-understanding and personal growth. Imagery can additionally be either 'guided', where one purposefully images certain things, or 'spontaneous', where one allows words and images to surface from within.

Self-directed imagery is a powerful way in which individuals can have more control over their own healing processes. Imagery can be used to contribute to the healing of physical problems and has been used extensively in the area of pain control. In one method, the individual allows an image for their pain to emerge. For example, an individual may come up with 'a red hot rod in my back between my shoulders'. Once such an image has emerged, the individual then creates a second image that (s)he feels

would counteract the pain image. This might be 'a cool, thick, blue liquid that would bathe my back and gradually cool down and then melt the rod'. Once the images are formed, the individual would then use a relaxation or meditation technique to open access to the levels where her/his self-healing power resides, and imagine the healing image. This could be repeated as often as necessary, allowing changes in the healing image that might either spontaneously appear, or be appropriate if the image associated with the pain were to change.

Individuals can contribute to the healing of an injury or illness by using imagery. The image used could either be a literal representation of what the body physiologically needs to have happen next for the ailment to heal (for example, imagining the cells of bones growing together), or the image could take more symbolic form. The most generaly symbolic image used for healing is white light (see Exercise 1). White light has been used as a healing image throughout the ages, by many cultures. It is the combination of all colour vibrations, and thus is a generalised healer. It heals on a vibratory level, as does medically-accepted ultra-sound. One can use the white light healing image by breathing it in through the top of the head from the universe straight into the affected body area with each inhale, and then with each exhale sending it down the body, out the bottom of the feet, and way into the core of the earth (see Exercise 5). Alternatively one could breathe the white light into the heart on the inhale, and on the exhale send it from the heart down the arms and out the hands, into the affected body part, on which the hands rest. In this second way, white light could also be used for the healing of another person. This author's 'imagery slogans' are: 'When in doubt, use white light', and 'White light is the disprin of the New Age!'

More specific images than white light have also been used as the self-help component in the treatment of illnesses, ranging from the mild (for example, minor infections) to the serious (for example, cancer). Carl and Stephanie Simonton of Texas brought the use of meditation and imagery for cancer self-help to popular attention with their excellent book, *Getting Well Again*. They emphasise several aspects characteristic of a powerful healing image: that the image be created by the healee her/himself; that it involve as many sense modalities as possible; and that it have as much dynamism and energy behind it as possible. The image must be vital, for it is the vitality of health and life that the image both represents and stimulates (see Exercise 8).

Images can be literal (for example, the actual cell action needed for healing) or symbolic (for example, blue liquid or white light) or some combination of both. The image can represent the healing process (for example, the next step that the body would have to take in the process of disease resolution . . . see Exercise 7), or represent the end state of total health (see Exercise 9). This author currently prefers symbolic images that represent the desired end state, as long as such an image is acceptable to the healee.

Self-directed imagery can also be used to stimulate personal growth and change. By repeatedly entering a relaxed or meditative stage and strongly imaging oneself behaving in a new desired way (for example, behaving assertively), one can help bring the desired behaviour into being. Similarly, by repeatedly imaging oneself as having already achieved a desired goal (for example, having a slim and fit body), the deeper mind gradually accepts this new self-image, and works to bring it into reality. Once again, it is of most value, initially, to work with this technique under supervision, to insure that any other factors that might work *against* change are also dealt with. Afterwards, steadfast use of such imagery gives one great power to help oneself to become the person one wishes to be.

Imagery can be of help on both physical and emotional levels, by aiding individuals to relax and 'centre'. The 'private place' image combines both guided and spontaneous imagery for this purpose (see Exercise 4). In this image, the individual is guided to find her/his special 'private place', preferably outdoors in nature. The individual is then led on an exploration of her/his place: 'What is on the ground?' 'What does the ground feel like?' 'What does the sky look like?' 'What does the air smell like?' 'What is the temperature of the air?' 'What do you see around you?' etc. Once this place is discovered, the individual is invited to return to it at any time on her/his own, to relax, be by her/himself, and be nourished.

Another self-directed imagery experience that uses spontaneous imagery is the 'inner guide' (see Exercise 11). This is an imagery technique which helps individuals to contact their 'internal healer and counsellor'; their own inner knowing or inner wisdom, in the form of an 'inner guide'. To meet this inner guide, the individual is directed to her/his private place. There (s)he invites a being to appear, whom (s)he can ask questions. This being (person, animal, spirit, whatever) is her/his inner guide who can help with healing and self-understanding. The guide can be asked questions, and answers will just appear. After the initial meeting, the individual can consult the guide on her/his own at any time, about any subject. The responses are most often amazingly wise and helpful.

The inner-guide image is an extremely valuable imagery technique that individuals can use themselves to add greatly to their self-understanding and to stimulate personal growth.

Most of the other imagery techniques used for these purposes are other-directed techniques. They are used with the guidance of an experienced imagery worker with a good background in psychology. The guide directs the image to a certain point, allows spontaneous imagery to emerge, and then may offer some further direction depending on what has emerged. These images are specifically designed to tap deep unconscious levels of the mind, and to bring to the surface resident thoughts, feelings, and beliefs. Since this area of our being is largely uncharted territory for most of us, and has powerful inhabitants, working with an experienced facilitator is very important.

Since unconscious thoughts, beliefs and feelings significantly affect our lives, there is great value in bringing them to light, so we can understand better what directs us, and have more choice in our lives. An example of one imagery sequence that might be used for this type of exploration would be one which leads to the discovery and opening of an ancient treasure chest buried beneath the ocean floor. This type of exploration usually involves a series of ten to twelve individual or group imagery sessions. Other-directed imagery can also be used, in ways such as helping to acquaint us with our 'subpersonalities'; the different characters within us who emerge now and again and affect our lives, or helping us to discover and perhaps transform our deep attitudes towards important issues, such as death. This type of imagery can be used in workshop situations to advantage when there is a skilful leader.

Many books which explore the use of imagery for healing are currently available. Two classics in this area are *Seeing With the Mind's Eye*, by Samuels and Bennett, a beautiful history of the uses of imagery for healing, and *Creative Visualization*, by

Shakti Gawain, an excellent review of imagery principles including a collection of healing image scripts. Multitudes of cassette tapes designed to take the listener through healing imagery experiences for every imaginable ailment are also commercially available. Some of these are excellent and represent another step in the direction of placing powerful healing techniques, and responsibility for one's own health, in the healee's hands.

Clearly, the use of imagery for self-healing and growth has many benefits. It allows us access to those parts of ourselves which are running much of our lives, and thus can offer us more conscious choice in our lives. It puts the power and responsibility for health and well-being back in our hands — there is a *lot* we can do for ourselves for our own healing and growth! And, as an added benefit, the more we use the language of imagery, the more we 'dance in its world', the more familiar it becomes and the more aware *we* become of internal and external image experiences. Much inspiration and creativity comes in the form of imagery, and by developing our sensitivity to images we are opening up these channels. Also, in expanding beyond the limits of the verbal, we transcend the restrictions of the human, and once again enter the realm of the more universal essential energies of life.

SELF-HELP IMAGERY EXERCISES

As explained earlier, imagery exercises are always preceded by a relaxation exercise, or meditation. This brings the person to a state of consciousness where (s)he has more access to, and communication with, the deeper levels of her/his consciousness, *where the imagery acts*. For optimum effectiveness, from ten to thirty minutes of relaxation is recommended before imagery is used, and the more consistently one works with such a relaxation or meditation technique, the more effective it becomes. When using a 'progressive relaxation' technique such as the following, it is best to have the instructions on tape. Several such relaxation tapes are commercially available *or* it is possible to make your own, with appropriate pauses and soft voice.

RELAXATION EXERCISE

Lie down, or sit down with both feet on the floor, in a comfortable position. Loosen any tight clothing, and make sure you will not be interrupted. Close your eyes, and take a few slow, deep breaths. With each exhale, allow any tension that may be in your body to start melting away, down and out of your body, as you continue breathing, slowly and deeply. Now focus your attention on the top of your head allowing, with each exhale, any tension that may be in the top of your head to start melting away, down and out of your body, as relaxation spreads through the top of your head. Continue breathing, slowly and deeply. Next allow your attention to go to your forehead, allowing any tension that may be in your forehead to start melting away, fading away, down and out of your body, as your forehead becomes more and more relaxed. Continue breathing slowly and deeply. Then allow relaxation to spread to the rest of your face, your face becoming more and more relaxed. Now the back of your head becoming relaxed, more and more relaxed with each exhale. Now your neck relaxing; with each exhale any tension that may be in your neck melting away. Now your shoulders becoming more and more relaxed with each exhale, as you continue breathing slowly and deeply. Chest relaxed. Stomach and abdomen relaxed. Upper back relaxing with each slow deep breath. Middle back, lower back relaxing. Buttocks relaxing with each exhale, genitals relaxing. Now your upper arms relaxing, elbows relaxing, forearms relaxing with each slow, deep breath. Wrists relaxing, hands

relaxing; the tops of the hands, and the palms, relaxing. And fingers relaxing, as you continue breathing, slowly and deeply. Now your thighs relaxing; the fronts of your thighs and the backs of your thighs. Knees relaxing; the fronts of your knees and the backs of your knees. Calves relaxing; the fronts of your calves and the backs of your calves, relaxing. Ankles relaxing, and your feet relaxing — the tops of your feet, your heels, the soles of your feet, relaxing more and more with each exhale. And now, your toes relaxing. Feeling with each exhale any remaining tension flowing out of your body. And now, as you continue breathing slowly and deeply, make a gentle survey of your body, and if there is any area that is not yet quite totally relaxed, allow that area to relax more and more with each exhale. As you continue breathing slowly and deeply, allow yourself to enjoy this pleasant state of deep relaxation.

The following are imagery exercises that you can use for your own healing and growth. They are best directed by one person and simply received by others. You could also make tapes of them for yourself, being sensitive to the pauses necessary between instructions, and the importance of a soft quality of your voice, except when energetic images are being described or formed! Purchasing at least one pre-recorded imagery tape could be very helpful, as a model.*

* The author makes tapes leading these various images, upon request. Inquire or order by writing to Janna Fineberg, Imagery Tapes, 149 Keen Street, Lismore, NSW 2480, Australia through December 1985. From 1986, contact Dr Fineberg c/o *Nature & Health* magazine, PO Box 60, Dee Why, NSW 2099, Australia.

GUIDED IMAGERY FOR HEALTH MAINTENANCE

Exercise 1 'White Light Circulation' To nourish, cleanse, and tune your body, mind and spirit. For a pick-me-up. To maintain good health, and peace of mind. Imagine that just above your head is a ball of white light, like a little white sun. It is vibrant, full of energy. With each inhale, draw some of this white light in through the top of your head, into every cell in your body. Feel the light cleansing, nourishing, healing, every cell in your body. Feel the light revitalising every cell. Then with your exhale, send this light and along with it anything your cells no longer need, down your body, out your feet, and way into the core of the earth. Once again with your next inhale, draw in more white light from the ball above your head into every cell of your body, energising and revitalising, cleansing every cell. And with your exhale send it down, out of your body through your feet, and way into the core of the earth. Continue circulating this white light with each breath for five minutes.

Exercise 2 'White Light Protection' To protect yourself from outside influences, for example noisy, busy streets, individuals who are hostile towards you, individuals whose illness you do not wish to absorb. Imagine once again the white ball of light above your head. Now with each inhale, draw white light in, through the top of your head, into your heart. With each exhale, send the light outwards from your heart in all directions, until you are enclosed in a circle of white light about two feet from your body.

You are surrounding yourself with a circle of white light that gets recharged with your every exhale. Spend several minutes establishing this circle of light around you. Only energy that is good for you can come in through this white light protection; nothing negative can get through. You are safe to exchange only love through this protective shield.

Exercise 3 'Running Energy —Grounding' This is to bring you out of your head, your mind, and into your feelings and your body. It will help you get your feet back on the ground if you feel 'spaced out'. It will bring you nicely back to reality if you spend too much time in fantasy; it will bring you back to today, here and now, if you spend too much time in memories of the past, or fantasies of the future. It grounds you in present reality.

With each inhale, draw in energy through the top of your head, in from the universe, or the sky above you, into your heart. With each exhale, send this energy down your spine, down your legs, out your feet, and *way into the core of the earth*. Once again, with your inhale draw in energy from the universe in through the top of your head into your heart. With each exhale, send the energy from your heart, down your spine, down your legs, out the bottom of your feet and *way into the core of the earth*. Continue running energy in this direction for three to five minutes.

Exercise 4 'Private Place' This is especially for those with busy lives, to bring in relaxation, and 'centring', or bringing you back to your sense of yourself, separate from outside influences. This exercise combines guided and spontaneous imagery.

Think of a place that is just the kind of place that you enjoy and can relax in. Preferably a place outdoors, in nature. It can be a place you have actually been to, or a place that you are creating in your mind. Allow an image of this place to form, knowing that there will not be anyone else there. And now in your mind, allow yourself to go to this 'private place', which is just exactly how you want it to be for you to relax in and enjoy yourself. Now let's explore this place. What is on the ground? And what does the ground feel like? What is in front of you? Behind you? To the left? To the right? Now look up. Can you see the sky? What does the sky look like, or whatever is above you? What is the temperature of the air? Is there a breeze? Are there any smells in the air? What sounds do you hear in this place? What else do you notice about your private place?

Now find a comfortable spot to sit or lie down. Feel yourself really relaxing. Know that this is your special private place, that no-one else can come here unless you invite them. You can come here any time you wish, to just relax, and enjoy it. It is your spot, and always available to you. Do come and visit it for at least five minutes a day for a while, so you don't forget it. It is always there for you, when you need to relax, to be by yourself, and to be nourished. Enjoy it awhile. When you are ready to leave, say goodbye to your place, and let it know that you will come again soon to visit. Allow its image to slowly fade from your mind. Take a few slow, deep breaths before you open your eyes.

GUIDED IMAGERY FOR SELF-HEALING

For Injuries:

Exercise 5 'White Light Healing' Imagine a ball of white healing light above your head, like a little sun. With each inhale, draw in some of this white healing light in through the top of your head, into the injured body part. Do this for several inhales, charging the injured area with white light. Then begin with each exhale, sending the light, and along with it any trauma and damaged cells resulting from the injury, down your body and out through the bottom of your feet into the core of the earth. Continue bringing healing white light into the injured body part with each inhale — light that soothes and heals, irradiating the injury — and then send the light and with it any trauma and damaged cells down and out of your body into the earth with each exhale. Do this for ten minutes, several times a day. Be sure, with each inhale, to really see and feel the injured body part becoming irradiated with healing white light.

Exercise 6 'Reverse Image' Allow a detailed image to form for the injury, involving as many senses as possible, for example, exactly where the injury is located, exactly how large an area it covers, what it feels like, what the temperature is, what it smells like, what colour it is, what texture it is. For example, if it is a burn, it might be on the arm, just above the elbow, tennis ball size, sizzling, orange-red, burning hot, rough and irregular. When you have this image, then allow an image to form that would counteract the injury image; that would be soothing, healing, and normalising to the injury image. Again involve as many senses as possible. For example, the healing image for the burn might be a thick, cool, blue liquid, smooth, with a flower smell. Then imagine, with each inhale, some of this thick, cool, blue, smooth, fragrant liquid is being poured on the burn, cooling, soothing, and changing the colour of the burn. With each inhale imagine more of this healing liquid being applied to the burn, and really imagine the burn gradually responding to this treatment by changing colour, temperature, texture etc. Keep the blue liquid coming for ten minutes, allowing the injury image to be transformed at the pace that it will. It cannot resist treatment from an appropriate healer! This 'reverse image' can be used for pain relief and/or healing at any time during the day, even for 30 seconds. Should the image of the injury itself begin to change, allow the healing image to change correspondingly.

Exercise 7 'Literal Image' With this one, you imagine that exactly what needs to happen physiologically in your body for the injury to heal, is happening. This may require a little research! For example, if you are healing a bone break, you imagine as

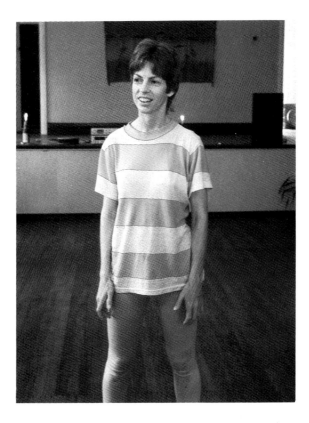

vividly as possible, the cells of the bone knitting, and the two pieces of the bone becoming one. You would also imagine the surrounding blood vessels bringing blood to the area with exactly the nutrients needed for the ideal healing.

For Illnesses:

Exercise 8 'Dramatised Literal Imagery' This type of imagery was popularised by the Simontons of Texas, and their work with cancer sufferers. With this one, as in Exercise 7, you find out exactly what needs to happen in your body physiologically for the illness to heal. For example, with an infection, your bloodstream needs to bring lots of white blood cells to the infected area; the white blood cells need to absorb the invading bacteria, and then your bloodstream needs to take the refuse away. With this kind of imagery, the individual then creates a fanciful dramatised image of this process, for example, flying saucers whizzing to the needed spot from outer space, creatures with mouths like vacuum cleaners emerging and sucking up all the bubble creatures that were invading earth, then getting back into their ships, and with a loud engine sound, whizzing away. Any image the individual comes up with spontaneously is perfect, and preferably it will include sounds, smells, different textured images, vibrant colours, and generally, *lots of energy*. Then, imagine it happening — it's like going to an exciting movie in your body!

Exercise 9 'Total Health' Here, you imagine yourself *totally healthy. Really feel* what that would feel like in your body. See what you would look like, totally healthy, and see and feel yourself doing the things you would do if you were totally healthy. What would you smell like? What would your voice sound like? Imagine every aspect of what being totally healthy is like.

For Excess Emotions:

Exercise 10 **'Reverse Emotion'**   This exercise can be extremely helpful in emergency situations, and with habitual emotional responses. If the emotional response persists, counselling can be extremely beneficial. This one is much like 'Reverse Image' (Exercise 6). Locate the feeling of the emotion in your body. Where do you feel it? What does it feel like? Allow an image or several images to form for the feeling of the emotion in your body, using all sense modalities (please see Exercise 6 for elaboration). Now allow an image to form that would counteract the image of the sensations connected with the emotion. With each inhale, use this 'reverse image' to reduce, or transform, the sensations associated with the emotion — and allow the emotion to dissolve. Continue the imagery until you are calm and peaceful, or at least the emotion is significantly reduced, and tolerable.

GUIDED AND SPONTANEOUS IMAGERY FOR SELF-KNOWLEDGE

Exercise 11 **'Inner Guide'**   Go to your private place (see Exercise 4), and spend a few minutes enjoying yourself there. Now invite a being to join you there; to appear in your private place. Do not direct what kind of being this will be or how (s)he will appear; just allow it to happen. This being is your inner guide. (S)he is a friend to you, someone who has much wisdom in many areas of life, and (s)he can be very helpful to you. Say hello to your guide, and thank your guide for coming. Introduce yourself, and ask the guide's name. Wait for a response. Show the guide around your private place. Tell the guide that you really appreciate her/his coming; that sometimes there are things about your body or your life that you are not clear about; that you have questions about. You have heard that this guide has much wisdom, and you would like to know if when you do have questions, if you could call upon the guide to meet you in your private place and ask her/him some questions. Let her/him know that you understand that since you will be asking her/him for help, that sometimes the guide will want you to do things for her/him, and that you will be quite willing to do these things, because you know they will always be good for you.

It is rarely the case that this being is not agreeable to help you in this way, but if (s)he says no to your request, you have not yet met your true inner guide. Visit with this being a bit to learn why it appeared, and then ask it to leave your private place, and call once again for your inner guide to appear.

Once you have met this true guide, you can invite her/him to come to your private place to discuss things with you any time you wish. For now, thank the guide again for coming and for being willing to be available to guide you. Say goodbye for now, and allow the guide to leave, knowing that any time you wish you can call on her/him to meet you in this place. It least for the next week, visit with your guide in your private place once each day, and ask any questions you wish. Just allow the answers to appear. You have now met an invaluable, wise friend and counsellor.

GUIDED IMAGERY FOR SPECIAL USES

Guided and spontaneous imagery can be adapted for many uses. One lovely use is for expanding our hearts/love, and sharing this love with a partner or others.

Exercise 12 **'Circle of Love'**   Sit facing your partner, or in a circle if there are more than two of you. Sit close enough so that you can easily reach out to hold hands when you are instructed to do so. Close your eyes. With each inhale, draw in pink light from

the universe around you, in through the top of your head, and into your heart. With each inhale you are drawing in pink light, love light, from the abundant universal source above your head and all around you. You are drawing it in through the top of your head, and into your heart. Play with this image for a few minutes, as you fill your heart with breath, with pink light, with love. Feel the vibrant, warm light in your heart — feel its fullness. Stay with that feeling for a few moments.

Now join hands with your partner or around the circle, opening your eyes minimally and only momentarily to do this, if necessary. Hold hands with your left palms facing upwards, and your right palms facing downwards. Now with each exhale, send some of the pink light, the love, from your heart, down your right shoulder, down your right arm, out through your right hand and to the person next to you. With your inhale, draw in pink light, love light, in through your left hand from the person on your left, up your arm and into your heart.

Continue. With each inhale you are receiving love (pink light) into your left hand from the person on your left, and drawing it up your arm and into your heart, and with each exhale you are sending love (pink light) from your heart, down your right arm, and out your right hand to the person next to you.

Everyone try to all inhale and exhale together, by doing so loudly, and perhaps choosing someone to lead the breath. Continue circulating pink light around the circle with your breathing, forming a circle of love, a sharing of love. After a few more minutes, allow the pink light image to fade. Feel how you feel within, after having received and shared love. Now slowly open your eyes and look at the others, still being aware of your heart feelings and what you have just all shared.

CHAPTER 3

CONTROLLING PAIN THROUGH IMAGERY

Kym Forrestal

Imagination is superior to all nature and generation, and through it we are capable of transcending the worldly order, of participating in eternal life and in the energy of the super-celestial. It is through this principle, therefore that we will be liberated from the bonds of fate itself.

Iamblichus, c.290 AD

TIMELESS THERAPEUTIC IMAGES

In centuries past and present, the power of the image has exerted tremendous force in many areas of life. Story tellers, mythmakers and artists have intuitively honed the greatly important skill of image-creation. Shamans and yogis have diligently practised the most necessary skill of image-concentration, and modern multi-media experts and film-makers have effectively utilised imagery as a rapid means of communication and persuasion. In this century, Freud, Jung, Assagioli, and more recently other researchers, have touched upon the power of the positive image for health. A rapidly growing body of scientific findings from psychology, psychiatry, and neuropsychology have found that rapid and extensive emotional, physiological and psychological change can occur through mental imagery. As events are seen in the mind's eye, the consequences are often as real as the 'reality', and for those able to follow the path, imagery promises great rewards. The surging scientific interest has confirmed the intuitive knowledge about imagery. It is indeed timeless and therapeutic: the silent language of experience and change.

In dealing with pain, imagery can be purposefully used to establish two-way communication between our conscious self and our unconscious aspects in an attempt to both discover the causes of our pain, and to unlock the deeper meaning behind it. The imagination when it operates outside of our conscious control, can be a potent source of anxiety and can generate stress-related dis-eases. However, when used skilfully, it can lead the way to a greater sense of well-being, self-knowledge, and control over one's health.

Pain is a complex phenomenon involving both physical and psychological factors. Imagery is a potent diagnostic and therapeutic tool in the management of these syndromes.

PAIN: FRIEND OR FOE?

Medical experts still do not know exactly what causes pain. However, research has shown that it is not merely a sensory phenomenon, but also includes many psychological factors. According to the International Association for the Study of Pain, 'Pain is a warning sign to the body that some part of it is being damaged'.* As we know all too well, there are numerous ways in which we can damage ourselves. Many of us have experienced the pain of cutting, tearing, crushing, burning, freezing, and bruising. These usually result in what is called acute pain (for example, a sprained ankle, a broken leg, a laceration), and are often the result of specific and readily-identifiable tissue damage. In these situations, a professional is usually consulted about the acute problem, and after following specific advice, the pain is relieved and does not persist beyond a reasonably short period of recuperation. Chronic pain, on the other hand, usually begins with an acute episode, but lasts beyond the expected period of treatment. The most common forms involve low back pain, headaches, neck and shoulder pain, abdominal pain, pain in arms or legs, joints and in various other localised areas.

In addition to the pain produced from acute and chronic complaints, feelings of anxiety associated with acute pain experiences usually increase as the pain increases, followed by a reduction in anxiety once proper treatment begins. Research shows that this reduction in anxiety generally results in a corresponding decrease in the pain sensation. The cycle is quite different for chronic pain sufferers. For these people, the initial anxiety associated with the pain persists, and may eventually evolve into feelings of helplessness and despair in spite of the healing professional's attempts to alleviate it. Without relief, the person suffering from chronic pain begins to feel fatigued from the constancy of it and the loss of sleep that results. In addition, he or she feels hopeless and frustrated, and cannot see an end to the suffering. This increasing anxiety and loss of vitality has the effect of escalating the perceived level of pain.

Chronic pain can result from a clearly identifiable cause, for example, arthritis. However, in many cases no specific origin of the pain can be found. For example, if patients present themselves to their doctor complaining of severe neck pain and, following a comprehensive series of x-rays and medical procedures, no physiological evidence can be found, it is usually assumed that emotional and psychological factors are its primary cause. Pain of this type is called psychogenic pain, and is often observed in certain types of psychological illness.

Pain due to muscle tension caused by obsessive fear or worry would be one such example of psychogenic pain. For the patient, this type of pain is no less real than pain which can be traced to identifiable sources. In cases of psychogenic pain, the patient is often referred for psychotherapy which can serve to unlock the more subtle and unconscious causes, especially when it is related to muscle tension.

Research clearly shows that pain also involves behavioural and environmental factors, as well as attitudes, beliefs and expectations, based on prior experiences. In moving beyond the pain experience, we can benefit greatly from a holistic approach, to discover the causes and their underlying meaning in our lives. Common to these latest holistic approaches to healing is the recognition that the body, emotions, mind and spirit are one inseparable system. This means that everything we think and believe and feel is experienced in our bodies. We all know that when we are afraid we may shake, feel weak or nauseous, blush when we are embarrassed, or yawn when we feel bored. If we can accept that our thoughts, feelings and beliefs are reflected in our bodies, then we can see that if we consciously change them, we can in turn change our bodies. This implies, of course, that controlling pain, and in turn healing its cause,

* Dr S. Lipton, *Conquering Pain*, Sydney 1984, Methuen, p. 8

can only be effective when we choose to take an active and responsible part in the healing process, rather than playing the role of passive victim of the disease or its treatment. Medical experts tell us that the reason mental imagery works is that it promotes the release of pain-killing endorphins in the body chemistry, which act on specific pain receptors in the brain and spinal cord, much like pain-killing drugs. Imagery for pain relief is said to be about 60 per cent more effective than morphine. Each of us has within us an innate capacity to combat illness and its resultant pain, whatever its cause. However holistic healing approaches are not regarded as a total substitute for medical science, but rather as a beneficial enhancement of the healing process.

PSYCHOSYNTHESIS AND PAIN

Psychosynthesis is a holistic approach to healing, and offers a way of integrating the various aspects of human experience — the physical, the emotional, the mental and the spiritual (related to our inner essence, our deepest purpose and values and the function of will). The word, 'synthesis' comes from a Greek root, meaning 'to put together' and synthesis is the combining of various parts to form a coherent whole. The function then of bio-psychosynthesis is in recognising the close ties that knit the body (bio) and the psyche (our inner psychological world) and, through the use of active techniques, eliminating conflicts and imbalances between them, so as to bring about a state of total wellness.

Psychosynthesis is an effective tool for inner guidance and direction, tuning in to the needs of one's own body, emotions and mind. It was originated in the second decade of this century and developed over a fifty-year period by the Italian psychiatrist, Roberto Assagioli, whose work was far ahead of its time. Assagioli's concept of the whole person had its roots in many Western and Eastern traditions. Although a contemporary of Freud and a pioneer of psychoanalysis in Italy, Assagioli felt that the Freudian conception of the human unconscious was incomplete and expanded his own to include the higher functions of the human psyche: the transpersonal dimension, which he recognised played an important role in the healing of physical and psychological disorders. Assagioli's conception of the psycho-physical structure of the human being is illustrated in the following diagram:

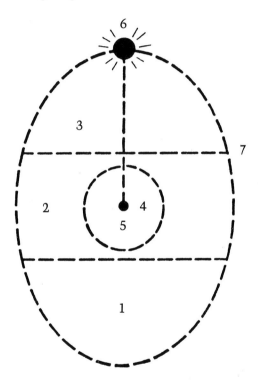

1 The Lower Unconscious
2 The Middle Unconscious
3 The Higher Unconscious or Superconscious
4 The Field of Consciousness
5 The Conscious Self or 'I'
6 The Transpersonal Self
7 The Collective Unconscious

The surrounding oval indicates the whole bio-physical human being; the circular area represents the field of consciousness; and the point at its centre the conscious self or 'I'. The rest of the area indicates the extensive field of the unconscious, which is divided into three zones:

1 The lower encompasses, first of all, the psychic activities, elementary but skilful, that govern our organic life. A number of biologists are now talking of a bio-psyche and regarding life and intelligence as inseparable. This zone is also the seat, or origin, of

the instincts, or fundamental drives, such as sexuality, self-preservation and aggressiveness. Within it, as well, are found the complexes having a strong emotional charge that are produced by traumas and psychic conflicts.

2 The middle zone is the abode of the psychic elements and activities similar to those of waking consciousness and easily accessible to us.

3 The highest area represents the higher unconscious or superconscious. It is the seat of, and from it come, intuitions and inspirations of a lofty, spiritual, artistic, philosophic or scientific nature, the creations of genius, ethical imperatives and the promptings to altruistic action.

The star at the summit of the superconscious represents what modern psychology — and pre-eminently Jung — designate as the 'Transpersonal Self', of which the 'I', the centre of self-consciousness, is a reflection. Outside the oval exists the boundless psychic world of the collective unconscious.

All the lines are dotted to show that a continuous exchange of elements and energies — a 'psychic osmosis', one might say — is taking place between any and all these psychic areas.

Roberto Assagioli — founder of Psychosynthesis

Assagioli believed that as all biological organisms exhibit an insuppressible tendency towards growth, there is a growth tendency in us as human beings which lasts throughout life. When this growth remains unrecognised, repressed, or frustrated by environmental obstacles, psychosomatic disturbances are produced.

Another specific contribution made by psychosynthesis is its reaffirmation of the importance of the human will, which is an attribute of our conscious self. The will is given a central position among the various psychic functions, which are represented in this 'star' diagram:

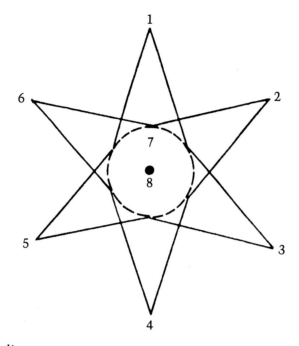

1 Sensation
2 Emotion — Feelings
3 Imagination
4 Impulse — Desire
5 Thought
6 Intuition
7 Will
8 Central point: the 'I' or conscious Self

Our will is a function of our inner 'Self'. Through the will, our 'Self' can act on the various psychological functions, regulating and balancing and bringing them into harmony.

Some people approach life mainly on the sensory level; others approach it on the feeling or emotional level. For others, everything has to be thought out, intellectualised: they cannot feel, they have to think how they feel. In these intellectuals, psychosynthesis would involve the development of the feeling function since it is undeveloped. The recognition and use of the will has great importance in psychosomatic medicine, and the success of many of the psychological and psycho-physical techniques requires the voluntary and active co-operation of the patient. So the will to be cured is essential. Without this willingness, any therapeutic technique remains ineffective. We can say to ourselves 'I *wish* I was well', but when we say ''I *will* to heal myself' we engage the dynamic power of our will. Experts in holistic health today tell us that disease is largely psychosomatic. We can wake up from the dream of victim consciousness when we recognise that we create our own experience of pain and disease. If we consider ourselves a victim we are likely to become dependent upon the healing professional to 'make it better', and to 'get rid of' the symptom rather than to explore the meaning of the pain and to co-operate in the healing process.

AM I IN PAIN? OR IS PAIN IN ME?

Assagioli deplored the tendency of diagnostic medicine to equate people with their illness. Instead, he viewed the person as a whole and considered that pathological complaints were only one aspect of the whole person. His perspective was one of growth and tended to view symptoms not so much as something undesirable to be 'gotten rid of', but rather as an energy blockage that needs to be explored. His emphasis was on releasing the constructive forces within us which would often cause symptoms to fade away.

The concept of dis-identification is a central one in psychosynthesis and is probably one of the most important contributions to recent psychological thought. It can be understood best in relation to its opposite: identification. When we are closely identified with something, then it is as though our sense of identity is bound up in it. Some of us are so identified with our cars, for instance, that if the car is scratched, we experience it as though we ourselves have been personally defaced. A woman who is identified with the appearance of her body may feel that her worth as a human being is lessened if she develops wrinkles on her face, or gets grey hairs. It is as though these people believed 'I am my car' or 'I am my body'.

In the work of healing ourselves, we need to integrate the various aspects of ourselves and dis-identification plays an important role. We must for instance be able to 'stand back from' our pain and disease in order to understand them more clearly, and to find a vantage point from which we can do something to transform them. Doing this enables us to feel less victimised or threatened, and allows us to explore the cause and meaning more clearly.

In his book *What We May Be*, Dr Piero Ferrucci uses the following diagrams to illustrate this principle:*

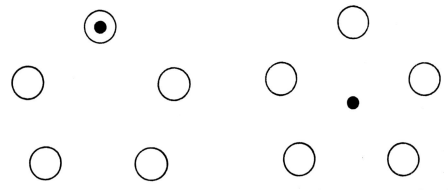

1 Empty circles indicate contents of consciousness: feelings, sensations, ideas, and so on. The point indicates the *self*. The self passes unintentionally from identification to identification throughout the day: 'I am in pain', 'I am tired', 'I am happy'.

2 It is possible to experience the self as pure consciousness, apart from any content: 'I am'. From this psychological place, the self has a panoramic view of all the personality contents instead of being identified with just one of them at a time.

* Dr P. Ferrucci, *What We May Be*, Los Angeles 1982, Tarcher, p. 64.

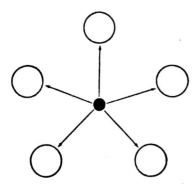

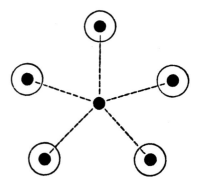

3 In the psychosynthetic conception, the self is neither the passive spectator extraneous to the show nor the actor completely involved in it. It is the producer, who stages the whole show with expertise, good timing, and tactful handling of the actors.

4 When clearly experienced, the self can decide to identify fully and easily with any personality content, from romantic love to furious anger to physical comfort, but it is also able to *dis-identify* from the content. The experience of self allows choice at all times. Thus the whole personality is available to the self.

When experiencing pain we often announce 'I am in pain', when in fact only a portion of our being is experiencing it. In relating to pain in this way we are unwittingly identifying ourselves even more deeply with the experience, and submerging ourselves in it. This in turn serves to accentuate the pain by feeding it a disproportionate amount of energy. It would be more accurate to say 'pain is in me' or 'I am aware of a sensation of pain within me'. In such a way we are able to dis-identify or to 'step back from' the pain and bring it into a more manageable perspective.

Chronic pain patients often carry on an inner dialogue, telling themselves how terrible and utterly hopeless their situation is and how helpless they are to do anything about it. Replaying these kind of messages to themselves reinforces the attitude which in turn heightens the pain. By reminding ourselves that we are a conscious 'self' we can choose to say: 'I am not my pain', 'I am in control, not the pain'. Assagioli stressed the principle that we are dominated by everything with which our self becomes identified. We can direct and control everything from which we dis-identify ourselves. For example, every time we identify ourselves with a sickness, we become more and more dominated by it. By focusing on the sickness, we succeed in chaining ourselves to it. If we can say: 'A sensation of pain is trying to submerge me', the situation becomes quite different, because on one side you have the pain and on the other you have the 'self'. Now, this does not suggest the Pollyana attitude of denial and repression which says: 'Oh! I'm not in pain' while gritting one's teeth at the same time. I do not advocate the attitude that everything is fine. Rather, it is recognising that: 'Yes, I *have* pain, but *I* am *not* my pain'. This allows us the flexibility, then, to deal with it more effectively. Our pain is not the whole of us, it is only part of us. The basic psychosynthesis exercise of dis-identification from one's pain and illness can be practised daily, so that the skill of moving into the 'self', our centre, is strengthened.

Chronic pain sufferers often carry on an inner dialogue

This following exercise in dis-identification, described by Dr Robert Gerard in *Psychosynthesis: A Psychotherapy for the Whole Man*, has been modified for use by pain patients.

Allow your body to find a comfortable and relaxed position, and with eyes closed, affirm to yourself:

'I have a body, but I am not my body because, after all, within a few days all the cells of my body will no longer be the same, it is constantly changing, and yet I experience a sense of continuity. At times I am tired, at times I experience pain, at other times I am more full of energy. Because there is so much change, how can my identity reside in that? I have a body; I use it just as I use a car, but I am the driver, I am not my car. Similarly, I am not my body, and I am not my pain.

'The same thing can be said of my emotions. Sometimes I feel depressed, sometimes I feel elated, sometimes I feel hopeless, sometimes irritated, sometimes very loving. The moods change; now where in that is my identity? These are all passing moods that I feel, but I am not my feelings. Nevertheless, they are extremely useful and helpful

in my contact with other people. I need emotions to sense through other than intellectual ways how others react and also to express love and affection. I have my emotions, but I am not my emotions.

'And I can go one step further and think of all the ways that my thoughts, my intellect, my ideas have changed and evolved over the years; that I have sometimes changed my point of view. So how can my identity reside in that? I think, but I am not my thoughts. I have an intellect; it is a tool, but I do not raise it above its rightful place. It is just a tool; it is an intellect, it is a way of resolving questions and thinking. But I am not my intellect.

'Who am I then? I am a self. I am a point of self-awareness, the essence of myself. It is the permanent factor in the ever-varying flow of my personal life. As the self, I possess dynamic power and am capable of observing, directing and harmonising all my psychological processes and my physical body. I can, therefore be in control of my pain and discover ways to go beyond it and to heal myself.'*

PAIN, FRIEND OR FOE?

We in the West are probably the most pain-conscious people on the face of the earth. For years we have been conditioned — in print, on radio, over television, in daily conversation — that any hint of pain is to be banished as though it were the ultimate evil. Consequently we become pill-grabbers and hypochondriacs, escalating the slightest headache into a searing ordeal. Dangerously, pain-killing drugs conceal pain without correcting the underlying condition. Our bodies can pay a high price for this suppression without regard to its basic cause. When we develop pain, anxiety, depression, or any of a host of physical symptoms, it is nature's way of telling us to pay attention to some neglected aspect of our lives.

A symptom calls for some adjustment to be made in the way we are taking care of ourselves. We can learn to understand its meaning, and plan a course of action that will lead toward better health and freedom. In this way we can view pain as a friend making us aware of imbalances, rather than as a foe.

In beginning the task of self-exploration, we need to look at the secondary gains we may be deriving from our pain. We may find many benefits from our illness, such as getting more love and attention, being taken care of, or escaping from a difficult situation we cannot cope with. We may also be using our pain as a diversion, or an excuse to avoid looking at an emotionally painful issue. In these cases, the physical pain is being unconsciously substituted for emotional pain, since the physical pain is often more bearable.

However, this pattern of behaviour can be altered if we could just give ourselves permission to request the love and attention or relaxation and release from inner stress we need.

ANSWERS FROM THE UNCONSCIOUS

The new developments in depth psychology have made it possible to approach the realm of the unconscious from an inherently affirmative and constructive point of view. The new holistic sense of depths is not conceived in terms of the malfunctioning of personality, but rather in terms of what man's nature requires him to become.

Ira Progoff

Within each of us there exists an intuitive part, which knows how to create harmony. In recent years numerous techniques using mental imagery have been developed. They

* Dr R. Gerard, *Psychosynthesis: A Psychotherapy for the Whole Man*, New York 1964, Psychosynthesis Research Foundation, p. 7.

are powerful methods for exploring the unconscious by using our intuitive self. One that can be used by pain sufferers is known as 'Answers from the Unconscious'. This can be used to gain information, guidance and a better understanding of our pain.

The basic idea is to formulate a question, addressing it to one's unconscious, and allowing the answer to emerge spontaneously in the form of mental image. The answer may come as a visual image, or in the form of a word or a phrase, or one may simply experience a feeling, or a sense of the answer.

The first step in this technique is to achieve a state of relaxation. One can do this by using the previously mentioned dis-identification exercise, in order to centre oneself in the experience of the self, and thereby dis-identifying from the pain. Since pain is so often linked closely to tension and fear, many people experience a decrease in pain after beginning to use relaxation and mental imagery techniques regularly. Other basic relaxation techniques outlined in this book would suffice in preparing for the imagery processes. Recorded relaxation tapes are also widely available for achieving this preparation stage.

A number of doctors suggest that patients enter a dialogue with a mythical figure, or a very wise and loving person, who knows the answers to all the problems they face, which they then discover in themselves. The purpose of this dialogue is to unlock the meaning of the disease — what the physical symptoms represent — and then to point the way to release through a re-ordering of the person's life. One may ask questions such as: 'What is the meaning of my headache?' or 'What changes do I need to make in my life to overcome this illness?'

In contacting your inner guide be aware that the quality of the dialogue with your advisor is a reflection of what is going on inside you. If your advisor acts in a timid or frightened way, it may be a reflection of your own timidity about exploring your self. If your advisor is sarcastic, it may reveal your own cynicism. If your advisor won't talk to you, it may suggest you don't want to face what is really happening inside that is making you sick. Your intuitive self is constantly striving to communicate information to you. This simple imagery simply allows you to gain access to that source, through a symbolic advisor. As fantastic as this technique may sound, it does work, not instantaneously, although for many relief does come quickly.

The limits of our beliefs define the limits of our reality. It is important to be open to all possibilities. If our minds are closed to the availability of inner guidance, then no amount of techniques will produce it.

However these techniques should not be used to replace medical consultation. If you are ill, you should see a doctor, but you can assist them by promoting your own healing process through imagery.

In their book *Getting Well Again* the Simontons suggest the following inner dialogue:

Prepare yourself by using a relaxation process:
1 *Visualise the pain as a creature of some sort. Try to see the pain-creature very clearly.*
2 *Establish a dialogue with the pain-creature. Ask it why it is there, what message it has, what purpose it serves. Listen very carefully to its answers.*
3 *Now ask the pain-creature what you can do to get rid of it. Listen carefully to what it has to tell you.*
4 *Open your eyes and start to follow its advice. Notice whether or not your pain is reduced.*
5 *Congratulate yourself for helping to relieve your pain and resume your usual activities.* *

* C. and S. Simonton, *Getting Well Again*, New York 1980, Bantam, pp. 184–85.

SUBSTITUTING PLEASURE FOR PAIN

A number of pain patients derive great relief from their pain and its associated distress by using a very satisfying approach — substituting pleasure for pain. In *The Act of Will*, Roberto Assagioli lists the 'technique of substitution' as one of the basic psychological laws,

according to which attention centred on an object gives it energy, making it more important in our awareness. Continued attention tends to increase interest and interest in turn reinforces the attention, thus creating a positive feedback loop. When the unwanted thought or image draws our awareness, it becomes like a magnet that captures our attention and continues to draw energy from it . . . by deliberately building another such centre of attraction, we can easily use it to liberate our captive attention.*

When one is willing to transcend pain and be more comfortable, this technique can alleviate or even eliminate pain and its distress. Another prerequisite is a state of relaxation, where the body and mind are free of tension, which allows the unconscious mind to be impressionable to new, positive images.

Our negative beliefs can keep us stuck in the pain and illness. One visualisation that is used to counteract old beliefs is as follows:

By Creating in your mind's eye a blackboard, complete with chalk and eraser, you can imagine erasing from the blackboard any of the following negative messages whenever they enter your consciousness. 'I'll never get well', 'I can't', 'if only I wasn't in pain'. We can erase negative beliefs and write up new ones such as 'I will to get well', 'I can', 'I can go beyond my pain'.

Yet another method for substituting pleasure for pain is to relive in your imagination a time before your present illness began, when you were well and pain-free. Sense how

* Dr R. Assagioli, *The Act of Will*, London 1965, Penguin, p. 67.

you were then: how you breathed, felt, moved. You may re-experience camping, dancing, swimming, or enjoying favourite TV programmes. When visualising, you need to see and feel the experience from within your own body, instead of passively looking on. Try to feel the breeze on your skin, yourself running, the touch of others, the joy in your body. By recreating energy images from times when we were not in pain, it produces a shift in energy within us that can overcome the preoccupation with pain.

Here is another visualisation useful for controlling pain, from *Seeing with the Mind's Eye*, by Mike and Nancy Samuels.

Close your eyes, breathe in and out slowly and deeply. Relax your whole body by whatever methods work best for you. Then let your ideas of all disease symptoms become bubbles in your consciousness, now imagine that these bubbles are being blown out of your mind, out of your body, out of your consciousness by a breeze, which draws them away from you, far into the distance until you no longer see them or feel them. Watch them disappear over the horizon.

Now imagine that you are in a place you love. It may be the beach, in the mountains, on a desert, or wherever else you feel fully alive, comfortable, and healthy. Imagine the area around you is filled with bright, clear light. Allow the light to flow into your body, making you brighter, and filling you with the energy of health, enjoy basking in the light. *

Adelaide Bry, in *Directing the Movies of Your Mind*, suggests the following two strategies:

1 *Visualise the pain diluting and diffusing throughout the body, and then leaving the body through the skin. A variation on this is to breathe in with each inhalation soothing, relaxing nourishment and breathe out with each exhalation the tension, tightness and discomfort. Each time you inhale, bring twice as much healing oxygen into your system. Each time you exhale, remove twice as much tightness, pain, or discomfort. Actually see the pain leave.*

2 *Focus very closely on your area of pain. Then experience its geometric shape. Then see its colour, and then estimate how much water it could hold if it could hold water. Repeat these three steps until the pain is gone. It works, so don't give up when it hasn't seemed to work after a few go-rounds.*

Bry also outlines strategies for helping with any medical therapy you may be receiving:

1 *Visualise the medical treatment you are getting doing exactly what it is supposed to do. For example, visualise the drug that's been prescribed for you moving through your bloodstream to the site of the disease, and then doing what it's meant to do — such as destroying viruses or depressing the pain receptors. It would be helpful for you to find out exactly how the drug you're using works in the body.*

2 *If you are receiving a treatment such as physical therapy, massage, or even radiation, you can help it by simultaneously visualising the process working. Allow yourself to be receptive to its healing effect. See it doing what it's supposed to.* **

Also from the Samuels' book *Seeing With the Mind's Eye* is the glove-anaesthesia visualisation,

that has been used for years by hypnotists. For example, to induce glove anaesthesia in a woman, a therapist tells the subject to imagine that her hand is relaxing, falling asleep, or immersed in cold water. When she feels tingling and numbness, she is told to concentrate on that sensation and deepen it. Within a short time, most subjects will not feel pain from a pin-prick, they will feel pressure, but no pain. A subject can then

* M. and S. Samuels, *Seeing with the Mind's Eye*, New York 1975, Random House, p. 235.
** A. Bry, *Directing the Movies of Your Mind*, New York 1976, Barnes & Noble, pp. 97, 98.

move the feeling of anaesthesia to other parts of her body by placing her anaesthetised hand on an area and allowing the feeling of anaesthesia to flow out from her hand to that area.*

Here is an extension of the glove anaesthesia technique which is particularly useful for pain that extends throughout the whole body. This involves visualising slipping slowly into an anaesthetic blue pyjama suit or overalls, and as you slip the suit on, the painful areas are 'put to sleep'. Finally, when the suit is fully on, one can feel total comfort and relaxation and fall asleep if one desires, being able to waken at will.

In severe pain cases, removal from the immediate scene through fantasy may also be used.

One can, at the onset of pain, develop, in imagination, moving away from one's sick or pained body, and going into another room to watch TV or to engage in some other chosen activity, free of pain, while the suffering body remains in the bedroom. In doing so we again dis-identify from the pain.

Visualisation can also be used to reverse the psychological effects of acute injuries, by removing the ill effects of the emotions associated with the upset. If, for example, you've burned your hand removing a hot skillet from the stove, review in your imagination all the things that happened just before, during and after the accident. Repeat this sequence for some minutes until the pain subsides. This reduces the fear associated with the event and subsequently the level of perceived pain.

Visualisation has also played an important part in modern obstetrics and natural childbirth. Grantly Dick-Read, world-famous British obstetrician, says that women exposed to negative images about childbirth, are likely to create psychological tension and fear which in turn produce real physical pain. Dick-Read believes that an important part of natural childbirth involves educating the mother towards a positive image of childbirth, preventing the fear-tension-pain syndrome.

Relaxation and visualisation techniques, practised prior to the birth, and used when needed, enable the mother to have a less-painful delivery and enjoy the birth experience more. The baby is not drugged and has a far better chance of breathing spontaneously.

Visualisation and relaxation are not only useful for labour and delivery, but also for other discomforts experienced during pregnancy, including overcoming morning sickness. By firstly relaxing deeply, visualise yourself happy and well, and in a scene in nature that you enjoy a great deal. It may be the beach or alongside a mountain stream. Let yourself experience all the auditory, tactile and visual stimuli in this place including the sun's warmth. Remain in this pleasurable place as long as you wish.

Assagioli stated that when we create a mental image of health and a lack of pain, chemicals are released in the body which help to realise that image in reality. This also works in reverse: if we imagine being ill and in pain, we can create that in our bodies too.

Healing and wholeness includes all parts of one's life, the physical, emotional, mental and spiritual. We must assume responsibility for healing ourselves, knowing at the same time that we do not live in isolation and that the love and support of those around us can provide the necessary strength to encourage us in our endeavour. The techniques presented here should be used in conjunction with professional healing strategies, not necessarily in lieu of them

The success of each method depends upon one's own attitudes, beliefs, use of the will and creative use of one's innate powers. We create for ourselves what we ask for — sickness and pain, or life, health and wholeness.

* *Ibid*, p. 236.

CHAPTER 4

RELAXATION TRAINING & BEHAVIOUR MODIFICATION
The Health Benefits of Video

Andrew & Jacqueline Staite

The woman lounges in front of a television set. She is wearing headphones so that she is not disturbed as she enjoys the soothing music and mellow voice. Her sleepy gaze is held by coloured waves and spiral effects. She is losing weight. In six weeks she has already lost 16 kilograms — without calorie counting, willpower, forbidden food lists, or strenuous exercise.

Other clients watch programmes for anxiety abatement, stopping smoking, or to develop learning abilities and overcome examination nerves.* The common aim of all the programmes is to teach a healthy and appropriate management of stress.

Stress has become a modern obsession. Everyone seems to be jogging, saunaing, meditating or pill-popping because of it. But what is stress?

The term was brought into use by Professor Hans Selye, Director of the Institute of Experimental Medicine and Surgery of the University of Montreal. He said stress was 'the rate of wear and tear on the body'. Confusion has continued to this day as to whether stress is the factor that causes the wear and tear, the process of wear and tear, or the resulting damage done. Selye more specifically used the term 'stress response'. He also called it the 'General Adaptation Syndrome' (GAS) which has three phases: an alarm reaction, a stage of resistance, and a stage of exhaustion. A stress cause, or stressor, mobilises the GAS by activating the sympathetic part of the autonomic nervous system. Hormones bring about marked physiological changes in the body, often referred to as the 'fight-or-flight syndrome', because our ancestors could utilise the burst of energy involved to fight off an attacker or run away.

'Fight-or-flight' is often inappropriate in modern, Western life, for example when stress results from the arrival of the phone bill. In fact it's a rather inappropriate term, because the syndrome referred to occurs as a reaction to pleasant, as well as unpleasant stimuli. For example, if we were to win first prize in a lottery, our physiological response would probably be the same as if we had just been threatened by a gunman.

Selye said that he worked best, himself, under stress. He divided people into 'hares' and 'tortoises' and said that people in the hare group needed stress and a fast pace of life. He therefore classed beneficial stress as 'eustress', and detrimental stress as 'distress'. One man's eustress is another man's distress.

Later research has shown that the stress response occurs to some degree in any novel situation, because novelty is stimulation. It produces the orienteering response — that

* This video system is marketed by Autogenic Relaxation Training Programmes, in Australia, and by Therapeutic Visualisation, Ltd, in England.

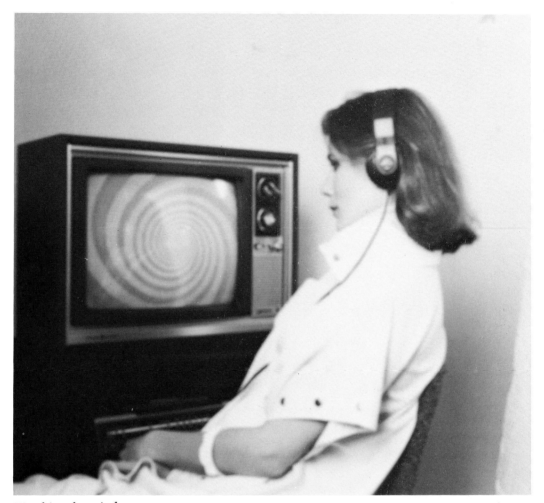

Watching the spiral pattern

is, we pay attention. We assess for usefulness, edibility and danger. It appears that our stress response is essential because, deprived of all stimulation, as when placed in a sensory deprivation tank, we invent our own stimulation by hallucinating.

When the stress response is minor, we do not notice any symptoms. The greater the stimulation, the more symptoms we notice. Holmes and Rahe's scale of life changes is a guide to the amount of stress attached to events — such as marriage, moving house, emigration, loss of a job, death of a spouse — which can so quickly overload our ability to cope. It seems that within a period, such as any year, we only have tolerance for a certain amount of stress before exhaustion sets in, and the accumulation of countless little stresses — Christmas, broken shoe laces, the TV news — all add up and use up tolerance.

In *The Human Zoo*, Desmond Morris shows that modern humans are engaged in the 'Stimulus Struggle': 'If we abandon it, or tackle it badly, we are in serious trouble'. We are trying to maintain the optimum level of stimulation — not the maximum, but that level which is most beneficial, somewhere between under- and over-stimulation. The bank clerk, the machine operator and the housewife are all vulnerable to under-stimulation, or boredom; the airtraffic controller is vulnerable to overstimulation, which he calls stress. Those who are bored seek excitement, those who are 'stressed' seek relaxation. The person with a stressful job only wants to relax when work is over, but the person with a boring job can't wait to get on with something exciting after work. It ought to be simple enough to achieve a balance, so why are so many of us so extraordinarily depressed or anxious? According to US scientists, 'stress is now known to be a major contributor, either directly or indirectly, to coronary heart disease, cancer, lung ailments, accidental injuries, cirrhosis of the liver and suicide' (*Time*, 6 June 1983). Why does our species have especial difficulty in coping with stress?

Desmond Morris points out that, in zoos, some specialised creatures, such as the eagle, adapt very well to under-stimulation as long as the ideal form of food is provided daily. They need only one essential form of stimulation — the eagle is satisfied as long as he can sink his claws into a freshly-killed rabbit.

Another group of animals he dubs the opportunists. These suffer greatly in zoos because they have evolved to thrive on novelty. The opportunists include dogs, raccoons, monkeys, apes and man. They all have an insatiable need to explore and investigate. Any new phenomenon may provide food, or be useful for survival. They have curiosity built into their nervous systems. Man, in particular, has a very high need for stimulation.

In modern cities man has tried to control every facet of the environment. He regulates room temperatures, locks his doors and relies on law and order for security. The welfare state ensures that he will not starve. His monotonous modern diet is easily obtained from the supermarket. As his nervous system cries out for stimulation, he may create unnecessary problems — getting in late for work and rowing with the boss, having affairs and breaking up marriages. Above all, he decides to pursue inessential material possessions — cars, furniture, stereo equipment, boats — even if (perhaps especially if) he has to get into debt for them. His entertainment becomes more and more exciting — video libraries abound, with pornography and thrillers most in demand. (He can be terrified in the security of his own armchair.)

So is stress good for us — in the right amount? In *Magical Child* Joseph Chiltern Pearce states: 'Stress is the way intelligence grows'. He explains that, under stress, the brain immediately grows massive numbers of new connecting links between the neurons which enables learning. However, 'bear in mind that, although the stressed mind-brain grows in ability and the unstressed one lags behind, the *overstressed* one collapses into physiological shock'. Something is essential to maintain the optimum level of stress. This, of course, is relaxation.

If Hans Selye was the guru of stress, then Herbert Benson must be the guru of relaxation. In his Harvard Medical School research, Professor Benson showed that relaxation is a physiological response which may be induced at will and in *The Relaxation Response* his research results indicated that excessive stress could cause, or aggravate, hypertension (high blood pressure) and its related diseases, atherosclerosis, heart attack and stroke. He then examined the nature of the relaxation response, showing that physiological changes as remarkable as those seen in the 'fight-or-flight' response occur during true relaxation, including lowering of oxygen consumption, metabolism, heart rate and blood pressure, and increased production of alpha brain waves. A marked decrease in blood lactate was found. Blood lactate is a substance produced by the metabolism of skeletal muscles and of particular interest because of its association with anxiety. Pitts and McLure, of Washington University School of Medicine showed that blood lactate injections increased anxiety attacks in anxiety neurotics.

Learning to cope with forays into the unknown

Basically, the relaxation response is the reverse of the stress response — relaxation reduces the activity of the sympathetic nervous system. The stress and relaxation responses need to be balanced, like yin and yang. Prolonged relaxation can lead to a desperate need for stimulation; prolonged stress can lead to exhaustion, or 'nervous breakdown'.

During novel situations, or stress, our brains prepare to assimilate information as we learn to cope. This process converts the unknown into the acceptable known, so increasing the stable base of familiarity from which we can make forays into the unpredictable. This is why most people desire a home — it is the physical embodiment of the known. As we grow and learn, our base, with which we are more relaxed, grows too, allowing us to explore more areas of unpredictability (stress-producing). Ideally, the stress response is regularly reversed by the relaxation response. The more often the relaxation response is invoked, the less violent are the swings back and forth, between anxiety and exhaustion.

It appears that each of us is born with a certain genetic tolerance for stress and that low or high tolerance is passed on in families. (Studies are complicated by the undeniable environmental factors, particularly that overstressed parents overload their children with anxiety and teach poor coping mechanisms.) Similarly, we have a muscular potential, but the interchange of contraction and relaxation must take place regularly and frequently if the muscles are to develop to that potential. (A weight lifter can only contract a muscle for a short period of time, or damage to the tissue makes further practice impossible — too much stress makes the muscle weaker.) In the same way, the use of both stress and relaxation makes the mind stronger, the person more adaptable to change.

Most of us can produce the stress response in ourselves easily enough, and in doing so we are fulfilling a vital need. However, we have become inept at producing the relaxation response, and have come to depend on periodic bouts of exhaustion or on chemical aids, such as alcohol and tranquillisers. We have even woven all of these into our social fabric, in the form of weekends, holidays and social drinking. Tranquilliser popping has not yet become quite fashionable but, as a very large number of any general practitioner's patients in the waiting room are there for tranquilliser prescriptions, it has become the norm. A US president's wife and a host of Hollywood stars have already made attendance at withdrawal clinics fashionable. And another type of pill-popping has grown popular lately — the 'natural remedy', B-complexes, anti-stress formulas and herbal teas. While these are preferable to drugs, the belief that stress is a disease which needs to be cured conceals the value of stress when balanced with relaxation.

Professor Benson's research into the relaxation response covered several efficient techniques of relaxation training, including TM, Autogenic Training, Progressive Relaxation, Hypnosis, and Sentic Cycles. He found that these methods had four common elements; a quiet environment; an object to dwell upon; a passive attitude; and a comfortable position. Whether called meditation, contemplation, quietude, prayer, yoga or autogenics, methods of relaxation training have existed in all cultures in all ages. Some are more effective than others, some are easier to learn.

The system is based upon the observation that most of us in Western society have already come to accept television as a conditioning medium. Benson's four common elements are easily achieved by television: isolation from distraction in the TV room; the TV screen to focus attention; the passivity of the TV-watcher; and the comfort of a soft armchair.

Whereas normal television programmes are designed to excite attention — if not to provoke with controversy, to thrill or to amuse — the Autogenic programmes are designed to relax. In order to keep the attention of the viewer without causing stress, they avoid soporific boredom and stimulation. Abstract images of colour and motion maintain passive concentration while a soothing voice guides the subject through muscular exercises (carried out while reclining in a chair). Traditional progressive relaxation or reciprocal relaxation, pranayama yoga and other breathing exercises are combined with Professor Schultz's autogenics.

A neurologist, Schultz discovered that repeated visualisation of some of the sensations associated with relaxation — particularly those of heaviness and warmth in the limbs — could bring about the relaxation response at will. Guided imagery should be used at first to form mental pathways, after which relaxation at will becomes a reliable mechanism. As the aim is to be able to produce relaxation from within the self, he called the technique autogenics, meaning self-generated. In the 1950s, with

Professor Luthe, he added colour visualisation to the system and it was shown that such visualisation can be used to alleviate anxiety.

Some people, especially those who complain that they cannot relax, may find colour difficult to visualise. This is why coloured images are provided during the Staite programmes. It has been found that visualisation abilities can be developed by first concentrating on the appropriate image in the external world. The use of colour in the right way is also an excellent relaxant. It is used in the same sort of way that Dr Manfred Clynes uses Sentic Cycles. (Sentic Cycles is a technique by which the subject passes through a variety of emotional states, such as anger, grief, joy and love, in order to improve emotional control and the relaxation response.) When colour visualisation follows the spectrum, dwelling on certain hues, anxiety abatement is remarkable. Generally, red is energising; yellow, cheering; green, healing; and blue, soothing. Violet can be used to bring about a meditative trance-like state of altered awareness.

In the Relaxation Series of video programmes, visualisation exercises develop feelings of self-worth, prosperity, security, and power over negative thought. They may be used in the home, but visits to a licensed centre are preferable so appropriate counselling may be given. Doctors, psychologists, and other therapists have incorporated these programmes into their practices.

The first programme in the series, Creative Visualisation, is a pleasant guided fantasy which introduces the subject to visualisation and uses the most reliable biofeedback device — one's own sensations — to develop relaxation skills.

The second programme, Health and Vitality, combines Eastern and Western visualisation and suggestions for physical well-being and the promotion of healing.

The third, Confidence and Optimism, which has proven very popular, is effective in developing a more positive outlook and self-image. This programme is very useful when incorporated in Slimming and Stop-Smoking courses.

The fourth programme, Emotional Growth, is deeply relaxing. It uses a long colour visualisation sequence combined with suggestion to reduce anxiety and develop self-awareness. Because it increases receptivity to positive affirmation, this programme in particular promotes liberation from dependence on alcohol, tranquillisers, tobacco and other drugs. Suggestions to this effect are made while another suggestion associates a simple gesture with instant relaxation, thus enabling the practised subject to relax at traffic lights, in the bank queue, or at the work bench.

Another course, the Study Series, is designed to enhance learning ability and improve examination performance. Used in conjunction with the Relaxation series, it has proven of great benefit to secondary-school and tertiary students. The first programme, Successful Studying, shows how to use the relaxation response to aid concentration and improve motivation. The second, Overcoming Examination Nerves, explains the benefit of using stress as energy, while controlling it by relaxation to the optimum level, so maintaining clear reasoning and factual recall. Both programmes employ visualisation to develop confidence and memory, and to reduce anxiety. They were prepared with the aid of a practising school psychologist and have produced excellent results.

The type of visualisation exercise used in all Autogenic Relaxation video programmes is already accepted into psychotherapeutic orthodoxy. Visualisation, for example, is the basis of the system devised by Carl Simonton, to aid chemo- and radio-therapy in the treatment of cancer. (He requires the patient to imagine his defender cells hunting down and killing off the tumour cells, using whatever imagery is most acceptable to the individual, such as white knights and dragons.) At the Seattle Children's Orthopaedic Hospital, Dr William Womack pioneered the use of relaxation and visualisation to help youngsters overcome migraine. In fact, more and more clinics around the world are using this approach, whether in the treatment of gastric ulcers, colitis or Raynaud's disease (a circulatory disorder causing painfully cold extremities). The English psychic and healer Matthew Manning similarly teaches self-healing which he calls Creative Visualisation.

The use of video has many advantages over other techniques. Most subjects are much less apprehensive about sitting and watching television than in joining in classes or one-to-one sessions with a therapist. Classes may induce anxiety over performance, as each person falls into the pupil role and tries to relax correctly. It is difficult to let go completely while being observed, and perhaps judged, by an instructor. In the one-to-one situation irrational fears of hypnosis — owing more to fiction than reality — may make relaxation impossible. A TV set, on the other hand, is non-judgemental and cannot have evil designs upon you. The standardisation of sessions is reassuring, as each subject knows that many others have previously been through the same session. Headphones improve the quality of a session, by excluding outside noise and interruptions and by enhancing the sound effects. At a centre, screens may be used to provide privacy for subjects watching the same programme.

To encourage regular practice of the relaxation response and continue support of behaviour modification, the Staite system also provides audio tapes to accompany each course. These give shorter sessions which may be enjoyed once or twice each day, in the home. Regular practice of relaxation is essential. Professor Benson proved the claim of TV meditators that two short sessions daily maintained improved health and emotional benefits. He also showed that such a routine could utilise any of various relaxation techniques effectively, but when the routine was broken for only a few days, benefits diminished.

Meditation is a bit like jogging — it is usually begun with enthusiasm but soon forgotten. Both practices tend to be goal orientated, pursued in order to become healthier or smarter. The actual process can become boring, and if this happens rationalisations arise — 'I'll do it tomorrow' — and soon the routine is lost.

Video and audio induced relaxation, on the other hand, can avoid this pitfall. While the subject pays conscious attention, the feelings and imagery are sufficiently pleasant. With repetition, it may happen that the conscious mind ceases to pay attention, but the subconscious continues to benefit, as is shown by the results.

With the Relaxation course, most subjects are interested in improving their ability to relax, or in alleviating the symptoms of over-stress. The success of the method must therefore be judged by their subjective reports. However, the Slimming series has given rise to very tangible results. Many clients have lost large amounts of weight, without dieting or calorie counting.

Earlier, it was mentioned that many people, desperate to be able to relax, turn to alcohol or tranquillisers. Both of these cause tremendous problems of addiction in our society, but perhaps even more widespread and addictive is compulsive eating.

Compulsive eating may be the oldest of all tranquillisers. Chewing has a soothing effect (which accounts for the popularity of chewing gum in the West, and betel in the East). Having a full stomach relieves the discomfort caused by the overproduction of gastric fluids resulting from anxiety. The drowsiness known to most of us after a heavy Christmas dinner is a very noticeable sign of the hormonal changes brought about by overeating. This effect can become addictive.

The whole process of eating and digestion occupies the parasympathetic part of the autonomic nervous system. The parasympathetic and the sympathetic systems are like opposite sides of a set of scales; when one is occupied the other is also affected. Or to use another simile, when the parasympathetic is engaged, the sympathetic gear becomes disengaged. As it is the sympathetic that manifests the stress response, stress may be reduced by eating. This is a simplification, because, if food is excitingly different both systems may be involved. But a remarkable thing about compulsive eaters is that, although they appear obsessed with food, during eating they become inattentive — they hardly taste the food and eat more quickly than normal. While relaxed by the eating process, they may daydream about what they are going to have next.

So compulsive eaters, especially if they nibble all day, should be more relaxed than other people. Yes, some do show higher than average stress-tolerance. They fit the traditional fat and jolly stereotype. However, fat is no longer culturally acceptable. The giant slimming industry pours vast amounts of money into making fat people feel ugly.

The ideal model is very slim — even skinny — and film stars who put on weight write their confessions for the papers and talk about the latest diet that will make them sexy and lovable once more. Overweight women in particular, as women are still primarily judged by their sexual attractiveness, suffer shame and despair. Over and over again they try the miracle diets that will transform them from frogs into princesses. Each diet works — if at all — only temporarily, because it is only a symptom remover. Like taking aspirin for a headache, which takes away the pain for a while and diverts attention from the cause, dieting confuses the issue. The real problem is overeating and dieting does nothing to remove the cause of that problem, whether it be anxiety, conditioning, habit or social pressure.

The typical compulsive eater is trapped within a cycle. When he or she eats, anxiety decreases a little. Later guilt adds to anxiety, and the temporarily anaesthetised stress response becomes painful. The trusty coping mechanism comes automatically to mind, and a craving for food must be satisfied.

Pressure from well-meaning family and friends leads to another diet. For a short time the pain of guilt is lessened by the pride of achievement, but soon the misery of 'cold turkey', the drudgery of counting calories and weighing food, and the resentment and feeling of victimisation as other people enjoy normal food ostentatiously all around, causes binge eating or abandonment of the diet. Worst of all, dieting can change tastes, leading to an obsession with the most fattening of foods (forbidden fruit).

Even that small minority that actually lose weight and keep it off for a while, must continue to resist temptation. They 'watch their weight' and weight-watching can develop into a neurosis akin to paranoia — 'The world is full of demon foods, and I am weak and afraid'. To seek support in numbers, they flock to groups. They are taught that it is possible to diet forever — it is only a matter of habit — but for the anxious eater the only way that it can become a habit is if it replaces eating as a coping mechanism to deal with stress. Some people do manage this. Whenever they are anxious they starve themselves even more and, in extreme cases, die of anorexia nervosa.

The medical profession now largely disapproves of crash dieting. It recommends a sensible, slow diet, paying close attention to nutrition. On the face of it this is an improvement, but it is only like substituting paracetamol for aspirin. It still treats only the symptom. In fact, 'sensible' diets remain unpopular because they prolong the misery of dieting and promise no magic results. As the urge to overeat has not been removed, willpower is still necessary, and people are prepared to use willpower for short periods only.

There is an alternative, however. It involves treating the cause of overeating, not the symptom. Relaxation training, in itself, can bring about remarkable changes in behaviour. As the subject learns how to relax at will, the need to control stress by eating diminishes. However, eating is a complex business; everyone has eating habits; some people have food allergies; many are addicted to sugar. All of these problems are dealt with specifically in the Slimming video series. Emotional recall, well-being and aversion visualisation change deeply-rooted habits and attitudes. As compulsive eaters tend to pay little attention to the taste and texture of food as they eat it, they are taught to enjoy these more, eating more slowly so that the appetite centre in the brain has time to register that hunger has been satisfied.

Anxious eaters are usually delighted with the course because, as well as losing weight, they lose anxiety, become more relaxed and able to cope with life. One reported that she was pleased to have lost weight but even more pleased that she was no longer terrified of heights. This is not to suggest that all compulsive eaters are anxiety cases.

Some have merely been conditioned since birth, usually by overweight parents whose concept of normal body size is like their own. In such an environment, large meals are served without question, and the wrong sort of food is staple fare.

Overfed (especially bottle-fed) babies develop more fat cells, which makes it easier for their bodies to store fat, and in adulthood they may complain that they put on weight if they so much as look at a cream bun. It is their idea of normal eating that is the problem. After a few sessions of the Slimming course they find they are eating less and that this feels quite normal.

Some older subjects have gradually put on weight over the years. These people are not, strictly speaking, compulsive eaters. They may only be eating a little more than they need, but it is enough to accumulate. This problem shows up particularly in middle age as energy needs decrease.

Our modern way of living by the clock has affected our eating patterns. Instead of eating whenever we are hungry — and stopping as soon as hunger is satisfied — we tend to eat because it is mealtime. We eat 'the usual amount', yet our bodies' needs vary from day to day, according to biorhythm, energy output and, in women, the time of the month. Eating by the clock conditions us into being able to eat whether hungry or not. Other stimuli, such as the sounds and smells of cooking, television commercials, coffee breaks, alcohol and socialising may all trigger off a craving for food — a false hunger. Just as Pavlov's dogs became hungry and salivated at the sound of a bell after they had learned to associate that sound with mealtimes, so we have learned to feel hunger although our bodies don't need food.

Even if the original weight problem can be traced back to parental conditioning or 'false hunger' habits, overweight people usually become anxious eaters once they begin to diet. Dieting may begin in the teenage years, when the conflicts between parental values and those of the rest of society are strongly felt. Sexual anxieties, a trouble to most teenagers, are acute for those who feel unattractive because overweight. Dieting is a heavy burden for these youngsters, as they see their friends apparently revelling in junk food (junk food advertisements are mainly aimed at teenagers).

Relaxation training can remove false urges to eat, whether these come from past conditioning, habit or anxiety. Stress levels can be controlled by the natural process of relaxation, instead of the unnatural one of overeating. Ingrained attitudes and rationalisations can be removed by appropriate visualisation and suggestion. Subjects report that they are slowing down while eating, and enjoying eating more when they are hungry. They are forgetting about food the rest of the time. They become more aware of their own inner feelings, whether these are stress and relaxation or true hunger demands. Self-image is subtly altered until the subject no longer identifies with the overweight group. Feelings of predestined failure disappear as self-confidence grows.

One subject summed up her own progress this way. 'I've lost about 20 kilograms, but the really important thing is I'm not dieting anymore. I don't think about food all the time. If I feel like having a piece of cheesecake, I have it. But I only have one piece. I don't eat the whole cake anymore. Sometimes I have a chocolate biscuit. Why not? I'm *normal!*'

Food preferences are changed by the course. Many subjects no longer want even one chocolate biscuit. They have lost their main problem — the craving for sugar. Many nutritionists now believe that sugar is addictive. Certainly it seems that the more people have, the more they want. Sugar is added to a huge number of processed foods and the quantity consumed per person in the last century has increased alarmingly. It has been linked to health problems such as heart disease, kidney and urinary problems, diabetes and hypoglycaemia. In 1815, each person ate about 7.0 pounds (3.5 kilograms) per year. By 1960, it had increased to 120 pounds (54.5 kilograms) per year, and since then sugar has been added to even more products.

Hypoglycaemia has been called the disease of Western society. It means low blood sugar. At first it was recommended that patients eat more sugar but this only made the problem worse. Now sugar is forbidden, and a high protein-complex carbohydrate diet is prescribed. But to a person used to high sugar consumption, such a diet can be very hard to tolerate. The stressful nature of any diet, as it entails a forced rejection of the dieter's habitual coping mechanism of overeating, leads to a rise in the stress hormone epinephrine (adrenalin) in the bloodstream and thus to a lowering of glycogen in the liver and muscles (the energy store) and therefore to a greater craving for food.

Relaxation training is essential to reduce this effect. The behaviour modification made possible by the use of visualisation and suggestion can successfully alter habitual food preferences and develop an enjoyment of healthier wholefoods.

Another video course is Stop Smoking. It has a remarkably high success rate because of its emphasis on relaxation, rather than on the perils of smoking. Surveys have shown that most smokers consider relaxation to be a prime motive for smoking. At least, they claim that it reduces tension although this subjective judgement is at odds with findings on the chemical effects of tobacco smoke. Nicotine, in particular, is a stimulant and one theory has it that, in response to the irritation of nicotine, the body produces its own morphine-like endorphins. Although the effect is not sufficient to produce the relaxation response, endorphins may be addictive. If so, the withdrawal symptoms a smoker begins to feel after an hour or two without smoking may be complicated — withdrawal from a stimulant as well as a relaxant.

The physical withdrawal effects do not last longer than two or three days, however, and do not account for the prolonged craving that is felt by most would-be ex-smokers who are trying a willpower method of giving up smoking.

The tension reduction that smokers notice after lighting up may first be attributed to an easing of chemical withdrawal, but other forms of nicotine supply, such as nicotine chewing gum or tablets, have proven very unpopular. A more adequate explanation of the tension reduction effect is a psychological one. It has been found that all animals relieve their tensions to some extent by performing repetitive actions which, because they have become familiar, have also become comforting.

The routine of smoking — twenty, thirty or forty times a day — is just such a repetitive action. And that is why every smoker smokes more at times of greater stress, and less when relaxed.

When a subject begins the Stop Smoking course he is told that he is not expected to give up smoking straight away. The first thing is to learn to relax at will. Interestingly enough, during the first few sessions, even if these use only the Relaxation series, the subject's smoking decreases markedly. However, to remove the smoking habit altogether, the Stop Smoking video programmes take the subject through appropriate guided imagery and suggestion. For example, one's earliest reactions to smoking are brought to the surface so that the insensitivity of habit is reduced. In particular, self-confidence is increased to overcome negative feelings and rationalisations. The subject begins to identify with non-smokers as his peer group. Recovery from the poisoning of the body is promoted by cleansing health visualisation.

This course contrasts markedly with willpower techniques, especially the group system where lectures and films on the horrors of lung disease and other terrors are supposed to strengthen resolve, but also serve to raise stress levels. (Smokers who fail

to give up smoking after attending one of these horror shows may actually be in greater danger of contracting a smoking-related disease than before, because over-stress reduces the body's immune response.)

The Relaxation course also contrasts with aids such as drugs and acupuncture, which, although they can reduce the urge to smoke temporarily, do nothing to change deep-rooted habits and coping mechanisms. The Stop Smoking course is so successful that it has been featured in the press frequently, and is recommended by many doctors, psychologists, naturopaths and health departments.

More programmes will be added to augment the existing range of courses, but what the Staites have produced so far is a very useful, rounded psychological health package suitable for home use, or in the office of a therapist. It is an aid to other forms of therapy, and has proven itself effective in breaking dependence on tranquillisers, alcohol, tobacco, sugar and overeating. Each programme is about half an hour long, yet achieves rapid and deep relaxation through the use of soothing visuals, the beautifully mellow voice of Ramsay McLean, and the 'anti-frantic' music of Steven Halpern.

Audio tapes are also available, to supplement the training given by the video programmes or as an independent relaxation aid. One of these, Child's Dreamtime, is designed to be enjoyed by children from four to fourteen, and develops self-confidence, learning skills and stress management. One side of this tape can be used to get children off to sleep when they are overexcited, and helps to reduce night fears and bad dreams. Hyperactivity in children is a syndrome resulting from a variety of causes, some of which will need orthomolecular or other treatments, but it has been found that Child's Dreamtime can reduce hyperactivity in many cases. Some four-year-olds are already able to respond to the Relaxation video series.

The Relaxation Training work has been summed up by psychotherapist Peter Houghton, Director of the Birmingham Settlement, who said, 'Therapeutic Visualisation Programmes are excellent for relaxation and an essential first step towards health'.

CHAPTER 5

NEURO-LINGUISTIC PROGRAMMING

Christopher R. Collingwood
& Alex Nicolson

Neuro-linguistic programming is the study of the structure of subjective experience and a study of the process by which we make sense of our world.

It emerged as a result of the work by Dr John Grinder, a linguist, and Richard Bandler, a mathematician who later became a Gestalt therapist.

They spent several years studying the interactions of some of America's most successful therapists, including Milton Erickson, regarded as the father of modern clinical hypnosis, Fritz Perls, the originator of Gestalt therapy, and Virginia Satir, a world-renowned family therapist, author, lecturer and consultant.

NLP was a by-product of this research into language structure and Bandler and Grinder, with their associates, drew on many modalities including cybernetics, linguistics, Gestalt and psychology in formulating the NLP model. They found that these communication patterns were useful, not only in the field of therapy, but also in business, education, and appropriately, in the areas of negotiation and mediation. As a tool for inner healing and transformation it is, without doubt, an exciting and innovative model. *Psychology Today* (1979), for example, has described NLP as 'the most powerful vehicle for change in existence'.

WHAT IT IS

The title itself takes us part way to an understanding. 'Neuro' comes from the Greek for neuron or nerve and indicates the neurological process implicit in all behaviour; 'Linguistic' from the Latin for language and pertains to the structuring and sequencing of behaviour through communication. And 'Programming' refers to the process of organising our behaviour to obtain specific outcomes. Together they imply a rounded approach to achieving mastery of our often habituated behavioural and thought patterns.

And for many of us, much of our behaviour is habitual, often patterns of behaviour learned early in life and now merely responses to unseen stimuli — failing to satisfy our needs or to get the outcomes we desire. So, if disease, depression, anxiety, lack of self-esteem or states of being in which we experience less than optimum health and/ or the ability to function anywhere near our peak are accepted as part of the human condition, then we lay cause for our ailments on a wide variety of external factors.

As a consequence there are unbelievably vast amounts of money spent on health care, insurance and research, and more knowledge of disease is available and more varieties of healing techniques are available than ever before. Yet, in spite of this, and

Neuro-linguistic programming analyses our gestures

not for a moment detracting from the many magnificent breakthroughs in disease control, very few of us experience a predominantly satisfying state of being. And of course, the results of our inability to experience in a meaningful and satisfying way can be pain, sorrow, depression and physical and mental disharmony.

The unique contribution of NLP is that it is presented as a model, a description of how something works — in this case, the process of behaviour or the context in which behaviour occurs. Its uniqueness lies in that it deals with what is useful, with what works in relation to our ongoing experience and not with theory or explanations of why things work.

It is based on sensory-grounded experience of the individual and can thus be applied to any behaviour or any individual. It makes no attempt to comment on or judge behaviour and in NLP exercises the subject doesn't even have to reveal his or her experience. Rather, it enables us to experience more choice in our behaviour and to have access to more useful abilities and latent potentialities and thus gain more satisfactory outcomes in our daily lives. In fact one of the most elegant aspects of NLP is that it deals with context rather than content. So, at the 'neuro' and the 'linguistic' levels, it helps us become aware of specific sensory details in our everyday experience, start to expand our horizons and become more attuned to our own rhythmic cycles.

Although NLP is not the panacea for all of mankind's ills, it is certainly one of the most positive and powerful new innovative approaches available today for initiating change and transformation in a satisfying and lasting way.

Previous attempts to describe and/or understand human behaviour have invariably based their methodology on the hard sciences, that is with the scientist or observer looking 'out there': the effect of the observer was not considered to have any bearing on what was observed. NLP, on the other hand, takes into account the presence of the observer and that the actions and responses of the observer influence what is being observed. The NLP practitioner, in working with a client, is himself in a relating interaction and is thus open to experiencing change himself. While acknowledging his own boundaries, he is able to observe closely the behavioural and linguistic patterns of the client and he is trained to 'locate' what Bandler and Grinder termed deletions, distortions and generalisations. These patterns of language and behaviour are a guide to the way we represent our experience of reality and, using the 'meta model', derived from linguistic theory and of which more later, the NLP practitioner becomes the navigator in effectively guiding clients through limitations in their representations, thus allowing for more choices in their behaviour and the ability to generate more satisfactory outcomes.

Before discussing this linguistic model, however, we must pay some attention to the concepts of 'calibration' and 'anchoring'.

CALIBRATION

The greater part of our ongoing experience is determined by the manner with which we internally represent our world.

If we wish to open ourselves to new experiences or to succeed by choice with things which previously only happened 'by chance', to systematically experience more positive outcomes, or to eliminate outmoded and unsatisfactory behaviour, NLP offers a variety of useful tools.

'Calibration' is a very useful starting point. NLP practitioners are trained to observe minute behavioural cues which externally represent internal states. For example, we may experience fluctuating emotional states without being aware of any external cause. Something, either an out of awareness external factor, or an internal state has triggered the feelings. There are certain behavioural patterns that accompany differing emotional states and while it is possible to generalise these, each of us will display unique individual traits. NLP suggests that it is useful to monitor very carefully our behaviour which is the apparent external representation of our internal state.

We would like to mention here that becoming aware of our own behaviour and opening ourselves to change can be a little scary. To break familiar patterns and take that first tentative step into new territory can be accompanied by uncertainty and anxiety. However, we would suggest that by having read this far you have taken that step. We can only say from personal experience that new choices and flexibility in our lives outweigh any initial insecurity which is only a signpost on the pathway to new learnings.

As an introduction to calibration, we would like you to try the following procedures. You can either do this on your own or with another person.

Sit in a comfortable position and as you access the following emotional states we wish you to observe carefully the following.

Firstly, your breathing, the location and rhythm — and any change.

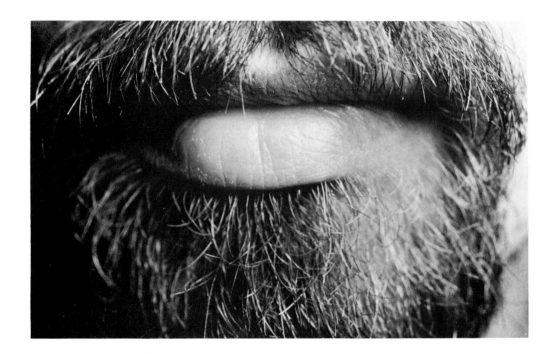

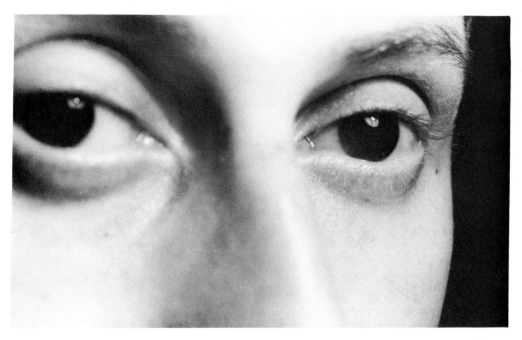

Secondly, muscle tension; any tightening or relaxation in your jaw, your stomach, your forearms and hands, your shoulders; or any desire to move your feet or cross your legs. Where do your eyes look (even if closed), and does your head follow?

Thirdly, any internal sensations, especially in the abdominal area; also the neck, jaw and mouth; and also check your palms for perspiration.

If you are doing this with another person, look for breathing shifts, facial tension or relaxation, skin colour change and even lip-size change.

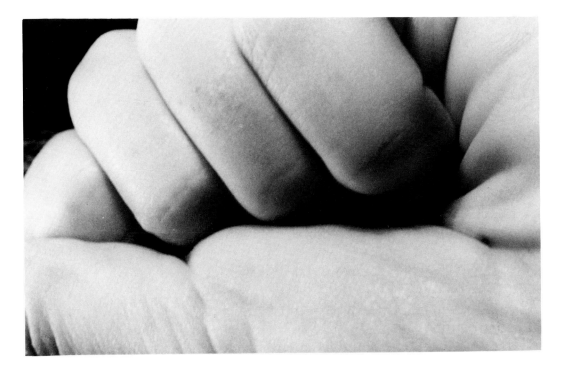

To start with we would like you to remember a time when you were angry: imagine/ listen, etc. Take your time and monitor any body sensations that occur as you sit with that experience. Then think of a time when you were really happy. Again just be with the experience and monitor the changing sensory awareness. Repeat this with the experience of being sad, being loved or nurtured, frustrated, exhilarated and any other emotional states you wish to try.

If you are doing this with someone else you may also try the following. One of you think of someone you like very much for a few minutes and then someone/thing you don't like. The other person monitors very carefully any change in the external behaviour, however minute. After a bit of practice you may ask questions like 'Who was the person of the two who you saw most recently?' and be able to determine which one it was simply by observing the calibrations.

The usefulness of calibrating is that, by having this awareness of our external behaviour, we have the choice to alter these body cues and thereby change our internal state. You will no doubt all be familiar with having taken a big deep breath when feelings of anger or frustration started to arise. This dissipates the feelings somewhat and allows you more time to assess the situation and choose your response.

Also, we are all familiar with other people's behaviour. We can tell what mood someone close to us is experiencing by merely observing their outward behaviour. For example, it is not the time to ask the boss for a salary increase when he is stalking about like a caged bear with his head down, his jaw set and his fists clenched. He doesn't have to verbalise that he is upset. He shows it.

So our outward behaviour expresses our inner feelings and it is useful to observe situations where we don't achieve our desired outcomes, or where something holds us back from doing something we think we would like to do, and calibrate our sensory behaviour. Often, by acknowledging limiting feelings when confronting certain situations, we are halfway to successfully changing them. Being open and honest with our own feelings, both the ones we like and the ones we don't like, is the pathway to accepting ourselves as human and as humans subject to emotions and feelings. But as Virginia Satir says in her book *Making Contact*, 'the universally used patterns of behaviour were learned and were not in our genes. Since they were learned, then at any point in our lives we can change'. She goes on to say that 'one change already influences other parts'. That means we can start anywhere.

Calibration is a feedback mechanism. A good comedian is possibly one of the best examples of someone who utilises calibration skills. By monitoring audience response he knows when to change his jokes or offer more of the same. But perhaps most importantly, he perceives the right timing for the punchline: the audience possibly thinks that he has a natural gift, but more usually this skill is the result of much practice with a wide range of audiences. This art of calibrating audience response can make all the difference between an ordinary comedian who on the right night gets lots of laughs, and the really great master who can manipulate any audience at will.

By having an awareness of our own behaviour through calibration we then have the opportunity to change behaviours that are not working to achieve our desired outcomes. The next section deals with 'anchoring', which provides the flexibility to change our behaviours. That includes our internal states, emotions, feelings, etc. By using this tool we have the power to manipulate ourselves to achieve well-being.

Flexibility in behaviour can be disconcerting because many of us identify with our behaviour. For example, the phrases, 'I couldn't do that, that's just not me', or 'This is the best way to do that', imply lack of choice, or being in a stuck state. We are not suggesting that you change a behaviour that is getting your desired outcome, but rather that you observe how closely you identify your behaviour. Because we do something stupid once in a while, that does not make us stupid. Conversely we may be competent at certain things but utterly useless at others. Can we then be identified as competent? A friend of ours is an electronics expert, but his cooking ability stops at buttering a slice of bread.

So for many of us, we tend to limit our experiences to those areas where we are competent, where we feel secure, and not to attempt things where we might get to feel foolish or insecure. With anchoring and other tools of NLP we can often cross into areas of experience without the pain or fear that stops us now. By gaining this flexibility in our behaviour we can enhance our self-image and expand our experience, opening up pathways to a more rewarding and fulfilling state of being. This is what we understand as inner healing. We are suggesting that personal growth comes from new experiences, learning to do something new, or doing something familiar in a new way.

ANCHORING

Anchoring is the NLP term for a process that is fairly easy to comprehend and which in fact most of us experience unconsciously all the time.

At any given moment of our experience we are accessing information through all our five senses: visual, auditory, kinaesthetic (feeling), gustatory (taste) and olfactory (smell). Because these last two senses are not as dominant in the process of gathering and sorting information, Bandler and Grinder classed these together under the heading olfactory and then used the mathematical term 4-tuple to describe these four aspects of sensory experience.

An anchor is a stimulus which consists of one or more (in which case read anchors) part of the 4-tuple of a previous experience. This stimulus of any part of the 4-tuple allows access to all the other parts. We may or may not experience all or any of these other aspects of the 4-tuple in consciousness. And in fact we do not: if we did our conscious mind would be overloaded.

One of our favourite analogies is that old romantic saying — 'Darling, they're playing our song'. For many of us a certain tune will evoke nostalgic memories. As part of this memory we may experience pleasant feeling and may even have an image of the original experience. For others the feeling may be more poignant. Whichever way they are, they are another aspect of the 4-tuple which was triggered in this analogy by an auditory anchor. Given the appropriate conditions we could recall all aspects of this or any other experience. In an unfamiliar situation, such as is encountered by travellers, some people experience homesickness. Lack of one's usual surroundings (anchors) may precipitate internal memories (anchors) of an environment in which one feels more secure. This is often the best choice a person has for coping with the unfamiliar, even though this experience may be unpleasant.

Many of us experience some portions of our lives as unpleasant or disharmonious, indicating inflexibilities in how we respond to certain stimuli. We actually delete, distort and/or generalise portions of our experience in order to cope. Anchoring is a tool which, when used effectively, can allow us more choice in our behaviour. More choice and greater flexibility allow us to cope with our ongoing experience in a more meaningful and satisfying way.

Another useful point here is that experiences in any one representation — visual, auditory or feeling — share the same neural pathways, whether generated externally or internally. By creating a desired experience, internally (that is, in our mind), seeing, hearing and feeling ourselves performing the behaviour we would like to have, we are generating our experience which the unconscious mind does not differentiate from our actually having that experience.

One of the authors used this technique to learn to beach start on a single water ski. In his words:

I had been skiing for some time on two skis and had reservations about going on to one ski. Beach starts looked incredibly difficult. My inner voice kept telling me I couldn't do it.

One Sunday I sat and observed very carefully several experts beach starting. I observed carefully their body position at the moment of weight transfer. That night, lying in bed I put myself into deep relaxation, lying on my back, breathing slowly and deeply and moving my awareness slowly through my body. I then recreated the picture of people beach starting, but put myself in the picture. I felt the water and the rope and the weight of the ski resting on the water. I heard the noise of the boat as it started accelerating and at the critical moment, as the rope came off the water, I moved my weight. My body tightened as I came up onto the ski. It felt great. I practised two or three times and then dropped off to sleep. The next Sunday I tried it for real. I missed the first time through overreaction, but the second time . . . away. The feeling of exhilaration was great and it was a skill I never had to relearn.

We can all apply this process to any behaviour we wish to change, improve or develop. It is necessary to create all representational systems, make pictures, hear the sounds and experience the feelings.

Some of us have representational systems which are not as developed or of which we are not consciously aware. The following exercise to create what Bandler and Grinder call an 'uptime' anchor is useful both as a future resource and to enable you to find out if any of your representational systems are less developed in your conscious awareness:

An example of minimal changes in muscle tone which can be 'calibrated' to an individual's changing mental state

Find an environment in which you are comfortable. You can sit down or walk around. Start by observing, seeing the whole picture, including shapes, colours and movement. Observe detail, specific flowers, trees, shades of colour contrasts.

Start actively listening. You may or may not wish to close your eyes. We suggest you try it both ways. Tune into voices, traffic noise, bird and insect noises, the wind moving the trees, dogs barking, or any sounds in your environment. It is often more effective if you are very still.

Become aware of tactile feelings. The feeling of your body on the ground or the chair, the clothing against your body, the temperature of the air, the wind moving past your skin. Then notice any smells and tastes. Breathe slowly through your nostrils, noting carefully the changing smells, the freshness of the air, or any odours, scents or fragrances. Spend several minutes with the experience and each sense, and longer on any you have difficulty with.

To apply an 'uptime' anchor you may use either of the following: squeeze your thumb and a finger together, or grasp one wrist with the other hand. As you experience each sense, apply increasing pressure corresponding to the intensity of the recall of the experience. Practise until, by application of the anchor, you can access the sense. You can anchor each sense separately using different fingers, or try simultaneously experiencing combinations. You now have a resource with which you can at any time focus all your attention upon your external environment.

This same exercise can be done accessing internal pictures, sounds, feelings, smells and tastes. Bandler and Grinder called this a 'downtime' anchor. It can be usefully employed to elicit internal states. We will discuss this in more detail later.

Some people encounter difficulty when trying to access certain of the sensory representations in the preceding exercises. Many of us operate without full consciousness of all our sensory channels. If this occurs we suggest to people that by developing the least consciously accessible senses they now have a unique opportunity to expand

Each person has unique calibrations. Other visual indicators are lower lip size and skin colour changes

and enhance their ability to access and utilise all their sensory channels, both externally and internally. As a result people generally experience increased flexibility and more conscious choice in their emotions and behaviour.

We now present an exercise to allow you to access positive emotional states:

Find yourself a quiet place where you can relax undisturbed. Think of an experience in which you felt good, positive emotions; maybe something from your occupation, your family, a hobby or a relationship.

Slowly recall this memory, paying particular attention to accessing all the sensory representation. Actually allow yourself to float into the experience rather than just seeing yourself in your mind's eye having the experience. This allows you to reaccess the good feelings of the experience rather than feelings you may have about the image. Pay attention to the noises, voices, smells or tastes associated with the experience. Pay particular attention to the feelings. You will know when you are accessing the same quality of feeling as during the real experience.

When you are satisfied with the intensity of the sensory recall, use an anchor as in the previous exercises. Do not use the same place to anchor this exercise. You can use the other wrist, other fingers, or squeeze your knee. But use a place where you can easily reach unobtrusively in the future. You don't want to be reaching down and squeezing your knee in the bus queue, or maybe you do.

We suggest you then take a few minutes' break and walk around a bit before repeating the exercise. Take another short break and then sit in the same position and squeeze the anchor.

What was the recall like? Did you have recall in all sensory channels?

Anchoring is an incredibly powerful technique and you can use this to recall at any time just about any emotional state. It often needs a little time to master, so we suggest you practise the first two exercises, honing up on any sensory channels that are not strongly represented in your conscious awareness.

The use of anchoring in NLP is very diversified. What we have presented so far is the basic essence of anchoring, with exercises to allow you to experience for yourself your own potential skills. The anchors used here are in the kinaesthetic (touch) representational system. Anchors can be and are used in all representational systems and their strength and duration can vary according to the individual, the intensity of the experience recalled or observed in the present, and, in therapy, the timing of the application of the anchor.

In therapeutic use, anchoring is a highly valued tool and its successful application requires astute perception and timing. The following is an example of one of the ways anchoring might be used in a learning demonstration.

The subject is asked to recall some memory which is associated with unpleasant feelings. Some experience which for them is uncomfortable. They are asked to see, hear and feel etc., their way through the experience and the practitioner anchors appropriately from feedback in the subject's non-verbal behaviour, i.e., calibrations. (As noted earlier, the subject does not need to reveal the content of the experience.)

Next, the practitioner would build and anchor in positive resources by having the subject think of a time when he or she were successful, happy, competent, or any combination of positive useful skills which we all possess — however infrequently we may use them. These would be anchored in a different place than the unpleasant feelings' anchor. Each anchor is tested, after installation, for strength and accuracy.

The practitioner would then have the subject recall the unpleasant experience and while it was recalled would 'fire off' both anchors simultaneously. The subjects usually experience some confusion at this time as the unpleasant memory they were recalling suddenly assumes a different quality — usually not unpleasant. Asked in the future to recall this memory the subject will certainly not experience unpleasant feelings associated with it again. In this way, habitual patterns of behaviour and emotion can be challenged and broken down.

THE META MODEL

The meta model is the quintessential basis of the NLP as it is used in therapeutic situations. It is primarily derived from Noam Chomsky's studies of linguistics and from Grinder and Bandler's years of observations.

The meta model specifies nine violations which are common in our everyday language and which indicate how we delete (information), distort (reality) and generalise, to such a degree that many of us become trapped in an impoverished and disharmonious perception of the world.

Our language, by its very structure, separates and allows us to make distinctions in the things we perceive. Unless we can see beyond the separate nature of entities which our use of language implies, to the cohesiveness, the wholeness, the unity and interdependence of all things, we are limiting our sensory perception and experiencing our reality in a fixed and limiting way. We can become stuck and find no way out.

Grinder and Bandler used the meta model to probe the client's surface structure (that is, the words spoken), and to arrive at the deep structure (that is, the deep meaning and context behind what we say). They would search there for deletions, distortions and generalisations and by the use of specific questions would guide the clients, enabling them to move through limitations and stumbling blocks in their own model of the world.

They used the term 'transderivational search' to describe that process by which we internally access our meaning of words. Given each person's unique personal experience, there is inevitably a diversity of understanding and meaning for any specific sentence. For example, the statement, 'I hate dogs', is one possible surface structure for a deep structure of: 'Dogs arouse fear in me as I have had several unpleasant experiences with them, especially in childhood. I am very wary of them.'

The surface structure, 'I hate dogs', communicated to another whose experience of dogs has been more pleasant would most likely lead to misunderstanding.

The use of the deep structure would allow room not only for understanding from another, but also allows for the possibility of a change in attitude in future encounters with dogs. The 'I hate dogs' statement is a fixed (stuck) state in which even the friendliest mongrel could find no place.

Whereas with dogs this may seem relatively unimportant, the distressing aspect is that we do this not only with dogs, but with each other and with our feelings and emotions.

We present now some examples of meta model violations. We suggest that you will find it useful to discover for yourself how frequently you use any of the following patterns in your own communication or your own thoughts. By being totally honest with yourself in answering some of the indicated questions we may begin to observe some of our habitual, self-imposed, limitations. But remember that, as we get in touch with our own feelings and emotions and begin to experience life in a more flowing way, we can also remember that if we did not have the capacity to feel discomfort, disharmony and dis-ease, we would not be able to feel contentment, satisfaction and what we understand as inner health.

Sentence: 'I *can't* change myself.'
Response: 'What stops you from changing yourself?'
The word 'can't' is used in this example as a limitation on change. This violation is called a 'modal operator'. Other examples of modal operators are 'should', 'shouldn't', 'have', 'haven't', 'ought', 'must', 'mustn't', 'don't'.

How often are you limiting your options in life by using this type of language violation? Every time you use or hear someone using the above words you can ask one of the following questions to find the limits in perception sign-posted with these violations: 'What stops me/you from X?', 'What would happen if I/you didn't/did X?'.

Sentence: '*People* hurt me.'
Response: 'Who specifically is hurting you?'
The word 'people' in this sentence is what is called a 'lack of referential index'. The speaker has failed to specify who specifically is hurting him/her. Other examples of this common language violation are 'they', 'them' and 'it'.

Sentence: 'I am experiencing depression.'
Response: 'How specifically are you experiencing depression?'
The word depression in this sentence is being used as an abstract noun. What the person is experiencing is being perceived as a fixed, unchangeable state. By asking 'How specifically are you experiencing X?', the speaker will recover or access the perception of the experience in sensory forms, that is, images, tape loops or feelings. This perception can then be altered to bring about change. For example:

One person may experience depression as 'a black cloud making the world seem dull'. Another person may experience depression as 'a heavy feeling throughout the body, especially heavy in the chest area'. By finding the deep structure (perception in images, sounds, and feelings) the speaker can be encouraged to change his/her perception so that in the first example the world becomes bright and clear again and in the second example he/she feels light and energetic in body again.

Sentence: 'Everyone is against my ideas.'
Response: 'Everyone?'

Sentence: 'Nobody loves me.'
Response: 'Nobody?'

This type of violation is called a 'universal quantifier'. It represents a generalisation to the extent of forgoing alternative possibilities in perception and experience of life.

Other examples are: 'all', 'every time', 'never', 'always', 'nothing', 'nowhere'.

When you or others use this type of violation, take the word and exaggerate it in a questioning tone of voice. The user of the violation will typically find some counter examples. For example:

Sentence: 'I'll never change my job.'
Response: 'Never?'
First Person Response: 'Well, I've changed my job in the past. I suppose I could possibly change it in the future.'

Another useful language violation to challenge is called 'mind reading', the case of claiming to know what another person is thinking without verification to find out whether or not we are correct in our assumption. Examples:

Sentence: 'You know what I mean.'
Response: 'How do you know that I know what you mean?'

Sentence: 'I know she dislikes me.'
Response: 'How do you know she dislikes you?'

These are only a few of the nine language violations. Please see the Bibliography for further study.

By asking the appropriate questions for each class of violations in the sentences you use to describe or think about a problem, you will quickly find the internal perceptions which are limiting your choices in the world. By enhancing those perceptions (enriching/changing the map) you will effectively change your experience of the world and move closer to experiencing inner health.

Grinder and Bandler used to say that NLP was all lies and its only usefulness is that it works. NLP is not reality, or an explanation or theory of reality, but a model. It gives us useful tools with which to explore our own unique perception of reality, our own possibilities or limitations, our choices or lack of them. We can recognise that others have a different perspective and we can join with them and appreciate them and their experiences. Having an awareness of the process by which we limit ourselves with our perception, and taking the necessary steps to change our perception of reality, will lead us to a new understanding and experience of inner health.

CHAPTER 6

CREATIVE SELF-EXPRESSION

Janna Fineberg

This chapter focuses on the role of 'Creative Self-Expression' in health maintenance. The model of health that the author has found most useful is a 'holistic' one. It views five areas of life as interacting and contributing to one's level of health and well-being. These are: nutrition, exercise, relationship with oneself, relationship with others, and creative outlet(s). The arts are clearly 'creative outlets', and thus artistic involvement can satisfy this requisite of health.

It is the author's experience that emotional and physical health cannot be separated as they intimately affect one another. The vast majority of physical ailments these days, have emotional components to their causes and these emotional causes are in the areas of relationship with self, relationship with others, and/or general stress. Thus any personal growth tool that works on these areas, also works to improve physical health. A creative outlet enables individuals to express their innermost, perhaps even non-verbal, feelings and this is important for health. Creative outlets, or artistic involvement, can also offer a release from stress, when used appropriately. This chapter will specifically explore how the arts can also be used directly for personal growth (to improve one's relationship with oneself and others). Thus, artistic involvement can potentially satisfy three of the five requisites for health (four out of five if the art one chooses is dance!). How rare to find a health-maintenance tool that is so efficient, and *enjoyable*!

THE ARTS AND PERSONAL GROWTH

Dance your sadness
Draw your pain
Beat your fear drum
Till they wane.
Act your anger
Fully be
Sing your love out
Till you're free.

Personal growth is both the fortune and the necessity of this period of Western culture. It is the fortune in that the basic survival needs of most of our population are met, and so we have the luxury of time to examine our characters, to refine ourselves. It is the necessity, in several ways. First, due to both our current international and environmental situations, unless we improve our ability to communicate and co-operate with others, and deepen our sensitivity to nature, we may be a doomed species. It is already crucial that we master techniques of dealing with the stress produced by the rapid changes that are now occurring in the environment, and that technology is currently making and about to make in our lifestyles.

On many levels, this is a time of great transition. It appears that quite a new world may be ahead, with changes in basic assumptions, lifestyle, diet, etc. Our ability to adapt to change easily is critical for our survival.

Personal growth is also a necessity in this age because, with more leisure time, it has become obvious that many individuals within our culture are in pain. Our culture's technological emphasis has resulted in rather barbaric birthing procedures, and production-oriented rather than human-oriented values, and the consequence is internal malaise. Personal growth is also critical at this time, because personal/ emotional conflicts are major contributors to physical disease, and physical disease is unnecessarily widespread. Fortunately, now, with the culture's growing recognition of the needs of its members, some powerful and even enjoyable forms of growth and healing are emerging.

In the past, participation in the arts was considered a rather frivolous leisure activity. 'Growth', in terms of traditional psychiatry, was intellectual, difficult work, and certainly not particularly enjoyable. Only now are we realising that even the thought that 'growth and transformation are painful and a struggle' is one of the thoughts that needs to be healed. Why shouldn't growth be fun? Creative? Even joyful? It does not have to be that the individual must first 'grow and change', and *then* can live and enjoy. The use of the arts for growth breaks down this separation between 'growth' and 'life' and the process of growth itself can be fun, creative, and an integral part of living.

Arts and growth form a natural marriage. An important aspect of health is a free flow of one's energy. Such a flow requires that one both has access to one's deepest feelings and motivations, and a form in which to express these deepest impulses. With expression, the energy moves; the impulses are given life, and naturally transform. Life continues — ever changing, ever flowing. Growth involves entering deeply within, and allowing the depths to emerge; art, the finest art, involves the expression of the deepest impulses. Art can express what words cannot. Art, from the deep place, serves the creator and the audience as well. For when we truly enter deeply, we reach what is within us all. Thus when art is used consciously for growth, the process is personally healing, and the product is universal truth, a healing expression for all.

The use of art for growth has several additional unique advantages. Most growth techniques, with success, free more of the individual's energy. Not much attention is paid, however, to what the person might do with this sometimes suddenly increased energy when it has been released. Unfortunately, many unprepared individuals, unable to handle the new intensity of energy, end up binding their 'excess' energy in addictions or negative relationships. The arts provide not only a tool for freeing energy, but at the same time an immediate outlet for its constructive use. Additionally, once an individual has learned how to use the arts for her* growth, she can continue the process on her own. Creativity has been tapped and expanded, and perhaps even a new area of life has been opened, offering many hours of future enjoyment.

DANCE: 'DANCE YOUR SADNESS'

Dance, one of the most beautiful arts, is also potentially one of our greatest healers, if used consciously for this purpose. This refers less to choreographed dance, with very specific movements involving practised technique, but more to pure movement and expressive dance. Dance and movement of the freer sort allow the body a natural path of opening.

Movement and dance used for growth can be of two types: 'directed', or 'expressive'. In 'directed movement', the individual is told how to move, either verbally or through a model. Most individuals have developed characteristic ways of viewing the world and being in the world, and these habit patterns are mirrored in characteristic ways of holding and moving their bodies. By asking individuals to move, consciously, in specific new ways, new possibilities are introduced into the nervous system (see Exercise 4). New muscles and brain cells are stimulated. The person's range of possible ways of being in, and relating to, the world is increased, since this very simple learning on the physical level is paralleled on the emotional and cognitive ones. The repertoire is expanded; response possibilities are expanded, and more choice becomes available. The more different movement possibilities the individual becomes familiar with, the freer and less rigid she becomes on all levels. And the movement experience is direct and immediate. The new possibility is introduced and immediately experienced.

Truths about life can be taught through directed movement (see Exercise 5). The nervous system can learn to become comfortable with the constantly changing rhythms of life, by practising moving in different natural rhythms (for example,

* For simplicity, the female form will be used throughout this chapter.

staccato, strong and flowing, chaotic) until the body is comfortable in each, as well as with rapid transitions (see Exercise 1). Then the natural flow of life can be experienced and channelled through ('danced') without resistance. Each phase can be experienced fully and thus complete itself and transform to another. It is resistance to Nature — to any of the natural rhythms — that causes suffering.

The emotions can also be artistically and therapeutically explored through dance (see Exercise 2). As we 'dance' (and sound) the different emotions, we learn how our bodies feel in each emotion. We learn where we are tense, where we tend to hold in that emotion. In this way we can increase our awareness of, and begin to identify, unexpressed emotions. As we continue to dance our emotions, we begin to fully express, and thus release. We dig into the crevices of our being, seeking out pockets of unexpressed feelings, and give the 'held' feelings the opportunity to be totally released.

As we become comfortable with the full expression of emotions through our dance (and voice), we learn to express fully each emotion in the moment it arises, thus allowing it to be immediately released and transformed. No more stiff resistance, inhibited life flow. As life brings us emotions, we become free to dance them all, fully. They move through us unrestricted, and we continually return to 'neutral', with no remnants: open, in the moment, and ready to ride the next wave of life.

Expressive movement, or dance, occurs when the dancer is allowed to create her own movements in the moment, initiated from within, usually stimulated by music (see Exercise 3). This type of dance helps the dancer develop self-awareness, awareness of internal impulses 'asking' to be expressed. It encourages spontaneity, and works to release self-consciousness. It is not long after dancing in a group of people all dancing their own movements, focusing within rather than without, that the dancer realises that no-one is watching, no-one really cares what she looks like, and she lets go and moves!

Expressive dance encourages individual expression. No two dancers dance the same way, in movement or feeling. The true expressive dance is individual, and encouraged to be so. Sometimes our movement in expressive dance comes from an inner emotion. Other times it is stimulated by a muscle that asks to be stretched, or a muscle that asks to be used. In this way expressive dance can be the most perfect individualised exercise, freeing one's body in exactly the right places at exactly the right time. Freeing muscles, reducing rigidity, increasing expressiveness and response possibilities. Expressive dance is a superb physical and emotional release. The mind quietens, the body moves itself, the breath is stimulated, life energy flows, and finds immediate expression. The more the mind quietens and the energy moves us, the deeper we go, the more we are healed, and life and art emerge together. The cosmic dance finds its channel, and we each discover our sacred dance. For when we totally let go, our body leads us to what it needs, and we are healed. And as we loosen and then totally let go, the universe expresses itself through us, and this is art.

Expressive movement teaches the participant additional important skills for life. It teaches one not only to become aware of, but also to rely on, inner impulses and intuition; to trust in one's own non-rational inner knowing. Expressive movement, when done in interaction with others, also teaches sensitivity. It teaches one to read and respond to body language and energy flow, rather than be distracted by words. Movement becomes communication, which is what it truly is — a universal, direct vehicle of communication. Expressive movement also helps participants develop comfort with the lack of external structures; an ability to find one's own way, an attribute that is truly important in these times of changing environment and culture. And beyond this, expressive dance accompanied by different forms of music (for example, tribal drums, aquatic music, space music) acquaints the dancer with different ways of being — different rhythms in the body; different experiences. And when we are comfortable with the new and unusual, we are ready for anything. Life can still surprise us, but we will respond and move to its new music, because we are fluid, responsive beings, comfortable with movement and change. We are prepared because we can flow with whatever evolutionary changes are afoot. We can dance to it all.

THEATRE: 'ACT YOUR ANGER'

Theatre, the healer.

Let us consider two different types of theatre, 'traditional theatre', and 'ritual theatre', and their healing properties.

Traditional Theatre   The actress in traditional theatre acts in a scripted play; taking on a given role. Acting in traditional theatre offers many growth experiences, and the more the actress 'grows', the more powerful her performance becomes.

Acting a role introduces the actress to the world of emotions. Many individuals, much to their disservice, tend to inhibit not only the expression of, but often even the experience of, particular (if not all) emotions. She must embody the emotions of the character being portrayed — experience them in mind and body, explore them from the inside out — in order to portray them powerfully in performance. This is a safer way to explore emotions — when they ostensibly belong to someone else, and are 'not real'. Yet quality performance comes from the making-real, the true experiencing, even for the moment. So theatre allows people to enter the world of emotions in a less threatening way. The recognition of one's own emotions, and how they feel and look in the body, is inevitable. And an outlet for their expression is provided in the performance (see Exercise 8).

Theatre also offers the opportunity to release self-consciousness. The actress must be *total* in her every word, every movement. No holding back, or power on stage is lost. This principle, of being *total* is basic both to quality performance, and quality living. To be 100 per cent involved in every movement, to do what we do fully, to say what we say fully, to commit ourselves totally to every moment — this is being truly alive.

Acting in theatre also demands, and thus helps develop, sensitivity to others. The exercise of understanding a character deeply, understanding the motives and personality of another person, is excellent training for the world. By understanding the deep issues of a character, an actress learns how to look deeply into others, to understand more fully why people act as they do. She can easily become more tolerant and understanding. Acting also develops another type of sensitivity. The actress must be aware of the movements and tones of other actors, and blend her performance to complement the others. Most theatre pieces are not individual performances, but a play among characters — individuals who must use and respond to each other, dance together. This is similar to life.

We are not individuals in the world on our own, but often in interaction with others. We need to develop sensitivity to others: when to talk softly, when to be quiet, when to move towards, or away. But in our traditional education, nowhere are we taught these fine arts of awareness and sensitivity: how to recognise what is needed by others, while still maintaining our personal integrity. Acting can aid in the development of these skills. Stage performance demands that the actress attune herself to the energies of the other actors and interact appropriately, while still maintaining personal presence. This is unique and important life training.

The modern growth movement has become more and more aware of the importance of the body. Whereas previously, traditional psychiatry emphasised the intellectual understanding of conflicts, it is now clear that habitual cognitive/emotional patterns are held in the body and that, by working through the body, growth can often come more quickly. In our mind-oriented culture, we tend to be very defensive on the mind level, and our ego strongly resists exposure and change. The body, however, cannot hide anything. Through the body we have easier access to observing and altering underlying causal issues. Change initiated at this level can be quite direct and most effective.

The first step of change is awareness. Becoming aware of how we hold our bodies can be the beginning of significant change. Acting makes extensive use of body language. The body expresses loudly and therefore must either go along with the situation and the actress' words, or be purposely contradictory. A quality actress must be aware of her body, and be free in her body, to express whatever needs to be portrayed. Any inhibitions in the body, which only parallel inhibitions of attitudes and emotions, must be released so the actress can become fully expressive without limitation, without carrying her personal limitations into her characterisations. Thus theatre work requires increased body awareness, and emphasises a released body, not stuck in any particular attitude, but able to express all attitudes as needed.

Another extremely powerful growth opportunity offered by theatre is the opportunity for the actress to 'try on' new ways of being. By assuming a 'role' she can come to understand what it feels like to express anger, to live without restrictions, to be a parent ... The actress gets the opportunity to experience new possibilities fully, making possible personal changes less unknown, and therefore less frightening.

Ritual Theatre Within ritual theatre are two types, personal ritual theatre, and universal ritual theatre.

Personal Ritual Theatre

Personal ritual theatre is quite different from traditional theatre. There is no script, and each actress plays herself. Personal ritual theatre, as practised by the author, is an extremely powerful growth form. The individual chooses an issue that is real for her in her life at the current time. A personal issue that she is exploring, an area of change or desired change. The individual is aided by the other members of the 'theatre group' (usually consisting of from four to six people) to explore this issue deeply, to look for the most essential conflict involved. For example, beneath the concern about a relationship might be one's fear of being alone — or one's fear of merging. Beneath a concern about a job might be the attitude that the world is a hostile place and there is not enough for everyone. Once the core issue is identified, the individual is encouraged to put the experience of the conflict into movement and sound. She is to embody the conflict by the positioning of her own body, and/or her position in relation to the group members. For example, if she feels that she is crowded by all of life's demands, she might start by being crowded into a corner by the others.

If she feels she is walking the line between two types of existence, then she might begin by walking an imaginary line. The 'actress' must bring the experience, the gut feel of the issue she wishes to explore and transform, into her whole nervous system — through movement, sound (chanting, drum beats), and words. For example, if an individual is frightened to take a leap into a new lifestyle, perhaps she would maintain whatever physical position represents the old style, speak about her conflict to the background of a mounting chant by the others of 'Jump!' and finally she might run and jump into the arms of others. Whatever represents the old, and the transition to the new; whatever represents the essence of the two states taken into the whole nervous system, is portrayed. The experience of acknowledging and exposing the essence of one's current state releases its hold. Experiencing the issue's resolution in the body energises change.

A complete personal ritual theatre piece is usually formed by an artful combining of pieces in which each individual in the group explores her issue, within a theme context created by the group for the opening and finale. Deep personal theatre touches upon the universal, for deep down, under all of our individual personality idiosyncrasies, we are all dealing with the same core issues. We are all just trying to live happily on this planet and make it work for ourselves and everyone else. We all belong to the human family.

The ritual aspect of this type of theatre is in its form. Issues are not detailed literally, but encapsulated symbolically in movement and sound. Chants and rhythm instruments are used. The theatre piece becomes a ceremony. Deeper levels of consciousness are tapped by the symbols and stimulated by the chants and rhythms. The effect is at a deep level; the play really proceeds at the levels where true transformation occurs. The transformative power of skilfully designed ritual theatre is awesome. And the beauty, again, of the use of art for growth is that the design of the theatre piece and the quality of 'acting' that maximises the result for the individual, also produces the power and edge that makes a superb production and a transformative piece for the audience.

Universal Ritual Theatre

This theatre form has many elements in common with personal ritual theatre. It differs in that its themes, rather than coming from individuals, are pre-selected because of their universality. Such rituals have formed an important part of many cultures, to help their members move through life's significant transitions (for example, birth rituals, initiations, marriage rituals). Somehow our culture has lost many of these aids and expects teenagers to 'naturally' and smoothly become adults; it expects individuals coming from a culture that stresses individuality and competition to be able to enter easily into bonded relationships. History has shown that these significant transitions need assistance, and that ritual is the ideal form. Rituals aid our passage through life's stages. Through participation in ceremonies that embody these transformations — that acknowledge the depth of the changes, and speak to the unconscious of the naturalness and importance of the passages — these life transitions can be smooth and natural, and can become anticipated privileges and celebrations, rather than difficult, imposed expectations.*

MUSIC: 'BEAT YOUR FEAR DRUM, SING YOUR LOVE OUT'

It does not take much convincing to perceive that music can be used for healing. Throughout the ages, music has inspired, expressed, uplifted, guided. The playing of music allows an expression of the inner self — an expression beyond words — of emotions, perceptions, experiences, and visions. Certain notes of the scale heal certain organs and cleanse certain chakras and so a consciously composed piece of music can be a specific healer (see Exercise 11). The improvising of music increases one's awareness of impulses, nuances of feeling, keeps one in the present moment, and increases self-confidence (see Exercise 10). The playing of different rhythms expands our horizons and increases our sensitivity to other cultures and life forms. Music creates the ritual and gives access to the subconscious, so deep healing can take place. Music inspires

---

*In this vein is the author's workshop series, 'Rites of Passage: Rituals for Life Transitions in The New Culture'.

us to try the new, to exceed limits. The musician can express, be inspired by her own expression, express this inspiration, be inspired once again, and so on — reaching greater and greater heights, exploring newer and newer places. Music brings us deep within, and high above. It stimulates the primitive and the spiritual. In music, nothing is fixed. All is possible. We can feel and hear what it is like to soar through space, to live underwater, to contract, to expand. Music can help both the listener and the musician become comfortable with change and the unknown.

The voice is also a great healer. Open your mouth and let the sound out! Singing teaches us not to hold back, but to express freely. For to emit pure sound, we must relax all the vocal passages. As sound and expression are no longer inhibited, spontaneity increases. To use the voice the breath must also be developed, and full breathing is the universal cleanser, healer and energiser. The singing of different notes cleanses and heals different specific organs, tunes and energises different chakras (see Exercise 11). Singing can be a creative way to express our emotions, either through the sounds themselves, or the content of our song. Powerful singing comes from full expression and, again, it is full expression which precedes transformation.

Full breath and the voice are also pathways to the spirit. With free sound, the soul speaks. And singing with others is one of the most precious unions. In song, we share the breath of life, and our spirits. We harmonise our vibration with others and the universe. This is peace and health.

VISUAL ARTS: 'DRAW YOUR PAIN'

The visual arts include many forms, having both unique healing elements and healing techniques in common. Here, we will simply consider painting as a visual arts example.

Painting is another art which enables the participant to express the inexpressible, express beyond words, beyond rational recognition, express from the non-verbal depths. This expression is profoundly healing. Energy is tapped, in expression it moves, and transformation is possible. Sometimes the painter herself cannot even identify what is being expressed, but below the mind, it can be recognised by others who are also served by the expression. Painting can also expand ways of viewing the world, and expand comfort with change, by expressing new forms. Recent research has indicated that the brain functions in patterns, and that visual patterns can carry information directly to the brain. This opens up another whole area of possibility in the connection between visual art and learning and growth.

Similar to the notes of a musical scale, each colour has been shown to correspond to particular organs of the body, and particular and energy chakras. Thus, by a conscious use of colour in art, specific healing can be energised.

Recently the value of imagery for healing has been rediscovered. When an individual, from a relaxed state, images a situation as she would like it to be, and feeds this situation with her energy, she is actually helping to bring the situation into reality. In this way, imagery can be used consciously for both physical healing and personal growth. Similarly, the individual can draw or paint a representation of a state she would like to bring about (perhaps in mandala form), enter into a relaxed state, and then meditate upon the picture. In this way art can be used consciously for growth (see Exercise 13).

The healing potential of each of these art forms has really been only touched upon, and there are other forms with significant healing properties that have not been mentioned. But the major principles are much the same.

The arts, because of their ability to tap depths and express the otherwise inexpressible, are unique healers. For when we reach in deeply and express, our energy moves, issues transform, and life and health increase. Additionally, the arts are fun and healing can, and should, be fun. Why not? Also, the arts, after having released more energy, offer a perfect use for the energy — participation in the further creation of art. And the more we grow, the deeper we go, the better art we create. Thus the rewards, and incentive, are doubled. And the very art that is the most healing comes from digging so deeply into ourselves that we have found the core, and thus the universal issues. Then expressing these through art heals others as well. Personally, I'd rather

Dance my sadness
Draw my pain
Beat my fear drum
Till they wane.
Act my anger
Fully be
Sing my love out
Till I'm free!

The arts are life, and give life. We can create to live fully, and then can live to create deeply. And with our energy flowing freely, we experience our healthy, true selves — the vibrant, creative beings we truly are.

The following are exercises that you can do, some on your own, some with a partner, and some in a group. They use the different arts, and are designed with personal growth in mind. Learn, and enjoy!

DANCE

Exercise 1   'Rhythms'   For one or more people. This exercise is based on the principle that there are various rhythms that are natural to life. We find these rhythms in nature, for example in the growth pattern of plants over the year, or in the wind. Most of us have gotten used to moving our bodies, and moving through life in one, or maybe two different rhythms. These have become familiar, and comfortable. The idea behind this exercise is that it would be beneficial for us to be flexible: to be at least familiar and comfortable with all the natural rhythms, even though we still might have preferences. This is because life will naturally, periodically bring us each of them. The main thing that causes problems in life is *resisting* what *is*. If we can move with what life is bringing us, rather than resist it, we will get through much easier. Thus, if, for example, our life just *is* chaotic at a certain point — life simply is bringing us chaos at that time — we're going to have a much easier time if we just accept the chaos and allow ourselves to be bounced around, than if we try to make it different. If we accept and go *with* the chaotic rhythm (in this example), it will also end that much sooner. What we resist, is prolonged. What we flow with, moves on. The five rhythms we play with in this exercise are 'Strong and flowing', 'Staccato', 'Chaotic', 'Light and lively' and 'Stillness'.

This exercise is best done to a live or recorded drum beat based on repetitive counts of eight, with four beats played and four beats silent (for example: beat, beat, beat, beat, wait, wait, wait, wait, beat, beat, beat, beat, wait, wait, wait, wait, etc.).* During the four beats, you move continuously in the rhythm you're working on. During the 'waits', you freeze in the position you were in on the last beat, and hold that position, focusing your awareness on how that rhythm feels in your body. Then, when the beats come again, you move in that rhythm again.

First, experience each rhythm for eight consecutive series of beats before moving to the next rhythm. When you have experienced each rhythm in this way, go through them again moving to each one for three consecutive series of beats. Now start mixing them all up, changing the rhythm you move with each new series of beats, in random order. Be *total* with each rhythm. (It is easiest to have someone acting as 'caller', calling out during the 'waits' the next rhythm to be moved. If you are alone, write the name of the five rhythms in large letters on separate large pieces of paper and tack them up around the room, so you can just look up to be reminded of another rhythm.)

Experience what it feels like to shift rapidly from one rhythm to another. It is important, in addition to experiencing each rhythm separately, to also become comfortable with this rapid shifting. Because that's also what life does — it sometimes changes pace very quickly, and it is best for you to be able to adapt and move with it.

When you are finished, walk slowly around the room, coming back to your normal breathing. As you are walking, one at a time, think of each rhythm, asking yourself 'Is this rhythm familiar to me in my life?' 'Am I comfortable with this rhythm?' For beneficial 'homework', spend three minutes each day for the next few weeks 'moving' in those rhythms which you found uncomfortable. It will serve you well to become comfortable with them all, so you can flow *with* them when life unavoidably brings them to you, as it sometimes will.

Exercise 2 'Emotions'   For one or more people. This exercise is similar to 'Rhythms', except it deals with five *emotions* that are natural to human life. These are sadness, fear, anger, joy, and love. Once again, many of us are more aware of feeling some of these emotions than others, and more willing to express some than others. Yet life periodically brings all of them to us. Unless we are able to express the feelings in some way, their emotional energy is held in, and this causes emotional or physical problems. This exercise increases our awareness of what each emotion feels like in our body so we can recognise it. It also introduces us to ways of expressing the emotions through sound and movement.

This exercise uses the same repetitive drum rhythm of four 'beats' and four 'waits' as Exercise 1. This time you express through movement *and sound* the emotion you are working on for the four beats, and then freeze in the position you were in on the last beat and hold that position during the four waits, becoming aware of how that emotion feels in your body. Try the emotions both subtly (for example, small movements and sounds) and in the extreme, where you really let the expression out! One suggestion with anger is that if you notice you are clenching your teeth and your fists, be aware of these signals that you are angry — but also be aware that these indicate the holding *in* of anger. In this exercise, *shout*, and throw your fingers *open* — let the

* Dr Fineberg produces tapes directing these exercises, upon request. Inquire or order by writing to Janna Fineberg, CSE Tapes, 149 Keen Street, Lismore, NSW 2480, Australia through December 1985. From 1986 contact Dr Fineberg C/o *Nature & Health* magazine, PO Box 60, Dee Why, NSW 2099, Australia.

feelings go *out*. Work with each emotion separately as you did with rhythms. Then work with the rapid changing from one emotion to another. This is a very important part of this exercise. When you experience and express an emotion fully, *totally*, it completes itself, and you *can* move right into another emotion. And sometimes life does move that fast.

At first, you may need to 'act' the emotions. That's fine, but while you are doing it, feel inside for remnants of the real thing, and allow the real emotions to take over and be expressed as soon as possible. Again, the expression can be subtle, or 'full on'. If, while you are working with one emotion it 'takes you over', let go to it. Stay in its expression until the expression has completed itself. Give yourself that opportunity for release. If the emotion is so powerful that it is frightening, some support and counselling could serve you well.

After going through the emotions individually, and then rapidly changing them, begin to walk around the room slowly as you return to your normal breathing pattern. While you are walking, review each emotion separately in your mind, asking yourself these questions: 'What did this emotion feel like in my body?' 'Am I aware when I feel this emotion?' 'Do I allow myself to express this emotion?' Know that it is very important for both your physical and emotional health to be able to express your emotions in some way. It may be by letting others know verbally how you feel, by letting others see you cry or jump for joy, or by going to the trees to scream and pound the ground in rage.

However you do it, emotions must be expressed. If you feel your emotions are excessive, some exploration with a counsellor into why you are responding this way might be a great help. But experiencing different emotions is part of human life, and you do need a way of expressing them. You might think of them like a dance.

Exercise 3 'Expressive Dance' For one or more people. Put on some flowing music, *without* a clear rhythmical beat to it. Simply move to it — feel the music inside your body, and allow your body to move in whatever way it wants. Try this with other, different types of music. Close your eyes. Feel the music inside. Allow the music and your body to move you.

Exercise 4 'Sharing Movements' For two or more people. Put on some music with a clear beat, but not too fast. Take a partner, and begin moving to the music, standing across from your partner. Keep eye contact if possible: you are sharing this experience! After doing your own movements for a few minutes, one person becomes the 'leader'. The leader then continues to do her/his movements very clearly, and the other person copies, or mirrors, the movements of the leader.

The leader can make this easiest by choosing one movement, repeating it for a while, choosing another movement, etc. Once the 'follower' has caught on to one of the leader's movements, (s)he is to become aware of how that movement feels in her/his own body. After the first leader has led about five movements, allow the follower to become the leader. After each person has led twice, begin to allow the leadership to change back and forth spontaneously. Then just play with each other through movement, respond to each other's movements, etc.

Exercise 5 'Hold on, Let go' For two or more people. Life is full of changes. One thing that causes problems for most people is their difficulty with letting go of the old, or the past. This might be letting go of a relationship which is no longer vital, letting go of what they 'expected' from some situation or person and surrendering to 'what is', letting go of parts of themselves which no longer serve them, etc., etc. Many of us cause ourselves problems by clinging to what has naturally passed, instead of simply allowing ourselves to feel the loss, while at the same time letting it go. This exercise explores our style of 'holding on' and 'letting go'. 'Holding on' can be either our way of being, of being with what is, or of trying to hold on to what is passing away.

Choose a partner for this (if there is an odd person, (s)he can be the 'caller'). Start by standing about four metres apart. The caller says 'hold on'. Both partners move towards each other, and hold on to each other in some way. After about 15 seconds, the caller says 'let go'. The partners let go of each other in some way. After 15 seconds, the caller says 'hold on' and the partners move towards each other again and hold on to each other. After 15 seconds the caller then says 'let go', and the partners let go of each other again. Each instruction is repeated approximately six times.

Each time you hold on, hold on in a different way. Each time you let go, let go in a different way. Explore different ways of holding on and letting go, and see how they feel. For the last round, explore a way of holding on and of letting go that feel really *good* to you. Then sit down with your partner and talk about the experience, and how it relates to how you hold on and let go of things and people in your life.

Exercise 6 'Park Bench' For two or more poeple. Choose a partner generally around your same weight. One partner gets on the floor on all fours — knees and hands on the floor, elbows slightly bent. Let your neck relax, your head drop down. Keep breathing. You are the park bench. The other partner has five minutes to explore what (s)he can do on you — sit on you, lie on you in all directions. Hang over you, slide under you, etc. Giving you their whole weight. After five minutes, switch roles. This exercise increases relaxation and trust, and is generally fun!

THEATRE

Exercise 7 'Unity Circle' For two or more people. This is fun, brings cohesiveness, and allows you to try on other people's sounds and movements. Stand in a circle. One person is chosen to start, and the leadership goes around the circle clockwise. The leader makes one repetitive sound and movement together. First, repeating it slowly, so the others can see what the leader is doing, and join in with the same sound and movement. Then the leader begins to intensify the movement and sound, building it up in speed of the movement and volume of the sound to a high pitch, with everyone doing the same. Then the leader starts to gradually slow and quieten it down again (with everyone following), until the leader just allows it to disappear. After a few moments, the person to the leader's left begins with a new sound and movement. Go around the circle twice.

Exercise 8 'Face emotions' For two or more people. Sit across from a partner. Choose who will be the 'actor' first, and who will be the 'observer'. (If there is a group of three, two will be actor together and observer together). You are again going to go through the five emotions explored in Exercise 2, but this time each emotion will be expressed purely through the face and eyes. It will be subtle — no overdone caricatures. To begin, the actors close their eyes and feel into the first emotion, sadness. They are to feel the emotion in their body, and to let it be expressed on their face. When they feel they have embodied sadness, they open their eyes, and look at the observer, saying nothing, but just staying with the emotion of sadness, and allowing it to be expressed on their face. After a few minutes they close their eyes again, take a few deep breaths as they allow the sadness to fade, and they return to emotional 'neutral'. Then they

move on to the next emotion. The observer simply observes. When all five emotions have been explored, and the actor has re-opened her/his eyes, the observer gives the actor feedback on what (s)he saw and felt, comparing the expression of the different emotions. Then the roles switch.

Exercise 9 'Personal Ritual'   For one or more people. This will be an example of what the author calls a 'ritual of release'. It is a ceremony designed to aid you in releasing some aspect of yourself that you would like to release. A ritual to help an aspect of you that is changing or that you wish to change, to move on to its next phase.

You will need a piece of cloth, coloured crayons, a large piece of paper for each person, a large inflammable bowl and matches, a candle, and incense and an incense holder. Preferably also a tape recorder and a taped piece of music that you all like to dance to. Spread out the cloth, and on it put the crayons and paper, bowl, incense and holder, and candle. Light the incense and candle to begin the ritual.

Everyone close their eyes, and begin to relax, allowing any tension that may be in your body to melt away, down and out of your body, with each exhale. Remind yourself why you are doing this: to further your own growth process. Now open your eyes, and all sing a short song together that you all like. Now each take your paper, and take about 20 minutes to draw a symbol of the part of you that you would like to release — to change.

When this is completed, all together, get up and walk around, expressing in your body and your voice how it is to be this way.

Now, one at a time, hold up the symbol that you drew. Say out loud what this part of you has meant to you— acknowledging how it may have helped you in the past. Announce, however, that you no longer want it, and intend for it to release its energy to change: to the growth of a new part of you. Invite your 'higher self' to hear your intention, and the strength of your 'higher self' to energise this change. Thank any other people who have helped you in recognising this necessary transition.

Now light the symbol with the candle, and put it in the bowl and watch it burn and release its energy. When it is finished burning, say the words, out loud, 'And now it is so'. When the last person has done this, all get up and walk around, expressing in your body and voice the new feeling: the new state that will take the old's place. Sit down and sing another song that you all like. Play the dance piece, and get up and dance to it. Put out the incense and together blow out the candle. Put all the items you used away. Bury the ashes in the earth somewhere (even in a pot plant!), or throw them in the ocean. All do this together.

MUSIC

Exercise 10 'Rhythm Instruments' For one or more people. This is to explore rhythms, to feel different rhythms in your body, to experience creating music, to increase spontaneity, and to harmonise with others. Each person needs a rhythm instrument. This could be a drum or a pot or bowl to hit; two sticks to hit together, shakers or a jar partially filled with dry beans or rice to shake, a bell or keys to jangle together, etc.

Begin sitting in a circle. Someone with a drum or an instrument that makes a resounding sound begins by setting up a continuous beat. One by one, going around the circle clockwise, each person joins those already playing with a repetitive sound.

First listen to what is already going on, hear and feel where you can join in in your body, and *then* begin to play. Each new instrument should be given the chance to really establish its contribution before the next instrument comes in.

Once everyone is playing, continue for a few minutes, and then everyone get to their feet while they keep playing. Begin to walk around to the music, especially to the rhythm you are playing, as you continue playing. Take what you are playing into your body movement.

When you have been moving your rhythms around the room for a few minutes, continue, but now also add your voices, doing anything you want with them. Use your voices as additional instruments. Play with this for awhile.

Now begin changing what you're doing with your instrument, remaining sensitive to what is going on around you. Improvise, and play around.

When it feels like you've been doing this for long enough, do something that seems like an ending and see if everyone can stop playing near the same time. You might want to try another piece, by someone just starting with a new rhythm. Enjoy yourselves!

Exercise 11 'Vocal Alphabet' For one or more people. Start by stretching out your mouth in all directions, and make a sound while you're doing it. Loosen your mouth and jaw muscles. The vibrations of the different vowel sounds and also of the different notes of the musical scale resonate with different bodily organs, and the different energy chakras. So whether you view the body on the physical or the energetic level, singing out the different vowel and different notes of the scale is healing to your body. It gives you a 'tune up', energising, healing, and balancing your system. For this exercise, we will add in an extra vowel sound, that of 'Ah'. So we will chant 'Ah', 'A', 'E', 'I', 'O', 'U', and then 'Ah' again.

Each person should start on a low note in *their* voice range, because you will be going up seven notes. You will *not* all be singing the same note at the same time; just the same sound.

All take a breath in together, and then sing out 'Ah' on a low note in your voice range. Wait until the last person has finished, breath in together again, and sing out 'A' one note higher up than you just sang. When the last person has finished, all breathe in together, and sing out 'E' on one note higher than you just sang. Continue through the vowel sounds including the final 'Ah', going up one note each time. Be sure with each sound to let your mouth move to form that sound.

When you are finished, sit quietly and notice any effects of this exercise. The effects increase with practice. This is a great exercise to do each morning, to energise, balance, and cleanse your system.

Exercise 12 'In the Mirror of Thee' For two or more people. This exercise is based on the concept that deep down, underneath all of the things which make us different, underneath all of our individual personality idiosyncrasies, we're all really pretty much the same. We're all basically dealing with the same issues in life, like security, self-esteem, relationships. We're all just human beings on this planet, trying to make it work for ourselves and for others. We've got more of the really important stuff in common, than we have differences.

For this exercise, create a very simple tune for the phrase 'In the mirror of Thee, I see me'. Sing it all together a few times. During the exercise, you will be singing this to each other: 'In the mirror of Thee, I see me'. When I look at you, its just like a reflection of me — another person dealing with the same basic things — life!

Now stand across from a partner. Look into each other's left eye ('the window to the soul'). All together now, standing in pairs, sing 'In the mirror of Thee, I see me' three times. Really look at this person, and absorb the reality of what you are saying; that they are basically just like you. You have more in common with each other, on more important levels, than you have differences.

After the third time, say goodbye to this person in whatever way seems appropriate, and turn around to find a new partner. When everyone is across from a new partner, all together start singing again 'In the mirror of Thee, I see me' three times, really understanding what you're saying. Then say goodbye, and move on. If you are in a large group, after doing this with about six partners, come into a circle, hold hands, and sing it three times to everyone.

Another way the mirror concept can be used is in recognising that if there is some-thing about someone that you really don't like, there's a good chance that they are just being a 'mirror' for you; they are reflecting back to you a part of yourself that you do not like. In this way, they are really serving you, showing you a part of yourself you might like to work more on. This isn't true 100 per cent of the time, but pretty close! So check it out. See if it's a part of you you're seeing and disliking in this other person. They are just being a mirror — thank them for that! Remember, our commonality is greater than our differences.

VISUAL ARTS

Exercise 13 'Mandala of Change' For one or more people. You will need a piece of paper with a circle drawn on it about 13 centimetres in diameter for each person, coloured crayons, and some tape.

As in Exercise 9, think of an aspect of yourself that you would like to change; that you would like to energise its 'transition to its next phase'.

Sit down or lie down, close your eyes, and take a few deep breaths, allowing any tension that may be in your body to start melting away with each exhale. Do this for several minutes, becoming more and more relaxed. Now think about this part of yourself that you would like to change. Think about the way it is *right now* — how it feels in your body, how it sounds in your voice. Feel into what it's like to be that way.

When you have felt this for several minutes, let the image and thoughts be released, disappear. Feel them floating up and away from you. Feel them releasing their hold on you. Feel yourself open to change. Return to your slow, deep, relaxing breathing.

Now focus on what it would be like with this part of you different. Really feel yourself different, just the way you wish to be, what that feels like. What it sounds like. What you look like. How you act with this change. What it *feels* like to be exactly the way you want to be in this aspect of yourself. Allow an image to form in your mind's eye, that symbolises the new you — that symbolises the completion of this transformation.

When this image has become clear to you, slowly open your eyes and get paper and crayons and draw this image in the circle. (Make a mark where the centre of the circle is, so that you will be able to recognise the centre later.) Allow this drawing to represent the change in you completed.

Take 20 minutes at least for the drawing and when it is complete, look at the picture, and once again feel in your body what this 'new way' is like.

Now tape the picture to a wall, so that when you sit in front of it the centre of the circle is at eye level. Sit in front of your picture and close your eyes. Take a few slow, deep breaths, and relax. Now slowly open your eyes, and simply gaze at the centre of the circle. Imagine that with every inhale you are drawing in the essence of the picture into yourself. Meditate on your picture like this for 10 minutes, with no particular effort.

After 10 minutes, close your eyes slowly, and once again feel how you feel inside. Feel how the image has filled you.

Now allow it to fade from active consciousness, and return to your slow, deep, relaxing breathing. When it feels appropriate, open your eyes.

Tape this picture up somewhere in your home where you see it frequently, and meditate upon it in this way for at least five minutes each day for the next 10 days. ENJOY!

CHAPTER 7
COLOUR HEALING & COLOUR BREATHING

Fai Chivell Hast

Colour Therapy (also known as Chromotherapy) is the art of using different colours to change or maintain vibrations to a frequency which will restore health and harmony to the human body and mind.

The colour rays are applied to the body either physically, through direct exposure to the light rays, or mentally, through techniques of suggestion, visualisation or meditation. Colour healing was probably the first type of therapy used by ancient man. All civilisations have worshipped the sun, for from the sun came light and colour which were natural phenomena for maintaining the balance and rhythm of the organism. Whether we acknowledge it or not, colour is basic to any and all healing systems.

The ancient Egyptians were very specific about their use of colour and associated the various rays with the Gods they worshipped. They believed that the colours blue, yellow and red were the activating forces of man's physical, mental and spiritual being. The blues were said to be most powerful in the morning and in the springtime and were

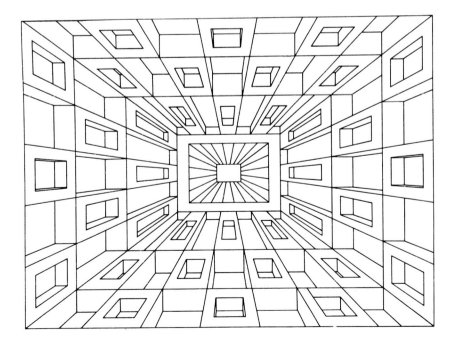

associated with the God Thoth. The yellow rays were associated with Isis, were most powerful at noon and in the summer, and were responsible for activating and stimulating man's mentality. The red ray assigned to Osiris was stronger in the afternoon and in the autumn and was thought to enter through the breath and gave man life. The Egyptians developed a healing technique of drinking solarised water.* This form of colour therapy is still practised by the Indians, Chinese and South American Indians.

Closer to modern times, many miracle cures were reported in the cathedrals of the Middle Ages and were attributed to the stained glass windows of red, purple, green and yellow. As the sun streamed through the coloured glass and on to the occupants, many ills were cured. In those dark, gloomy days it is no wonder that the bodies of the ill and infirm were stimulated by the beneficial colour rays.

These reports may have influenced the early experiments with colour during the eighteenth and nineteenth centuries. In 1878 Edwin D. Babbitt, MD, published *The Principles of Light and Color* and caused an uproar in medical circles. Babbitt utilised panes of coloured glass placed in front of ordinary windows. The coloured glass panes were moved to follow the sun and provided maximum benefit for the patient who was being treated while he/she was working or resting. Babbitt wrote: 'Long repeated colour therapy treatment plus proper diet produces wonders'.

Many therapists in recent times have substituted coloured gelatin sheets, like those used in theatre lights, and have achieved astonishing results. The gelatin filters are placed in front of a lamp with a 60–100 watt incandescent globe. The light is then focused on the area needing treatment. The person is treated either sitting in a chair or reclining on a bed in a warm darkened room, with as much of the skin bared as possible.

* To solarise water, place clean, clear rain water, river water or distilled water into a container; cover. Wrap the required coloured cellophane around the container and place in the sun for at least one hour, preferably longer. Keep in refrigerator till needed. Drink the colour-solarised water at room temperature. Be sure to sip solarised water slowly for maximum benefit. This is another way of introducing colour to your system. Blue solarised water is extremely cooling to the body on hot summer days.

All living creatures have a radiation sense. Some researchers say that the visible light of the sun acts directly on the superficial layers of the skin and has a definite metabolic effect.

The beaming of colours on to the body through direct application to the skin appears to be a form of 'feeding' colour to the body through light rather than through food.

Most people imagine light to be white. Light is in fact made up of all the colours of the spectrum. This is broken into seven bands of colours — the rainbow — which graduates from red at the long wavelength or low-frequency end of the scale through to violet at the short wavelength or high-frequency end. These bands are the seven qualities or divisions of pure white light. Colour is the *quality* of light — the seven distinct qualities being red, orange, yellow, green, blue, indigo and violet.

The red, yellow and orange rays fatigue and irritate sooner than the other colours. They are the heat-producing and exciting rays and a quiet, relaxed person will be excited or irritated by bright colours incorrectly combined. Blue, green and indigo are cool and soothing and a nervous, quick moving person is calmed by them. But colour does far more than evoke an emotional response in our subconscious mind; we not only see colour, we 'feel' it. We feel it by the reason of its action upon the millions of cells that go to make up the bones, blood, lymph, muscle and tissue of our physical body. Research has found that people will emphatically say they are colder in a blue room than in a red one. In fact, body temperature will drop even if the rooms are of identical temperatures. This reaction even occurs when subjects are blindfolded. Further tests have been conducted on people who were blind from birth. It was found that they were also able to 'feel' the difference and their body reactions were the same as those of sighted people.

At present, psychologists disagree as to whether our colour preferences are a result of education and training or whether we are born with them. However, colour therapists say that we are born with certain colour preferences and that these reveal certain personality types. In general, people respond positively to all colours and, if there is an outright rejection of any, this indicates a disturbed, frustrated, unhappy or ill person. Similarly, an overreaction to colour can be a sign of mental confusion, flightiness, poor direction or lack of discipline.

Our colour preferences can also alter as we grow and mature, signifying that a person's character is undergoing change. There is also a notable difference between those who are more sensitive to the warm colours — extroverts — and those who are sensitive to the cool ones — introverts. Those who prefer warm colours are characterised by their receptiveness to their social environment. They are emotionally outward-going, mentally alert, objective and assertive. People who prefer the cooler end of the spectrum are less likely to express themselves freely, may appear cold and detached and tend to be more subjective in their thinking. People with open characters and dispositions are more likely to prefer primary colours, whereas people who are more complex and selective usually express a wider choice.

Red and blue are the two most commonly chosen colours and are usually related to people with extrovert or introvert characteristics. Red for extroverts; blue for introverts.

The famous American psychic Edgar Cayce believed that a person's favourite colour revealed his/her major aura colour, hence the reason for being drawn to that particular colour or its variants.

The aura has been described as emanating from man's physical body. Humans have aspects other than the dense, physical body. This has been known throughout the ages by those who have studied the subtle forces of nature. These other bodies, seven in all, have been grouped in various ways and called by various names and are collectively known as the aura.

All seven bodies make up what we call man. Many people react to others' auras unconsciously. We all 'see' auras even if we don't consciously realise it. This is reflected in our language when we say red with rage, green with envy, blue mood, etc. In her book *Color and Personality*, Audrey Kargere, PhD, states:

There was a well-known judge who could often tell the general character of a speaker's thoughts, before they were even spoken, from the colours of the emanations he saw around the speaker's head.

The seven bodies are:

The Physical Body   This has dense visible matter and also finer physical matter not visible to the naked eye — the electrons and protons of the atoms. In effect, our physical body is condensed colour.

The Etheric Body   This body is often called the etheric double as it is an exact duplicate in every cell and organ of the physical body. It is the model upon which the physical body is formed, but is capable of great expansion and contraction and can extend beyond or out of the physical body, be moulded to any shape or form, take on any colour, and return to the physical body unchanged. It can draw out a long thread of itself and send thought-forms along this thread to any distance. The chakras or gateways reside in the etheric body.

The Vital Body   This is made up of millions of bristle-like fibres that resemble points of light or prisms similar to a mosaic. The vital body is the receiver and distributor of vital force, which is stored in the etheric body.

The Astral Body   This is the body of emotions and desires. It is in the astral that we experience dreams and out-of-body states. It can travel by a silver thread of 'force' to any distance.

The Lower Mental Body   It is where our waking consciousness dwells and is the vehicle of the reasoning, thinking, willing mind; its activity is in the action of brain-waves.

The Higher Mental Body   The vehicle of the higher mind and the intuitive faculties, it is from this body that we perceive phenomena of ESP, precognition, clairvoyance, etc.

The Spiritual Body   The body of spiritual consciousness links man with the universe. The colour of this body is called the major ray and represents the individual's spiritual development. This colour is usually stable, whereas the colours of the other bodies are continually changing according to the emotions and thoughts of the moment.

The aura is as much a part of a person as the face or liver — it is a protective shell, an armour of light and is completely individual.

Throughout each day every individual is continually creating thought-forms. These thought-forms direct the trend of one's life and are responsible for the form and appearance that the individual presents to the world. Negative thought patterns can imprison the higher self and cause disease, ageing and emotional and mental disorders. Through colour breathing we can eliminate negative thought-forms and bring about renewed vitality.

Colour breathing works through the action of the skin and lungs. The skin is a receptacle that can contain negative vibrations; its texture shows the trend of a person's thinking — fine or otherwise.

For example, in moments of embarrassment or shock we have all experienced the outbreak of perspiration along with a slightly tightening sensation. If we touch the skin at this moment it feels rigid with a stony-like texture. During this momentary action, we deposit minute particles of petrified matter within the skin layers. These particles are highly toxic; they cling to certain nerve ends in the skin which are connected to the nerve centres that have been stimulated by the emotional reaction. These nerve ends respond to specific colours.

The tiny particles of petrified matter which are deposited through emotional or mental reactions eventually clog the glands of the skin and in time this causes wrinkles and the appearance of age. It is the accumulation of faulty emotional and mental responses, along with bad dietary habits, that is responsible for the ageing of the body, not the number of years it has been functioning.

Through colour breathing one can destroy this shell of petrified toxins which are the result of emotional or mental 'storms', whether outwardly expressed or inwardly felt. Through the practice of colour breathing the individual can find renewed life and health.

All of the seven bodies have their part to play in our being, but in colour breathing practices we concern ourselves with the etheric body only.

As stated, the etheric body is an exact duplicate of the physical body, but it vibrates at a much higher rate. Metaphysical research has shown that in many cases disease actually appears or registers in the etheric body first and then moves into the physical. The physical body is a copy-cat and this realisation gives us a system whereby we can influence our physical body for health or appearance, via the etheric body.

The etheric body is a blueprint for the physical. In the following colour breathing exercises, the physical body becomes the servant of the etheric. The etheric body will faithfully reproduce in the physical whatever has been programmed.

Thoughts are things and the mind is the builder of our thoughts. We are the sum total of our thinking. We can be diseased today as a result of what we thought, felt or did yesterday, last week, or last year. This may be difficult to accept at first, so let's elaborate further. If a thought occurs accompanied by a strong feeling such as fear, this deeply impresses the etheric body and also animates the subconscious into action. This combination has a powerful influence in shaping our future.

Through colour breathing and visualisation we can transmute inharmonious thought-forms and feelings into more harmonious and positive ones.

The most important thing to remember with colour breathing is to visualise and feel what we *want*; not what we *don't want*. Colour visualisation forms our 'new' or desired blueprint in the etheric body. This is not done overnight. It must be repeated again and again until the blueprint has well and truly imprinted itself in the etheric. Negative and half-hearted thinking never accomplishes anything but negative and half-hearted results.

It is important to select the proper colour for each problem (see colour selection chart). If we seek out the colour of the thought-form we wish to destroy, then apply its opposite colour. This brings about change.

When first practising colour breathing it seems that not many people can clearly visualise purity of colour other than that of the colour group to which he/she belongs. Exceptions to this rule do occur, however, usually amongst people whose occupations are in the field of colour and whose appreciation and visualisation is highly developed. Without this sensitivity people may clearly visualise their own colour ray — red, say — but it is difficult at first for them to visualise clearly any of the other six spectral colours. It takes practice, but if you begin the exercise trying to visualise blue and all you seem to be able to see is yellow then you can be sure that yellow is your major colour ray. Every colour that is visualised appears to be tinged with the dominant or major colour. Consequently when a red person thinks of blue, he/she is prone to visualise a blue tinged with red, resulting in a purplish-blue. A yellow person trying to visualise red will produce a mental picture of an orangey-red.

Along with our major colour we have three others that are associated with activity, intellect and will.

The colour selected for activity is the one through which a person can best be activated. This colour is also the one through which a person can express his/her creativity. The colour of the intellect is the colour that a person responds to for rest and use of this colour brings about relaxation for tired nerves and body. The colour of the will is the colour of inspiration and meditation.

With colour breathing techniques we are not restricted to any one colour but can select different ones for different problems. To obtain a feeling of vitality, clean blood is necessary and is, in fact, the foundation upon which good health is built and maintained. The colours of vitality and energy are red and orange. Orange has a 'freeing' action which helps to break-up deposits of toxic matter and is excellent in relieving arthritis and bronchitis and for giving that little extra 'boost' that we all need now and then. For rebuilding health after an illness, visualise yourself bathed in the green, blue or violet rays. These colours assist in changing grey, dull or bitter thoughts into bright, cheerful ones.

When recovering from a physical, mental or emotional illness, it is beneficial to repeat an affirmation of positive thinking — for example, the healing ray of (colour) is filling my whole being with vital energy, health and peaceful vibrations.

The breathing in and visualising of the colour blue will alleviate pain. The colour to visualise is a clear, sapphire blue. For those who suffer insomnia, the colours to visualise are violet or lavender.

Pink works wonders for wrinkles, acne, sagginess, puffiness and looseness of the skin anywhere on the face or body. It is an excellent colour for eliminating scars caused from surgery or child-bearing.

Pale green is effective in improving vision and eye injuries. Indigo is helpful for cataracts. The beautiful blue-green turquoise ray has brought about changes in the circulatory system, relieved respiratory ailments, eased the pain associated with arthritis and is of vital importance to the re-growth of skin tissue. For any wounds or scars, visualise turquoise and relax. Turquoise is extremely helpful in losing weight.

Rose-pink is the universal colour for creating rapport with others and is beneficial in re-generating organs. This ray is a good therapeutic for those who do not like themselves. By visualising rose-pink, many people have begun to see themselves in an entirely different way. This brings about positive and dramatic healing and personality changes.

If you are ever in doubt as to the colour to visualise and breathe, use white. White contains all the colours of the spectrum and benefits all disorders. It is a powerful protector for yourself and loved ones.

Most people have tried meditation at some stage, and colour breathing gives you the opportunity to embark upon the adventure regularly. It is pointless trying it just once. Since your problems were not made overnight, it will take an effort from you to change. But regular practice of colour breathing will produce marvellous results.

Little notice is taken of our breathing habits in day-to-day living. Only when our breathing process is disturbed do most of us become aware of it. Ordinary breathing is not sufficiently attuned or rhythmic enough to bring about healing on its own. Through conscious effort we can alter our breathing patterns to boost the oxygen in our blood and therefore help clean and purify it. This is the first step to good health.

There are three types of breathing used in colour healing.

The first is inhalation-exhalation through the nose and is designed to introduce a contemplative state; air is drawn in and out at a slower rate. This has a great effect on the area above the shoulders.

The second form of breathing is the open-mouth technique which provides more air in a shorter period of time and is useful in external states of activity and has an effect on the body below the shoulders. Nasal breathing has its primary effect on thought processes while the open-mouth technique is effective when combined with physical activity.

The third form is a combination of both, achieved by inhaling through the nose, holding the breath while visualising, then exhaling through the mouth, holding the breath out while visualising a clearing out of the body. The diagram shows correct diaphragm-breathing action. This action should be applied whether lying, sitting or standing.

The first step in colour healing is to select a time when you will not be disturbed by door-bells, telephones, etc. This is your time and the only commitment you have is to yourself.

Adopt a relaxed state, either lying down, sitting with the spine straight in a comfortable chair, or standing straight but relaxed; at ease. Take your time. Do not expect instant results. Do not worry if at first you cannot visualise the colours. If they do not appear at first it is only because you are not used to imagining in colour. The colour will appear with practice.

After achieving a relaxed state, try to recall how you looked and felt at some happy time in your life. Don't get locked into the situation, just recall how you felt and looked. Imagine yourself being like that *now*. It is difficult at first and will take a little effort: old thought-forms die hard and you will need to keep a watchful eye on them slipping into your meditations. For those who just cannot remember ever feeling and looking good, imagine what you would like to be. Get a good picture of yourself since the stronger you can visualise the stronger the image will be that the etheric body receives. Hold this image but do not allow yourself to become tense. Stay in a relaxed state. Then visualise the colour you need and let it grow in your mind's eye. At first the colour may be muddy, mixed with your major colour, or unclear. Persist.

When you have achieved a reasonable degree of the colour you have chosen, then imagine your whole being bathed in its radiance. Keep your breath rhythmic and easy. Visualise the appropriate colour being drawn into your solar plexus (diaphragm) with your inward breath and spreading right through your body just beneath the skin. For specific areas, imagine the colour penetrating your solar plexus and then direct it to the area in need of assistance. With the outward breath, visualise a release of toxic matter from the body.

As you become more proficient at visualisation, try the 'four-four' breathing technique. As you visualise, breath in to the count of four, hold your breath for the count of four. When holding the breath this is the time to absorb and hold the colour, or to direct it to the problem area. Then slowly release the breath, also to the count of four, visualising a cleansing of the system. When the breath is released, hold it once again to the count of four and visualise your 'new self' — happy, healthy and peaceful. Repeat this as often as possible. Always finish your colour breathing with an affirmation of health and well-being.

Don't be disappointed if you fall asleep while colour breathing. This is normal and sleep is nature's way of making you relax. Practise colour breathing for at least 15 minutes each day. Increase this time to 30 minutes. The best results are obtained when colour breathing is done first thing after waking and last thing at night.

For those who wish to incorporate some form of exercise into their colour breathing, stand, sit or lie down as described before; relax and visualise. Then, with the inward breath, extend your arms up over your head and hold this position for the count of four. With the outward breath, lower the arms to the side, hold, then begin again.

Colour breathing can be done while practising Tai Chi, aerobics or related forms of exercise. There is no reason why we cannot condition ourselves to breath colour all day long and in all the things we do.

CORRECT DIAPHRAGM BREATHING

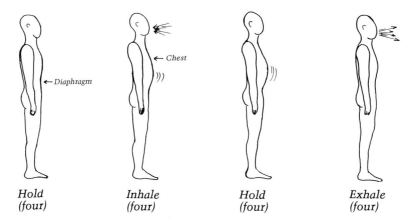

| Hold | Inhale | Hold | Exhale |
| *(four)* | *(four)* | *(four)* | *(four)* |

COLOUR SELECTION CHART

RED

Properties: Warm, the ray of strength and vitality, a stimulant

Opposite Colour: Blue

Therapeutic Action: Increases the temperature, heart beat, circulation and stimulates the liver and spleen

Use for: Lumbago, rheumatoid arthritis, sciatica, anaemia, colds, paralysis. Raises blood pressure, releases adrenalin. Stimulates hearing, seeing, smelling, tasting, touching. Exhaustion. Cleaning blood

Negative Action: Should not be used by alcholics or ruddy, overweight types, people with high blood pressure or on inflamed conditions

Red Foods: Beetroot, tomatoes, red cabbage, spinach, silverbeet, cherries, currants, watermelon, grapes, whole wheat, liver, radishes

Variants: *Scarlet* — courage, sex stimulant, helps potency and frigidity, raises blood pressure, renal, heart, kidney and adrenal stimulant

Pink — raises emotional vibrations, the colour of universal healing. Useful in rejuvenating the skin, removing wrinkles, acne, puffiness and sagginess. Removes scars caused by surgery or child-bearing. Reduces weight

Magenta — boost vitality rate, cardiac and adrenal tonic, stimulates genitals, revitalises spine

ORANGE

Properties: Warm, the ray of energy, a stimulant

Opposite Colour: Indigo

Therapeutic Action: Energises the thyroid gland, increases vital energy, depresses para-thyroid action, expands lung action, activates respiratory system. Has emetic effect. Can be used when red cannot

Use for: Coughs, colds, bronchitis, cramps or muscle spasms. Toning up digestive system, stimulating milk-production after childbirth, relieving asthma and ulcer conditions. Increases enthusiasm, stimulates pancreas

Negative Action: Should not be used in acute inflammatory states

Orange Foods: Carrots, pumpkins, oranges, peaches, apricots, canteloupe, mangoes, eggs and dairy products

Variants: *Orchid* — for spiritual attunement

Gold — for healing in general, helps put a gloss and shine to the hair

Colour breathing of orange ray will transmute brown and grey moods

YELLOW

Properties: Warm, the ray of intellect. It activates the motor nerves and generates energy for muscles. A stimulant

Opposite Colour: Violet

Therapeutic Action: Stimulates the mind, relieves lethargy, activates digestive system, liver and kidneys. Increases skin secretion. Acts as a tonic and blood cleanser. Activates colon and sluggish lymphatics

Use for: All sluggish conditions, for revitalising the whole system, for fluid retention, constipation. Increasing mental capabilities, strengthening the nervous system. For paralysis of all kinds

Negative Action: Should not be used in hyperactive states, over-excitement, nausea, diarrhoea, irritability or by those who suffer from insomnia

Yellow Foods: Corn, bananas, pineapples, lemons, grapefruit, parsnips, butter, eggs, cheese

Variants: *Lemon* — relieves colds, stimulates thymus gland, increases brain activity, blood cleanser, tonic, stimulates motor nerves. Removes toxic waste. Bone and tissue builder. Useful where congestion is present

GREEN

Properties: Cool, the ray of harmony and the master healer, a relaxant

Opposite Colour: Magenta

Therapeutic Action: A tonic, it strengthens without stimulating or sedating. Helps combat infection, builds cell tissue. Excellent for insomnia and irritability. Soothes stomach and liver inflammation. Improves vision. Calms nerves

Use for: Relieving exhaustion and inflamed conditions. Insomnia, hypertension, headaches, sore eyes, emotional upsets

Negative Action: Should not be used in anaemic conditions

Green Foods: All green vegetables, celery, asparagus, peas, beans, cabbage

Variants: *Turquoise* — cools fevers, reduces weight, prime skin builder, hastens formation of new skin, relieves pain, has quietening effect on overactive mental states. For treating sunburn, relieving itching and a general tonic to the skin

BLUE

Properties: Cool, the ray of inspiration and a relaxant

Opposite Colour: Red

Therapeutic Action: Relieves inflammation and fever, heals burns and pain of all kinds. It has a calming, soothing effect and is an astringent, and antiseptic

Use for: Burns, itching, eczema, laryngitis. Activating the pituitary gland and the etheric body. For pain of any kind. Lowers the blood pressure

Negative Action: Should not be used when fatigue, depression, paralysis or constipation is present

Blue Foods: Berries, grapes, prunes and plums

Variants: *Dark Blue* — mends bones

INDIGO

Properties: Cool, the ray of intuition and is a relaxant

Opposite Colour: Orange

Therapeutic Action: Has sedative and pain-relieving qualities. Stimulates the para-thyroid gland. Depresses the thyroid gland and respiratory system. Helps reduce bleeding and excessive menstrual flow. Stimulates formation of white blood cells in the spleen

Use for: Diseases of the eye, ear and nose. Cornea, styes, deafness and cataracts. Pneumonia, pain and inflammation. Swelling, convulsions, tonsillitis, whooping cough, haemorrhages. Toning muscles, nerves and skin. Relieving the pain of colitis

Negative Action: Should not be used when chills are present

Indigo Foods: Blueberries, blue plums, blue grapes

Variants: *Purple* — depresses the sex drive, activates without irritating the liver, lungs and kidneys. An inspirational colour

VIOLET

Properties: Cool, the ray of spirituality and a relaxant

Opposite Colour: Yellow

Therapeutic Action: Stimulates the pineal gland, sedates the mind and nervous system. A powerful bactericide and parasiticide. Encourages bone growth, activates white blood-cell production. Depresses lymph and motor nerves, maintains potassium-sodium balance in body

Use for: Bladder trouble, cramps, concussion, epilepsy, neuralgia, nervous and mental disorders, sciatica, dandruff, dermatitis. Lowering heart rate, inducing sleep. Soothing tired nerves and overactive adrenals

Negative Action: Should not be used when energy is required, when chills are present or when depressed

Violet Foods: Egg plant, red cabbage, blackberries

Variants: *Lavender* — eases tired nerves, relaxes the muscles. Induces sleep

CHAPTER 8

MUSIC &
SELF-TRANSFORMATION

Nevill Drury

THE POWERS OF MUSIC

Music has many wonderful and distinctive qualities. It can intensify our feelings, summon to mind associated images and memories, transport us into a state of awe or simply charm us through the delicacy of melody. In primitive trance rituals, frantic monotonous drumming can lead mediums into a state of spirit-possession, while in Indian music drones and mantras are used to focus the mind and lead it through its many distractions to a state of inner peace and unity.

Clearly, music speaks to us in a special way — and one of the core ingredients of music is rhythm. According to musicologists Manfred Clynes and Janice Walker, rhythm is intrinsic to animal behaviour — whether we are considering such activities as flying, walking, swimming or running — and the rhythms which characterise these movements are controlled by the programmes of the central nervous system.* In man, these rhythms have become linked with the imagination and can influence our moods, our attitudes, and the way we feel. Indeed, in the extreme example of trance dancing, rhythm expresses itself in movement and gesture in such a total way that there is a complete shift of consciousness — from the everyday, familiar world to the altered state of myth and magical transformation.

Inner health is also about self-transformation, but in a more composed and self-aware way. The trance medium who is possessed by a tribal god loses consciousness and is subsumed by the incoming deity. The sort of self-transformation we are advocating here is a broadening of the spectrum of inner events accompanied by full sensory awareness: a resolution of states of conflict and tension to achieve a new sense of integration and wholeness.

The Viennese writer Victor Zuckerkandl has suggested that 'words divide' whereas 'tones unite',** and it may be that while so many factors in the modern technological world urge us towards precision, objectivity and measurement, we need more than ever a way to channel our subjective feelings and emotions. These, after all, are also an important part of our human experience.

Exactly why music affects our state of consciousness can only be hinted at. Perhaps, for example, the experience we had as infants listening to our mother's heartbeat, and our subsequent awareness of the pattern of our breathing — a crucial factor of our

---

* 'Neurobiologic functions of rhythm, time and pulse in music' in M. Clynes, 1982:pp. 171–172.
** V. Zuckerkandl, 1973 (vol. 2):p. 75.

existence — are directly linked to our experience of rhythm. It also seems that our awareness of time is an important factor. For most people, it appears, a rate of less than 80 beats per minute is 'slow', whereas more than 90 beats per minute is 'fast', and as we all know our perception of rhythm can have an immediate influence on our moods and feelings. A more leisurely beat tends to relax and soothe, while an up-tempo beat exhilarates and excites.

However, music has several other important qualities apart from rhythm, and these affect still further the range and qualities of our perception:

Intensity and volume
These contribute power and impact. In music, intensity arises as tones are added layer upon layer — a characteristic, for example, of most types of orchestral music. Intensity is one of the ingredients of 'carrying power' — the ability music has to literally transport us into other realms of awareness.

Timbre
This is the quality of 'richness' in music. It is often linked to volume but also to the sonic structure of the composition. Rich and 'full' music tends to be more convincing and the images it summons to mind are correspondingly more 'real'.

Consonance and dissonance

Chords in music tend to be of two kinds — those which create tension (dissonance) and those which tend towards resolution or harmony (consonance). The presence of consonance and dissonance in music creates important dynamic contrasts which have a direct effect on the listener. For most people, a 'satisfying' musical composition is one which leads the listener through a range of tonal contrasts to a state of resolution.

Music and Health   From a therapeutic point of view the music that is of most use in attaining inner health tends to take the following forms:

• music which reduces stress or induces relaxation. This music allows us to enter a state of consciousness midway on the spectrum between normal alertness and sleep;

• music which summons specific images to mind and which can in turn be used to focus upon one's inner processes;

• music for encountering repressed or unacknowledged dimensions of the self;

• music which leads the listener through a transitionary process from one mode to another;

• music which lifts one's consciousness to a transcendental or blissful state.

Each of these categories of music can be valuable in the process of attaining inner health. However, at this stage it is appropriate to consider some of the varied visualisation techniques available for our purpose. The following approaches each lend themselves to musical adaptation or include the use of sound as an integral part of the technique. The systems described here come from quite different sources: from European psychotherapy, primitive shamanism and Indian mysticism.

GUIDED IMAGERY AND VISUALISATION

Guided imagery has been used extensively in psychotherapy since the pioneering work of Robert Desoille, Eugene Caslant, Carl Happich and Hanscarl Leuner. The work originated in Europe but has had a major impact on the Human Potential Movement, especially through popular adaptations like Robert Masters' and Jean Houston's 'mind games', the Silva Mind Control method and Alexander Everett's Mind Dynamics. It is also an integral part of the contemporary approach to cancer meditation therapy advocated by Dr Carl Simonton and Dr David Bresler.

Eugene Caslant, whose work is seminal to this process, emphasised the idea that certain meditative symbols had a particular psychological effect. Symbols of ascent like a staircase or flying chariot, for example, tended to lead the meditator towards a feeling of tranquillity and self-composure, while 'descending' in the imagination could produce feelings of anxiety and fear associated with the perception of darkness.

Like Caslant, Robert Desoille also believed that the idea of ascent and descent mirrored a psychological reality and that it was present even in our language. In *The Directed Daydream* he commented:

In both instances we are dealing with a basic law of the mind; it is expressed in everyday language when we speak of 'bright ideas', 'warm feelings' and 'lofty thoughts'. And, on the other hand, we recognise, 'shady deals', 'a cool reception' and 'low deeds'. *

Desoille developed the idea of leading his subjects through symbolic imaginal situations which would reveal aspects of their personal psychological makeup. This

* R. Desoille, 1966: p. 2

The patient must learn to control the 'archetypes' within himself, to be free of them, and thereby lose his fear of them . . .

involved patterns of both ascent and descent. For example Desoille might ask his subject to imagine himself at the foot of a mountain and then to start climbing. Some patients would find this an easy task and move along at a brisk pace, while others might encounter major or insuperable obstacles. Those experiencing difficulty would be subsequently assisted with the suggestion of 'helpers' of various kinds (friends, loved ones, or even supernatural beings). Other themes employed by Desoille included the following:

Purpose	Theme
Confronting one's more suppressed characteristics	For both sexes, a descent into the depths of the ocean
Coming to terms with the parent of the opposite sex	For a man, a descent into a cave to find a witch or a sorceress
	For a woman, a descent into a cave to find a wizard or a magician
Coming to terms with the parent of one's own sex	For a man, a descent into a cave to find a wizard or a magician
	For a woman, a descent into a cave to find a witch or a sorceress*

Here, Desoille employed mythic images rather than encouraged imaginal encounters with the actual people at the source of the conflict. He felt his patients would be less likely to qualify their answers and replies in dialogue with such 'imaginary' beings than with the real-life counterparts they represented.

Desoille's guided imagery approach was essentially conceived to help the patient overcome personal limitations. His approach can be summarised as follows:

*The patient must learn to control the 'archetypes' within himself, to be free of them, and thereby lose his fear of them ... The goal of the technique is to direct the patient toward the fulfilment of his human potentialities through the creative development of man's basic biological impulses into a higher and harmonic idea.***

For Desoille the state of religious awareness aroused in this process was the highest level of mental functioning.

Carl Happich published several writings on guided imagery in Germany in the 1930s and, like Desoille, made use of specific meditative symbols to produce a positive mental effect. These included: a meadow, a chapel and a bubbling fountain (as well as a mountain, used in much the same way as described above).

Happich used the meadow image to gauge the mental health of his patients: the balanced and happy person would invariably populate the meadow with children, flowers or images of Spring. The unhappy or depressed person was more likely to visualise dying vegetation or barrenness, and conjure other negative motifs to fill the landscape.

The chapel image, on the other hand, was a symbol of the sacred centre of being, while meditating on the bubbly fountain attuned the patient to the energy source of life itself.

Happich was opposed to the use of symbols like a snake or scorpion which could stimulate dangerous or negative emotions and preferred to choose motifs which he felt

* R. Desoille, 1966: p. 3
** W. Kretschmer 'Meditative Techniques in Psychotherapy in C. Tart, 1969, p. 224

sure had a positive and transforming effect.

Hanscarl Leuner developed the guided imagery techniques of Carl Happich in the 1950s and similarly advocated the use of 'positive' images. He commenced his therapy sessions with the scenes of the meadow, mountain and brook which, for most people, had an unthreatening connotation. Leuner's system, which he called 'Guided Affective Imagery' included several of the symbolic situations described above, as well as some new ones:

The Stream
More far-reaching than Happich's bubbly fountain, the image of the stream was used to represent the amount of psychic energy available to the patient, and the depth and width of the stream was taken to be indicative of character, eg. 'broad-minded', 'shallow'. Obstacles in the stream were symbolic of conflicts in real life.

A House
Leuner considered the house to be an appropriate symbol of the self. The patient might start by visualising a familiar house and then extend it or explore it in an imaginary way. The more imaginary the house, the greater the insights it provided into the makeup of the psyche. The size of each imaginary room in relation to the nature of its contents was indicative of specific personal qualities.

The Ideal Personality
The patient was asked to 'hear' in his imagination the name of a person of the same sex, and then visualise that person. Leuner found that the imaginary person often represented the qualities regarded as 'ideal' by the subject.

A Swampy Pool
Leuner would ask the subject to visualise a swampy pool in the meadow and look down into the waters. Human figures or animals that appeared in the pool, or which rose out of it, were considered to be symbolic of repressed sexuality.

An Erupting Volcano
Leuner considered this symbol an ideal gauge of inner tension. The degree of violence and the amount of material erupted were highly indicative of this inner conflict.

A Lion
Leuner asked the subject to visualise a lion and then imagine it confronting someone regarded as an opponent in real life. The reaction of the lion — eating the opponent or lying passively at his or her feet — was indicative of the subject's ability to express himself effectively and interact with competitors.

An Old Picture Book
The subject was asked to imagine a house, explore its cellar and then dig a hole in its earthen floor in order to find an old book buried there. The subject was then asked to describe some of the pictures in the book. Leuner found that his patients often referred to unresolved or unexpressed issues which had arisen in earlier sessions.

Leuner also introduced the notion of the 'inner guide' to his guided imagery work. For him this persona — whether it appeared as an animal or as a wise old man — represented the positive directions of the psyche, and the subject was encouraged to communicate with it. There were also several specific strategies for relating to images:

• in a confrontation situation the subject was encouraged to watch the encounter dispassionately rather than struggle to escape;

• the subject should ideally seek reconciliation with a hostile image rather than 'wound' or 'kill' it (after all, this counter-attack could rebound on oneself);

• 'magic' fluids or potions could be visualised to relieve pain.

As mentioned earlier, guided imagery is now used extensively as a health therapy in the United States. As Dr Dennis Jaffe and Dr David Bresler note in a recent article on healing imagery, we need to distinguish between the somatic and autonomic nervous systems for we can access each of these in different ways:

*Verbal thoughts most directly access the somatic nervous system, so, if for example you wish to stand up, all you need to do is think 'stand up, now' and your voluntary nervous system will co-ordinate the appropriate muscular activity. On the other hand, the language of imagery directly accesses the autonomic nervous system which regulates breathing, the heartbeat, blood chemistry, digestion, tissue regeneration and repair, immune and inflammatory responses, and many other bodily functions essential to life.** *

As a consequence, imagery can be used for a diverse range of health functions, from simply inducing the 'relaxation response' through to visualising the healing of ruptured blood vessels or containing — and hopefully eliminating — the spread of cancerous tumours.

On one level such visualisation has to do simply with focusing on positive outcomes: optimism is always preferable to negativity. However the visualisations can also be quite specific. Dr Carl Simonton, whose work with cancer patients is well known, uses imagery techniques to counteract the notion of cancer as 'some big powerful thing' about to overrun the body. Stimulating the patient's belief in his own curative powers, the cancer visualisation might involve the image of the patient as a warring knight successfully overcoming the cancer dragon within the body, or any other pictorial metaphor that might seem appropriate to the patient. The effect is for the person with cancer to engage in his own healing process. As Dr Simonton writes:

I try to get [the patient] to produce mental descriptions of all aspects of the disease. Through these techniques the patient begins to activate his motivation to be well and to arouse emotions and problems into consciousness. *

SHAMANIC HEALING

Introduced to the Human Potential Movement in the 1970s by American anthropologist Dr Michael Harner, shamanic healing incorporates visualisation techniques within a ceremonial setting. For our purposes the healing aspect of shamanism needs to be distinguished from the path of personal knowledge and power described in the works of Carlos Castaneda. The two approaches nevertheless spring from the same tradition — the Native American Indian vision-quest.

Harner's field research in the early 1960s took him among both the South American and North American Indians, including the Jivaro of the Ecuadorian Andes, the Wintun, Pomo, Coast Salish, Conibo and Lakota Sioux, and it was among these peoples that he learned shamanism first-hand. The method he presents is essentially a synthesis adapted for a Western audience, while still remaining true to the principles of mainstream shamanism.

Harner's workshops — presented at Esalen Institute and at other 'growth' centres in the United States and Europe — feature the beating of a large flat drum which the person taking the role of shaman uses as a vehicle to travel into the 'mythic world'.

---

* Dr D. T. Jaffe and Dr D. E. Bresler, 1980, p. 254
** C. and S. Simonton, 1976, p. 63

Michael Harner with drum

Forming the 'spirit-canoe'

In shamanic terms this is the domain of the spirits of disease and also the place where one's source of healing power may be tapped.

Using a technique which resembles the visualisation and guided imagery methods described earlier, the shaman travels in the mind's eye through a crack in the ground, a gateway, or down through the root system of a large tree to meet a force in the other world that is traditionally called the 'power animal'. The shaman discovers in this power animal his own source of vitality, and in many shamanic societies it is considered that no healthy person could survive in the physical world without such an entity as an inner ally.

Harner believes that the monotonous drum rhythms produced during a shamanic session activate theta patterns in the brain (associated with creative thought) and also simulate the rhythmic beating of the heart — the pulse of life. The shaman 'rides' the drum-beat in an imaginal way and learns to function consciously within the altered state of consciousness which now becomes his operative domain.

In Harner's shamanic healing workshops the favoured technique is that of the 'spirit canoe'. In this workshop the participants — ideally there may be between 12 and 15 — sit on the floor in a canoe-configuration and face the same direction. The person in need of healing — a person who in a true sense is dis-spirited — lies in the centre of the 'canoe'. At the same time one of the group members sits at the rear, ready to beat the drum. The drumming will enable the participants to focus their energies towards the healing purpose at hand.

The healer-shaman, meanwhile, uses a rattle to define the sacred space wherein the transformation will occur. Gourd rattles are used to announce the shamanising and to summon the 'healing spirits'.

Dancing the power animal

The shaman now enters the spirit canoe and lies down beside the sick person. His task, once the drumming begins, is to journey into the magical world to find a power-animal for his dis-spirited client. Having signalled for the drumming to commence the shaman focuses his consciousness, accompanied by the collective will-to-heal of the members riding in the spirit canoe, and prepares to journey to the 'other world'. As mentioned earlier, the shaman rides on the drum-beat and visualises a tunnel leading to the magical domain. Here he looks for an animal which, according to shamanic tradition, presents itself to view from four different directions.

Once the animal has appeared, the shaman's role is to clasp it to his chest and, imaginally, to return with it to the everyday world. He now kneels beside the sick person, signifying to the client to sit upright, and 'breathes' the animal into the patient's head. Then, lowering the sick person down to the floor again, he breathes the animal into the chest.

The shaman whispers to the client, 'I have given you a deer' or 'I have given you a hare', depending on which creature has presented itself, and the formerly dis-spirited person prepares to rise and 'dance' the newly received power-animal to the accompaniment, once again, of the drum-beat. For the recipient of shamanic healing the shamanising can produce a dramatic emotional transformation at this time. When the dance is concluded the shaman steps out of the 'canoe', signals to the four quarters with his rattles, and the healing ceremony is completed.

Shamanism is essentially a primitive religious form which utilises altered states of consciousness either for healing or for acquiring personal power. It differs from spirit-possession — the type of trance state associated especially with African and Caribbean cultures — to the extent that the shaman always retains consciousness, while the possessed trance medium does not. The shaman's journey is a vision-quest to the inner world — in psychological terms a venture into the subconscious mind. As with the visualisation methods employed by Dr Simonton, the shamanic technique makes use of powerful metaphors for tapping the positive, integrating forces which are accessible to man for healing. The symbolic transfer of energy from the shaman to the patient is an act of spiritual 'channelling', and in a workshop or ritual setting frequently stimulates self-renewal and healing in the patient. The final dance of acceptance and thanksgiving completes the shamanic process

MEDITATION

A popular misconception about meditation is that it is a type of passive introversion, a peaceful but ineffectual form of self-centredness. In fact, meditation as a technique of mind control has very positive benefits for health. Those who practise meditation systematically and regularly believe it leads to increased inner calm, heightened powers of creativity and decision-making, increased efficiency in the work situation, and decreased mental tension and negative emotions. Many ailments that are stress-related can be eliminated or reduced by meditation, including migraine and tension headaches, high blood pressure, heart trouble and menstrual cramps.

The meditative approach to life is traditionally associated with Hinduism and Buddhism although it is also found to a lesser extent in Islam and Christianity. It is fair to say, however, that meditative techniques have developed more systematically within the Eastern experiential traditions than in the Western creed-based religions.

The researcher R. K. Wallace, who studied Transcendental Meditation, has suggested that meditation in itself may actually be an identifiable state of consciousness — similar to, but distinct from, sleeping, dreaming and waking. Essentially, meditation produces heightened powers of awareness and deep tranquillity: it is a journey to the inner self.

Various meditation techniques have become prominent in the West in recent years. Among the most popular are the mantric method, advocated by the Maharishi Mahesh Yogi — founder of the TM movement — and the Siddha Yoga system developed by the late Swami Muktananda (see Chapter 9). The appeal of meditation is that it broadens one's sense of being. Personal anxieties, fears and tensions — which often underlie disease — acquire a diminished status and become less all-consuming than they once seemed. As Baba Ram Dass says, 'meditation frees your awareness' and opens new horizons for perception.

There are basically two approaches to meditation. The first focuses on powers of concentration, the second emphasises detached awareness.

The first approach requires that the attention be focused on a meditative symbol, a sound or chant, or on a body process like breathing. In some forms of concentration-meditation the teacher gives the pupil a mantra on which to meditate. The idea is to turn the processes of thought inwardly until the mind transcends thought itself.

With the second method, the emphasis is on what is happening *now*. The task is not so much to elevate the consciousness to a 'higher state', but to become increasingly

Maharishi Mahesh Yogi — founder of TM   Buddhist meditation — unification of mind

aware of the present moment. From that position one gains an awareness of the eternal ebb and flow of human experience.

One of the major disciplines of the Buddhist meditator, for example, is to eliminate distractions with the aim of attaining a 'unification of mind'. As the practitioner learns to meditate for a long period such factors as agitation, scepticism and doubt disappear and a feeling of bliss and reassurance begins to dominate. The meditator becomes absorbed in thought and moves deeper and deeper, finally acquiring an awareness of infinite space. In so doing, the meditator learns to break out of stereotypes of thought and perceives each moment of the everyday reality as if it were a new event. The ego becomes comparatively less important and the manifested universe is seen to be in a state of everchanging flux. This leads to the sense of detachment from the world of sense-experience, the abandonment of desire, and finally to the transcendence of the ego itself.

Concentration The first approach is exemplified by the well-known meditative system of Kundalini Yoga. According to this viewpoint, the body contains *chakras*, or spiritual energy centres, which align with the central nervous system. The meditator learns to raise the Kundalini — or 'fire serpent' — through the central energy channel *Sushumna* which passes through each of the chakras in turn. This entails sitting in the Lotus yoga position and arousing the energy from the base of the spine towards the crown.

Whole books have been dedicated to the system of Kundalini Yoga and it is not possible to summarise the method adequately in a few paragraphs. However, from the

Arousing Kundalini

perspective of sound and health which we are considering here, Kundalini Yoga is of considerable interest for several reasons:

1 the chakras correlate with different organs of the body and there is an implicit connection in yoga between states of consciousness and inner health;

2 the energy is aroused through a combination of visualisation and sound;

3 the approach is basically holistic because it encompasses all aspects of man: physical, mental and spiritual.

Of particular interest for visualisation purposes is the fact that the first five chakras are associated with the elements Earth, Water, Fire, Air and Spirit (the final chakras being essentially transcendent states of consciousness beyond specific imagery). As I have described in more detail in my book *Music for Inner Space*, and also in the workshop section of this chapter, one can practise a form of meditation to music which enhances the elemental imagery of the chakras and makes each symbol easier to focus on as an 'inner reality'. Over and above this aspect, there are also 'seed mantras' which should be intoned through the visualised chakra images and used to maintain the flow of consciousness from one energy level to the next. As we can see, the healing power of sound is an integral part of Kundalini Yoga.

The first five Kundalini chakras can be summarised as follows:

Chakra	*Location*	*Element*	*Mantra*
Muladhara	At the base of the spine, near the coccyx (associated with the pelvic plexus, testes and ovaries)	Earth	'Lam'
Svadisthana	Two inches below the navel in the sacral region (associated with the hypogastric plexus and adrenal glands)	Water	'Vam'

Manipura Three inches above the navel in the lumbar region (associated with the solar plexus, pancreas and liver)	Fire	'Ram'
Anahata Near the heart (associated with cardiac plexus and thymus gland)	Air	'Yam'
Visuddha Near the Adam's apple in the throat (associated with the cervical plexus and thyroid gland)	Spirit	'Ham'

Detached Awareness This approach is more abstract than the system of mental focusing described above and endeavours as its central aim to produce a state of inner stillness within the meditator. While experienced Kundalini Yoga practitioners often report feelings of transcendence and bliss — especially when arousing the Kundalini beyond the first five chakras described above — the technique of 'detached awareness' is more a shedding of images than a focusing of the mind.

In the context of inner health, detached awareness involves progressively letting go of anxieties and pent-up emotions in order to eliminate sources of stress which lie at the core of psychosomatic disease symptoms. The aim is to pass beyond the incessant swirling of mental impressions within the field of consciousness to a source of deep and profound peace in the heart of one's being.

Essentially different from the guided imagery technique of Dr Carl Simonton, the method of detached awareness is central to the meditation system advocated by Australian hypnotherapist Dr Ainslie Meares as a treatment for cancer.

Dr Meares' method, which he calls *mental artaraxis* (from a Greek word meaning 'absence of disturbance') involves leading the patient towards a state of inner stillness. Dr Meares encourages his patients to relax, often rests his hands on their shoulders to reassure them, and gently asks them simply to let go, to drift into a state of effortlessness, and to yield increasingly to a pervasive sense of inner calm. In reducing anxiety through meditation, Dr Meares believes, there is an actual physiological effect on the body. The cortisone level is reduced and the immune system strengthened. The self-regulating processes within the body are activated and begin to restore it to its natural, integrated state.

Achieving inner stillness in a modern urban context is, of course, easier said than done. As Dr Meares notes, even in meditation subjects tend to move in and out of stillness rather than retain a constant level. Effective meditation requires regular practice and might entail putting aside at least an hour each day for any real and lasting effect. Inner peace is attained as part of a gradual process and, by its very nature, cannot be hurried along.

There are, nevertheless, different ways of attuning oneself to the task. From my own viewpoint, detached awareness meditation can also be approached in a musical context.

In recent times there has been widespread interest in different forms of relaxation music, both in the United States and in Britain and Europe. The gentle piano music of Steven Halpern and the 'ambient' synthesiser sounds of Brian Eno are perhaps the best known examples of this genre but it also includes the tranquil flute music of Paul Horn and Larkin, the melodic synthesiser compositions of the Japanese musician Kitaro and the abstract sound textures of Nancy Hennings and Henry Wolff, who play Tibetan bells.*

---

* For a detailed overview of relaxation and ambient music see N. Drury, *Music for Inner Space*, 1985.

American flautist Larkin

The forms of inner-space music which lend themselves most effectively to detached awareness meditation are essentially non-intrusive: rather than assisting the mind to focus on mental images, the music should be chosen as a means of dispersing them. The most appropriate music, therefore, is tranquil, relaxing and abstract — without any pronounced melody line or distinct tonal qualities that could lead to the formation of associated ideas or images. In fact, the most suitable music for such meditation is as close to pure silence as possible and is used in meditation sessions simply as an adjunct to the 'yielding process'. Suggested recordings for use in this type of meditation are given at the end of this chapter.

RECOMMENDED MUSIC FOR VISUALISATION AND MEDITATION

Because music can be used to enhance the perception of imagery it is a valuable adjunct to meditation. One simply has to select sequences from existing musical recordings which relate to the specific visualisation process and, where necessary, make compilation tapes. It may be music to evoke an atmosphere, to provide a musical context for a specific image or symbol, or to transport the meditator from one imaginal locale to another. In each of the three meditative systems described here, different aspects of sound and music come to the fore.

1 Guided Imagery and Visualisation Since guided imagery leads the subject into an altered state, it is ideal to begin with a sequence of relaxation music and then to structure the session with a series of musical environments that pertain more specifically to the process in question.

Kitaro — music for relaxation

Within the genre of contemporary inner space music — which specifically caters for altered states — there is an enormous range of musical colour and texture from which to choose. This type of music also has an advantage over more traditional music in that, for the most part, it is abstract rather than melodic and is recent enough not to suggest distracting image-associations.

The following recordings provide possible musical environments for the main themes which have been described earlier.

Music for relaxation
Aeoliah and Larkin *Inner Sanctum* (Celestial Octaves)
Harold Budd and Brian Eno *The Pearl* (EG/Polygram)
Brian Eno *Discreet Music* (Side One) (Antilles)
Brian Eno *Music for Airports* (EG/Polygram)
Steven Halpern *Eventide* (Halpern Sounds)
Paul Horn *Inside the Great Pyramid* (Mushroom)
Kitaro *Silver Cloud* (Polydor)

Music for ascent
Gyorgy Ligeti 'Requiem' from the *2001* film soundtrack (MGM); Pink Floyd 'Echoes' (last section) from *Meddle* (Harvest); Klaus Schulze 'Bayreuth Return' from *Timewind* (Virgin); Tangerine Dream 'Rubycon II' (first section) from *Rubycon* (Virgin).

Music for descent
Rajneesh Foundation musicians 'Nadabrahma' (first two-thirds) from *Nataraj/ Nadabrahma* (Rajneesh Foundation International); Tangerine Dream 'Rubycon I' from

Rubycon (Virgin); Tangerine Dream 'Logos Part One' (opening sequence) from *Logos* (Virgin).

Music for the ocean
Fripp and Eno 'Wind on Water' (first half) from *Evening Star* (Island); Klaus Schulze 'Mindphaser' (first half) from *Moondawn* (Brain/Metronome).

Music for the meadow
Brian Eno 'Unfamiliar Wind' from *On Land* (EG/Polygram); Pink Floyd 'Grandchester Meadows' (first section) from *Ummagumma* (Harvest).

Music for the chapel
Gyorgy Ligeti 'Lux Aeterna' from the *2001* film soundtrack (MGM).

Music for the bubbling brook and stream
Edgar Froese 'Aqua' and 'Upland' from *Aqua* (Virgin).

Music for exploring the imaginal house/old picture book
Harold Budd and Brian Eno 'Their Memories' from *The Pearl* (EG/Polygram); Rajneesh Foundation musicians 'Nadabrahma' (first two-thirds) from *Nataraj/Nadabrahma* (Rajneesh Foundation International).

Music for a swampy pool
Brian Eno 'Lizard' and 'Tal Coat' from *On Land* (EG/Polygram).

Music for an erupting volcano
Ash Ra 'Sun Rain' from *New Age of Earth* (Virgin); Manuel Gottsching 'Echo Waves' from *Inventions for Electric Guitar* (Ohr); Laraaji 'Dance 1' and 'Dance 2' from *Day of Radiance* (EG/Polygram).

Music for confronting a lion
Philip Glass 'The Grid' from *Koyaanisqatsi* (Island).

2 Shamanic Healing This technique does not normally require recorded music since one member of the group provides the monotone drumming which enhances the altered state for the other participants. However, a taped recording titled *Drumming for the Shaman's Journey* is available from Dolphin Tapes, PO Box 71, Big Sur, California 93920 for those practising shamanic meditation individually. For further information, readers may contact The Centre for Shamanic Studies, Box 673, Belden Station, Norwalk, Connecticut 06852.

3 Meditation

Kundalini Yoga
It is possible to classify inner space music according to the five elements, thereby producing a range of Earth-music, Water-music, Fire-music, Air-music and Space-music. The following selections are suggested for preliminary sessions during which the meditator learns to familiarise himself with the Tattva symbols. The latter are integral to the visualisation of the chakras (see workshop).

Muladhara/Earth
Brian Eno 'The Lost Day' from *On Land* (EG/Polygram); Rajneesh Foundation musicians 'Nadabrahma' (first two-thirds) from *Nataraj/Nadabrahma* (Rajneesh Foundation International); Tangerine Dream 'Rubycon I' from *Rubycon* (Virgin).

Svadisthana/Water
Harold Budd and Brian Eno 'The Silver Ball' from *The Pearl* (EG/Polygram); Harold Budd and Brian Eno 'An Arc of Doves' from *The Plateaux of Mirror* (EG/Polygram).

Australian synthesiser musician Japetus

Manipura/Fire
Ash Ra 'Sun Rain' from *New Age of Earth* (Virgin); Laraaji 'Dance 1' and 'Dance 2' from *Day of Radiance* (EG/Polygram).

Anahata/Air
Fripp and Eno 'Wind on Wind' from *Evening Star* (Island); Japetus *The Great, Great Silence* (opening sequence) (Listen Music); Larkin 'Communitizing' from *O'cean* (Wind Sung Sounds).

Visuddha/Space
Brian Eno *Music for Airports* (last third of first side, second side) (EG/Polygram); Brian Eno 'An Ending (Ascent)' from *Apollo* (EG/Polygram); Manuel Gottsching 'Qasarsphere' from *Inventions for Electric Guitar* (Ohr); Rajneesh Foundation musicians 'Nadabrahma' (last third) from *Nataraj/Nadabrahma* (Rajneesh Foundation International).

Meditation on Detached Awareness
This requires music which is extremely minimal and ethereal, and substantially without focus:
Geoffrey Chandler 'Iris' and 'Penumbra' from *Starscapes* (Unity); Nancy Hennings and Henry Wolff 'Astral Plane' from *Tibetan Bells II* (Celestial Harmonies); Tangerine Dream 'Zeit' from *Zeit* (Ohr/Virgin).

WORKSHOP EXERCISES

1 Basic Relaxation This is ideal prior to visualisation work, shamanism and meditation.

Sit in a chair or lie down on the floor in a comfortable position. Breathe deeply following this pattern: breathe in to a count of four; hold for a count of four; release to a count of four; hold for a count of four (repeat).

Now gradually release the tension from all parts of your body in sequence. Imagine a soothing impulse entering your feet and working its way up through your ankles, your calves, your knees, your thighs and into your abdomen. Let go of any tensions and allow this calming wave to flow into your chest, your arms and your neck. But don't go to sleep! Focus your awareness in your head.

Appropriate music: see relaxation music listings. Several of Steven Halpern's recordings are suitable but *Eventide* is especially soothing. Brian Eno's *Music for Airports* is also an outstanding example of the ambient style.

2 Guided Imagery Select imagery sequences from Desoille, Happich or Leuner's visualisation therapies which you feel would be suitable meditations either for yourself or a group of friends. If in a group situation you may like to take turns as leader, guiding your fellow meditators into different symbolic locations in turn over several sessions. In order to do this you should write descriptive 'entry' material which can be read aloud to the group to establish the symbolic setting in each case. Make these descriptions as minimal as possible so that they allow the meditators' imaginations a broad scope for self-exploration.

Begin each session with the Basic Relaxation technique described above and ask each participant to record the 'inner journey' in a meditation diary after each session. You might like to have group discussions afterwards.

Select music from recordings available to you or, if you prefer, make your own compilation tapes.

Appropriate music: see music listings for different symbolic locations.

3 Shamanic Healing Take turns at drumming and familiarise yourself with the idea of 'riding' the drum-beat in semi-darkness. Michael Harner likes the drum-beat to be reasonably fast and unchanging. I personally like to vary the drum-beat patterns slightly, exploring the different resonances which arise. See what works for you . . .

You should also practise holding the image of the magical doorway clearly in your mind — whether it is a crack in the ground or an opening in the trunk of a large tree. As you become more proficient with these visualisations the 'canoe' exercise described in the text will take on extra meaning.

Note: Having a live drummer is always preferable to using a recorded cassette. The latter is very much a second choice because the sound is flatter and less resonant. The drumming should be powerful to fill the room but not too overwhelming for the meditators. The appropriate balance will emerge with practice.

4 Kundalini Meditation An important precursor to Kundalini meditation (which should ideally be undertaken in an ashram with the help of a guru when you feel ready to commence) is to familiarise yourself with the Tattvas, or symbols of the elements.

The following exercise should be practised for each of the Tattvas in turn, from the chakra *Muladhara* through to *Visuddha*. Initially, you might like to practise one Tattva each day, for 10–20 minutes.

Sit in a relaxed position, ideally in a full-Lotus asana or in a chair if that is more comfortable, and breathe deeply. Close your eyes and visualise the following Tattvas one at a time, persisting until you can hold the image clearly in your mind's eye:

Muladhara — a yellow square containing an inverted red triangle;

Svadisthana — a white horizontal crescent (points upward);

Manipura — an inverted red triangle;

Anahata — a smoky grey hexagram;

Visuddha — a white circle.

When you can visualise each of the Tattvas clearly, practise vibrating the seed syllable mantra through each symbol, using each tone as a 'bridge' from one Tattva to the next. The sequence is as follows:

Visualise the *Muladhara* Tattva . . . intone 'Lam'.
Dissolve the 'Lam' intonation as you begin to visualise the *Svadisthana* Tattva.
Visualise the *Svadisthana* Tattva . . . intone 'Vam'.
Dissolve the 'Vam' intonation as you begin to visualise the *Manipura* Tattva.
Visualise the *Manipura* Tattva . . . intone 'Ram'.
Dissolve the 'Ram' intonation as you begin to visualise the *Anahata* Tattva.
Visualise the *Anahata* Tattva . . . intone 'Yam'.
Dissolve the 'Yam' intonation as you begin to visualise the *Visuddha* Tattva.
Visualise the *Visuddha* Tattva . . . intone 'Ham'.
Dissolve the 'Ham' intonation into your own visualisation of the Kundalini serpent energy.

Once this has begun to work for you, practise the same sequence but visualise the Kundalini energy rising through the chakras in their appropriate position on the body:

Muladhara — the base of the spine;

Svadisthana — just below the navel;

Manipura — just above the navel;

Anahata — near the heart;

Visuddha — near the Adam's apple in the throat.

Since the Kundalini is often referred to as the 'serpent fire' you may like to accompany this exercise with Fire-music. Your selected music should be powerful and intense, suggestive of a current of life-force rising through the body!

Appropriate music: 'Dance 2' from Laraaji *Day of Radiance* (EG/Polygram).

5   Meditation for Detached Awareness   This is a more personal style of meditation since it involves not-doing rather than doing! As mentioned earlier, the music you select for your meditation sessions should be non-intrusive and suitable for leading you into a state of deep inner stillness. You may find the Basic Relaxation exercise a useful entry to deeper levels of meditation.

Since *Tibetan Bells II* is itself within the Eastern mystical milieu and contains no synthesised effects it is perhaps the most appropriate choice of meditation music. However, Tangerine Dream's early recording *Zeit* and Geoffrey Chandler's ethereal keyboard compositions on *Starscapes* are also highly recommended.

CHAPTER 9

MEDITATION
THE ESSENCE OF HEALTH

Christopher Magarey

THE NATURE OF HEALTH

Somehow we seem to have lost sight of the meaning of health. We have 'health foods' which are mainly dried fruit and nuts, herbal teas and vitamin tablets; and we have 'health clubs' where we can take hot and cold baths, do a little exercise and drink fruit juice with no added sugar. Somehow we seem to think that these will keep us healthy, even as we yell at the children and complain about the weather.

Health has to be more than this. The World Health Organization tried to define it in 1947 as 'a state of complete physical, mental and social well-being and not merely the absence of disease or infirmity'. This is certainly broad but still seems sterile and static. The ancient definition of Pericles is more lively: 'that state of moral, mental and physical well-being which enables a man to face any crisis in life with the utmost facility and grace'. To this we could perhaps add 'humour'.

The inevitable changes and set-backs in our lives have to be faced, even the deterioration of our bodies and death. We should find ways of achieving health in the midst of all this. We have to be able to adapt, to stand erect, and to feel a sense of purpose and serenity and humour whatever the circumstances of our lives. Seen in this way, health is more of an experience than it is a state: an inner experience of stillness, harmony and strength, independent of any outer turbulence.

When we understand health as an inner experience, and when we really experience inner health, then nothing can touch us. Nothing can affect us. We can remain strong, enthusiastic, light-hearted and loving in all circumstances. Not even disease or death can disturb us.

THE NATURE OF ILLNESS

So what is new? Do we not all spend our lives seeking happiness, contentment and love? Perhaps we find it in a hobby, when we are intensely absorbed in doing something that we love. Perhaps we find it in sport, especially in those moments of peak performance; those moments of perfect concentration and achievement. Maybe it is food, or music, or intimate physical contact that gives us the pleasure and enjoyment we are looking for, or if we can't find it in these, then perhaps cigarettes, alcohol, marijuana or heroin. We each have our techniques, our personal, individual ways of finding happiness.

But how much happiness do these pursuits provide? Can we continually do our hobby, and as we become good at it, doesn't it have to become more and more compli-

Health is an inner experience

cated, time-consuming and expensive? How often can we go skiing or surfing, and even when we do, how often are we actually skiing down that perfect slope or riding that perfect wave? How do we feel when there is no snow or no surf? How do we feel when we lose the game? How do we feel when someone else gets what we are wanting or when our boyfriend or girlfriend goes out with someone else? How do we feel the morning after the party? Most of the time we are waiting for the experience, striving for the experience, fighting for the experience, and even when it comes we cannot completely enjoy it because we know that it will slip away again so quickly.

Through these ordinary pursuits, then, we do experience occasional delight and momentary contentment but mostly we experience striving, stress, frustration, anxiety and exhaustion. And our bodies become filled with tension, aches and pains and disease. What started as a search for happiness ends in suffering and disease, because the search is in the wrong direction. When we depend on our outer circumstances for our enjoyment and happiness, we might find some for a few moments but mostly the circumstances fail us and we condemn ourselves to unhappiness, worry and disease. Illness is the result of dependence on external circumstances just as much as health is the experience of inner contentment.

INNER-HEALING POTENTIAL

So, every day, we spend our time looking for happiness in the external world. We do this, we eat that, we involve ourselves in so much every day, but the result is always the same. However much we enjoy ourselves, however much everything seems to go right for us, still, eventually, we always become exhausted. We cannot keep ourselves going. We want no more of the external world. All we want to do is to go to sleep.

What a mystery sleep is! When we enter the deep sleep state nothing seems to happen. We lie like a log and are unconscious and remember nothing. Yet, after six to eight hours, we wake up refreshed, rejuvenated, ready to do the whole thing again, and to exhaust ourselves all over again. What happened when we were asleep? We left the external world, we even went beyond our mental activity, and we went deeply within ourselves. There we found stillness, we found refreshment, and we found rejuvenation. Right within ourselves, every night when we sleep, we find all the peace and content-ment, fulfilment and enthusiasm that we spend our waking lives looking for. Yet in sleep we are unconscious. We go somewhere deeply within ourselves and have the perfect experience but we are unconscious throughout it and miss it. If only we could experience this state consciously, wouldn't that be something?

We do experience this inner state consciously, we do savour its delight, its beauty and its contentment whenever our minds are calm and concentrated. Whenever we experience pleasure, whenever we find happiness it is always within ourselves. Our own nature, the core of our being, is nothing but this experience, hidden by the cease-less activity of our minds. It was always there, is always there and always will be there for us to experience, whenever we penetrate the screen of the thoughts in our mind. When we absorb our mind in our favourite hobby it stops wandering and we drift beyond it to experience the contentment of our own inner nature. In our sports, too, in the moment of perfect play, in the peak experience our mind is so concentrated that it stops and, again, we go beyond it to experience the strength and the ecstasy of our own inner state. Even the pleasure of eating comes from inside ourselves. Do three slices of pavlova make us three times as happy as one? All of the activities that give us happiness and enjoyment are techniques for controlling the mind, for quietening the mind, so that the natural inner happiness is experienced spontaneously.

Even violence gives pleasure through control of the mind. On the Big Dipper or at the horror movie intense excitement comes welling up from within ourselves in the moment that the mind stops from sheer fright. When normal music doesn't work we can turn up the volume so that its sheer loudness drowns out our thinking and the mind lets go, leaving the experience of happiness and contentment exposed beyond it.

But we have already seen that these external methods lead to limited happiness and much more suffering and unhappiness. What is needed is a method for controlling the mind which does not depend on external circumstances. We need an inner method which can be used at any time, in any place so that we can delight in our own inner state, and be happy and content anywhere, at any time. This is meditation — the experience of our natural inner state through control and quietening of the mind. There are many techniques for this, and they all lead to meditation which is our own natural experience.

A simple meditation technique is the use of mantra. This sanskrit word, from *man* (mind) and *tra* (protect), means a sound which protects us from the mind. There are many mantras, and the most powerful have been tested and handed down through lineages of great sages and meditation masters for thousands of years. The mantra of the great Shidda lineage is such a one. It is 'Om Namah Shivaya' (pronounced 'om numaa shivaa-yuh') which means 'I honour my own inner state'. Anyone can use it. Just repeat it over and over in the mind, whatever you are doing, and observe how it centres you and opens up the experience of inner stillness, contentment and enjoyment. Keep trying it. The more it is used the more effective it becomes. It contains the key to healing — to perfect inner health. Practise this technique sitting quietly with your eyes shut for half an hour every day. Then repeat it with your eyes open whenever you can during the rest of the day.

THE NATURE OF THE WORLD

We experience everything through the power of the sound inherent in our own thoughts. Even the writing on this paper is just ink in certain patterns. We see the ink and make out letters and words. Then we make sounds in our minds and start having thoughts and then we experience this or that. Whatever we feel, whatever we experience, is the result of our thoughts.

When I was a child I saw a cartoon film called *Bambi*. The mother of the deer is killed in this film and I cried for hours afterwards. My mother could not reassure me that it was only a film — I had seen the deer die and I was convinced. Yet, of course it was only a cartoon, and I *thought* that there was a mother deer and that she had been killed. It was the *thought* that upset me. This is the story of our lives! We see something or we hear something, we have some thoughts about it and then we experience the result of our thoughts. We never really experience anything — only our thoughts about it. We only ever experience the world according to our thoughts. And then we think that we are right and everyone else is wrong! So again, conflict and suffering. Seldom do we experience peace and happiness in the world.

If our minds would only have pleasant, positive thoughts everything would be alright but, somehow, most of our thoughts seem to be unpleasant and negative. Whatever is going well, whatever is right about our lives we hardly notice. We notice whatever is going badly much more, no matter how small it might happen to be. This is the mosquito effect. There needs to be only one mosquito in the whole room and that is where our attention goes and our sleep is ruined!

Somehow, if we are going to improve the world, if we are going to be happy and to experience health, then we have to grab hold of our minds. We have to start thinking positive, beautiful thoughts. Then the whole world will become positive and beautiful. Better still, we can stop thinking altogether when we don't need to (and we seldom need to). Then we are free, free to see the world as it is, as a place of exquisite and divine beauty, existing only for our pleasure and enjoyment, which we can freely share with love.

THE NATURE OF THE MIND

When have we ever tried to control our minds? Have we every paused to understand our minds or to see just how the mind works and what it is made of? Try it! Just sit there for two minutes with your eyes shut, and watch your mind. Let it go wherever it wants but watch it go, from one thing to another. What is the mind? It is nothing but a bundle of slippery thoughts — one after another in never-ending succession. What are these thoughts? They are nothing but different forms or different vibrations of pure consciousness. If we watch carefully we see that each thought arises from the pure stillness of the consciousness within us and then, sooner or later, subsides back into the same consciousness. Our thoughts are nothing but the play of consciousness taking different forms — like the waves on the ocean. That consciousness (the ocean) never changes but it appears in so many different ways as different thoughts (the waves on the surface). And these thoughts create our whole experience.

When we see our minds in this way, as a play of consciousness; when we are aware of how insubstantial our thoughts really are — no more real than a movie projected on a screen — then we begin to delight in the play. No longer do we get caught up in our thoughts. No longer do we have to believe that the world is that way. We begin to become free — and our worries and stresses and our diseases begin to leave us. We become tolerant, we become resilient, and we begin to enjoy the graceful flow of our lives. We begin to realise our own beauty and the beauty of the world.

When you were watching your mind did you notice who was doing the watching? Did you become aware of who you really are? We are certainly not our bodies, which is a great relief. Whatever happens to our bodies, whatever goes wrong with our bodies does not need to disturb us when we are able to meditate and go beyond identification with the body. Neither are we our minds. We can watch our minds. We can watch all the amazing thoughts coming and going in our minds and yet we do not come and go. We stay. We are that inner stillness that peace and satisfaction, the consciousness itself which exists deeply within us, watching the mind. We are the witness of the mind. Never changing. Never affected by the worries of the mind. Never touched by the tension and suffering of the body. This is our true nature — our own awareness of our Self. This is the essence of health.

THE PROCESS OF HEALING

This is why the mantra has so much healing power. This is why meditation is the key to health. When we begin to focus our attention inwards towards the stillness and strength which is our own inner Self and we begin to realise who we really are, then we can watch our minds. We can watch the play of our thoughts and we can see them creating our experience of the world. Then we can begin to take control of our minds so that instead of creating stress and illness we can begin to create happiness and health. And as we begin to know who we really are we are less disturbed by the state of our bodies, or even our minds. We can see that our bodies are living out their lives

Calming the mind

and deteriorating, but we do not experience this as disease because we are in touch with the perfect state of health within. The meaning to us of health becomes more subtle and more real.

At the same time, of course, we stop having such stressful and destructive thoughts. We have no more need for these when we know our inner state of harmony. We stop creating so much tension and stress in our bodies and we allow the natural physical healing process to occur unfettered. The body has such power of healing that we may be amazed at what occurs when we let it. Scientific studies of the body during meditation have shown rest and relaxation responses even greater than those of sleep. The reserves of the body are renewed and released for healing.

HEALING

Even more than this, as we meditate easily and naturally, and experience our own inner calm and strength, we begin spontaneously to perceive these same qualities in others. We experience the fundamental similarity between all of us and feel a sense of oneness or profound empathy with others. As the barriers that we put up between ourselves and others dissolve we naturally experience the peace and beauty in other people and they begin to sense this experience themselves. Healing then takes place in them also.

Maxwell Cade, a London scientist, has studied this process in healers, using sophisticated electronic devices. He has studied medical and non-medical practitioners and his observations are the same in all effective healers. Their muscle tension falls, their electrical skin resistance rises and their brain wave activity includes the waves of the waking state and sleep at the same time. These are the changes found in meditation, and it seems that effective health practitioners meditate when they are healing.

Perhaps even more significantly, when Cade studied the patients of these healers, he found the same fall in muscle tension, the rise in electrical skin resistance, and the brain wave activity of meditation, even when the patients had had no previous experience of meditation. It seems that when a healer meditates, this state is passed in some subtle way into the patient who then also experiences meditation and its beneficial healing effects. A yogi whom Cade studied was able, by a single touch, to produce a state of inner peace or euphoria in Cade's wife, lasting for three days; an experience that she still remembers with delight. Just as we feel anger when another person is angry, and laugh when another person laughs, so too is the experience of meditation transmitted from one to another.

Meditation, it seems, is the key to understanding health and healing. There are so many healing practices, medical and non-medical, and they are so different from each other yet, in the hands of effective practitioners, they all work. The essence of healing is not in the technique applied. It is something that goes on at a more subtle level when any effective technique is applied, and when the practitioner meditates naturally in some way during its application. For example, what is the explanation of the remarkable results achieved in cancer patients attending the well known clinics of Max Gerson, Joseph Issels or Ernesto Contreras using a variety of unconventional methods? As well as special diets and exercises, and the encouragement of positive attitudes, unlikely methods such as coffee enemas, tooth extraction and tonsillectomy, and almond kernel extract (laetrile) were or are used. Tested by other doctors and scientists elsewhere, these methods have been found to be ineffective against cancer and have been officially condemned, but the clinics have records of many cures.

The real effectiveness of such clinics is not so much in their particular methods but in the personalities of the healers concerned. About Gerson it was written 'many were often led to a renewal of faith because of the living example of Max Gerson — who came as a stranger but who, nevertheless, demonstrated that divine compassion and unconditional love of which Paul spoke'. About Issels, the British Government's Department of Health and Social Security wrote, 'The doctor-patient relationship here is very remarkable. Dr Issels and his patient become partners . . . there is no doubt about their feeling for Dr Issels, amounting to devotion at times.' Contreras, too, takes a particular interest in his patients' spiritual awareness, conducting regular services, himself, in the clinic. All three men had or have a profound spiritual conviction and, whatever it may be called, any intense spiritual practice leads to the state of meditation. This is undoubtedly the key to their success.

Dr Ainslie Meares

Ainslie Meares, a Melbourne doctor, has published a series of remissions in cancer patients who he simply taught to meditate. His method is very relevant, and positively confirms Cade's research. He wrote 'I regress [meditate] with the patient and move from patient to patient immersed in the primitive state of being which I share with the patients'. If meditation has so much power that it can result in the permanent disappearance of advanced cancer, how does it really work? Such an event surely goes well beyond the established mechanisms of rest, relaxation and recovery.

SCIENTIFIC BASIS OF THE WORLD

Modern physics throws fascinating light on this problem. Its findings are so startling that even great physicists have found them hard to accept and most physicists continue to ignore the conclusions. No longer can anything in the universe be regarded as solid or even as an object at all. As things have been broken into molecules and these into atoms and even these into sub-atomic particles, nothing substantial seems to remain. Sub-atomic particles appear and disappear, and change from one into another in complex patterns quite unlike anything solid. In fact, they are not really particles at all but packets of energy or patterns of vibration. There is nothing solid in the universe, only masses of vibration, manifestations of energy in various forms.

The big questions in science now are 'What is it that is vibrating' and 'What is the basis of the energy of the universe?' Scientists are being forced to admit that it is consciousness itself which is vibrating and that consciousness is the basis of the universe. Sir James Jeans said, 'Today . . . the stream of knowledge is heading towards non-mechanical reality. The universe begins to look more like a great thought than like a machine,'' and E. G. Wigner said, 'It was not possible to formulate the laws of quantum theory in a fully consistent way without reference to consciousness'.

If this is true, there is only one, universal, consciousness. What we each think of as our Self, our own individual consciousness, our separate awareness of being, is nothing but a manifestation of the same consciousness that exists everywhere. In essence, we are not separate from each other or from the universe, we are all the same Self. When we meditate we focus our awareness inwardly on this very truth, on our own inner nature, that consciousness. When we meditate and experience this inner state we dissolve our boundaries and our sense of limitation, and we expand our sense of being. As we begin to identify with that consciousness which exists everywhere and which always exists we experience profound contentment, fulfilment and sense of belonging or love. Then we know that, basically, on the inside, we are so strong, we are so content, and we have so much love that we need nothing else to make us happy. Whatever seems to be going on in our lives on the outside is only a play of the mind, a source of amusement, which can never hurt or distress us, never affect us. Inside we always remain the same — complete, whole, healthy.

Yet, even when we know this to be true, even when we sometimes experience this inner state for a moment, we begin to have doubts again and to worry about things. Our minds are so restless, they continue to give us trouble. Only when our minds are still, only when they are under perfect control can we experience perfect health, spontaneity and freedom from doubts and fears. Science is giving us an understanding of the nature of the universe and of ourselves, but it lacks the means to give us the experience. Knowledge alone is insufficient for true healing to occur.

INNER HEALING POWER

The clue to true healing lies hidden in the symbols used by healing professionals, all over the world. Most, like the Australian Medical Association, have adopted the serpent and staff of Aesculapius, the Greek God of healing. Other healing associations, like the Royal Army Military Corps, have adopted the caduceus, the intertwined pair of serpents and staff of Hermes, the Egyptian God of harmony. The Clinical Oncological Society of Australia has adopted the Marryalyan, the staff and two serpent healing symbol of the Australian aborigine. The serpentine form appears also in other cultures such as the Barong of the Balinese and the Dragon of the Chinese, as the universal healing force. One might well ask why this symbol seems to be so universal, but in most cases the reasons have been forgotten, lost in antiquity. Only the Sanskrit scriptures remain intact, records of knowledge thousands of years old, wisdom whose importance is only now becoming widely appreciated. Here the serpentine form is called *Kundalini* (literally 'the coiled one').

The ancient sages knew of more than our physical bodies. They also described the subtle body, in which we dream, in which our minds are active. Of the 72×10^9 subtle channels comprising this body, the most important is the *Sushumna*. This passes, roughly, vertically from the perineum to the crown. The Sushumna is the repository of all our memories where nothing that was ever said to us or ever happened to us or we even thought is ever forgotten. We can recall past events in utmost detail. These memories, fears, desires and habit patterns are a constant source of mental activity, creating endless thoughts and worries and ways of reacting to our circumstances. No matter how hard we try, we can never be completely happy, we can never truly experience our inner state of health as long as these accumulated impressions remain in the inner recesses of our minds to disturb us. The mind never seems so active and disturbing as it does when we have a quiet moment. No wonder we have to keep ourselves active and occupied every minute. We exhaust ourselves. We push our poor bodies beyond their limits. In order to be still, to experience our own peace and contentment and health we have to be free from this material, and this is the role of the Kundalini.

The Sanskrit scriptures describe the Kundalini lying coiled at the lower end of the Sushumna, usually quite dormant. When awakened, it rises up the Sushumna, like a chimney sweep, cleaning out all the accumulated mental impressions. As it rises, it eliminates, progressively, all of our mental conditioning, all of our fixed ways of seeing things, all of our old habits until eventually we are free of them.

This surely is true healing. What a miracle it is when we can see the world as it really is instead of how we think it is, when we can accept each moment as it is and enjoy it as precious and unique. What a great day it is when we experience the truth of our own nature, as the Self of the Universe, complete, content, loving. There is nothing to fear, nothing to worry about, everything is perfect the way it is and no matter how much it changes it can only remain perfect. Then we realise for ourselves the truth of Saint Augustine's statement 'We spend our lives looking for God, until we realise that it is God who is doing the looking', and Swami Muktananda's, who said 'God dwells within you, as you'. When the Kundalini has swept away all false impressions and misunderstandings we know our own divinity and we see God everywhere. The whole world is nothing but the play of our own Self.

The awakening of the Kundalini is the goal of all spiritual, religious and healing practices. At the moment of awakening we have a glimpse of our own true nature, and

The late Swami Muktananda

Dr Christopher Magarey at the Siddha Yoga Ashram, Sydney

the process of inner healing begins. From that moment our lives are transformed as we experience the divine more and more clearly. So many practices are taught, so arduous, so lengthy and so uncertain, that can be undertaken to awaken the Kundalini but there is one practice that transcends all of these. It is the relationship with a great being, a holy person, a Siddha, whose Kundalini has already awakened and completed its journey, who knows that whatever the appearances, essentially, inwardly, we are all perfect, we are divine. Religion means, literally, 'tying together again' and yoga means 'union', when the individual sense of identity becomes the universal, when we experience our divinity. A holy person, a Siddha, awakens that awareness spontaneously and initiates the process of inner transformation quite naturally and effortlessly.

Religious scriptures describe many ways in which a Siddha initiates this awakening, through touch, through glance, through will, or through sound. The mantra 'Om Namah Shivaya' is such a sound. It is the mantra of a long lineage of great Siddhas, carrying in itself their power. Repetition of this mantra is a convenient but effective way of establishing the crucial relationship and awakening the inner power of healing. For example, while watching a television programme one evening on which a Siddha Yoga monk was teaching meditation and the use of this mantra a person noted:

So I thought that while I was watching it, I would just have a go. So, anyway, I relaxed a little like he said and chanted the words 'O Mia' something. I forget now, over and over silently to myself . . . and the sensation I got . . . and what I saw within myself scared me to death so I opened my eyes. But today has been wonderful. Something happened and I don't know what. I've never felt like this before . . . It's an inner peace. I thought, 'Why not?' So then I done it again this morning and I feel so good. I can sort of get on top of my problems and hassles . . .

Swami Muktananda's successors: Swami Chidvilasananda and her brother, Swami Nityananda

If this mantra can give such an experience in 30 seconds, what can it do with constant repetition and practice? What can an ongoing relationship with a Siddha lead to? Nothing but a total transformation of our lives. Nothing but perfect inner health. We, too, will become Siddhas. We too will experience truth, the beauty of the world as it is, the bliss that exists everywhere, the love that fills every person. We, too, can be free of all habits and conditioning; completely natural, spontaneous and appropriate in every situation. Not only will we experience our own divinity but we will see God in each other and everywhere. We have created this world for our pleasure. It is a beautiful garden for us to play together. Whatever each of our circumstances, whatever the state of our bodies, inside is eternal wholeness, unshakable health. We need only to meditate to discover it.

CHAPTER 10

CANCER AS A PATH TO ENLIGHTENMENT

Ian Gawler

This is a personal account of the effectiveness of meditation in treating cancer. It is included in this anthology as an example of how cancer patients can help themselves through achieving inner stillness, as well as assisting others in cancer support groups.

Dr Ian Gawler was born in Melbourne and in December, 1974 was spending 80 hours each week working in his veterinary science practice. Also an active athlete, he had run for his State three times in the decathlon and had a very busy life. However, in January 1975 bone cancer was diagnosed and his right leg was amputated as a result. When the cancer reappeared in November 1975, Ian was told he could expect to survive for three to six months. There was no medical treatment available that was likely to improve his situation.

Ian Gawler in earlier times

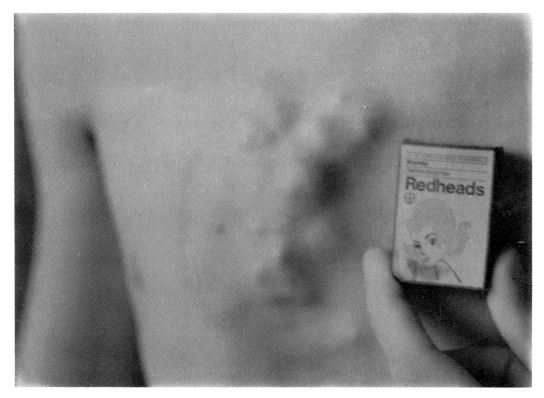

After Ian's leg was amputated bone cancer appeared in his chest. The matchbox indicates the size of the growth

Determined to find an answer, Ian embarked on a strict dietary regime and began intensive meditation with the world-renowned hypnotherapist Dr Ainslie Meares. This programme kept the cancer stable, but by February 1976 pain had become a problem. Unable to attend Dr Meares any more, Ian sought help from acupuncture and then from Dr Warren Hastings. Dr Hastings was able to alleviate the pain enough for Ian to marry Gayle, who had been the veterinary nurse in his practice and had remained by his side through all his problems.

Shortly after their marriage, Ian's right kidney became obstructed, and he suffered more pain, weight loss, night sweats and then jaundice. In desperation, the two headed for the Philippines. There, although the tumours were not removed, a healing process began. Ian's pain declined to manageable levels and his weight began to return. For the next six months they explored all avenues in a bid to re-establish Ian's healing processes; to get his body to heal itself.

By October 1976, Ian's physical condition was excellent, but the bone tumours were assuming very large proportions. Ian was aware of a mental block about things like diet, meditation and healing. In the hope of removing this, as well as receiving some physical benefit, he sought medical help again.

A two-year course of chemotherapy was begun but after two and a half months Ian and Gayle decided to stop it. The chemotherapist warned of an expected rapid growth in the still large tumours if the treatment were stopped.

Ian and Gayle left for the Philippines again, where they spent three months concentrating on good food and meditation as well as receiving healing. They spent a lot of

En route to Sai Baba . . .

time talking to the healers and photographing and studying them at work. The mental block was still very evident, and so Ian and Gayle now travelled to India and the holy man Sai Baba. He told Ian, 'You are already cured, do not worry'. This simple statement catalysed a major shift in Ian's thinking so that he was able to accept that he really would recover. He began to think of himself as a well person rather than one with a disease.

By the end of June 1978, Ian and Gayle were once again establishing a veterinary practice. Gayle was awaiting the birth of their first child but Ian seemed over-tired. Tests revealed the cancer was all clear — but in its place was tuberculosis. This condition had gone unnoticed for the past two years at least, but responded rapidly to treatment.

In 1980 the Gawlers moved to a farm at Yarra Junction in Victoria. The following year, they established the Melbourne Cancer Support Group as a means of sharing their extraordinary experience with other cancer patients and their families. They developed a twelve-week programme based on the self-help principles of good food, positive thinking, meditation and stress management — all carried out in a caring, supportive environment.

How is it that cancer patients who take responsibility for their illness can be expected reliably to say, as I do, 'Cancer was a turning point for the better in my life'?

For me, losing a leg brought a choice between order and disorder. Already I had experienced enough of life to know that to approach the wondrous complexity of

Nature and its exuberant creations as being the pallid product of random chance, was unfounded. I sensed a spiritual meaning in everything around me. So my basic life philosophy demanded an answer to 'Why me?' It had to do with me.

Initially I applied an orthodox religious perspective to my problems and felt my disease was either a sentence passed on past misdeeds or an opportunity to learn through adversity — the way we humans seem to prefer to learn best.

On reflection, I decided it was both. I could readily see errors in my past and I soon realised that I would learn so much through my new situation. Reflection also brought a greater awareness that I was a product of a body, mind and soul that was an integrated unit. A few months earlier, as an athlete, I had been preoccupied with my body and working to make it perform better. Now, as a cancer patient, I had lost a leg and, with it, one quarter of my bodyweight. And yet when I awoke from surgery, *I* still felt the same. Just less body. In my social life, my emotions waxed and waned, but always, *I* seemed to be feeling them. Although my emotions could lift me up or dump me down, I weathered it all and *I* felt the same. As a somewhat analytical veterinary scientist, I had been preoccupied with my mind — like trying to remember unending lists of parasites and microbes with impossible, double-barrelled Latin names. But, as my illness made me more introspective, there came the discovery that my mind was a tool that *I* used. I could observe it at work. What a revelation! There was something, or someone, who was aware of my mind's activity as it went about its daily tasks of thinking, deciding and directing.

Then, in meditation, came the direct experience of something beyond my mind. When the mind and the body entered into the stillness, I experienced my inner core, that more permanent purer part of being that is common between us all and links us with a principle I can only call Divine: our very essence.

This direct experience gave me the knowledge that my existence extended beyond my immediate, worldly personality with its temporary body, mind and emotions. I *knew* that there was a spiritual reality in my life and that it was the reason for being. I came to realise that the actions of the life I had been leading had moved me too far away from the path that my spirit had needed to follow. Not that I had been doing things that could be judged as unlawful or immoral by any worldly standards, but that my role in life was passing unfulfilled. My actions, while reasonable enough, were far removed from my attitudes. I came to know that my disease was useful as an opportunity to realign those actions and attitudes and that the attitudes were what really counted.

'Why me?' was easy. Now I sought answers to 'Who am I?', 'Where does happiness lie?', 'What is the purpose of life?'

Life offers the opportunity of experience. These experiences may loosely be grouped as physical, psychological or spiritual. In all of these areas we can experience separation or oneness.

Separation brings division, hence opposites and conflict. With separation comes fear. With fear comes stress, pain and disharmony. Separation brings disease and unhappiness.

Oneness brings unity and cohesion. With oneness comes peace of mind, relaxation, true pleasure, joy and harmony. Oneness brings health and happiness. To experience life with a sense of oneness, is our natural destiny. This comes through experiencing the inner man and with it the spiritual reality that each one of us is a unique part of a greater whole.

In meditation, stress is discharged

Our external manifestations are transient. No matter how seriously we take our body, our emotions, our minds, no matter how strongly we identify with their fluctuations from joy to sorrow, pain to pleasure, we can be confident that they will pass, leaving something much more important.

Man's natural quest then is to experience oneness. This quest often begins with the externals, seeking first to find harmony and health in the physical world, then on to seeking psychological balance. One does not have to travel far on this quest, however, to know that the urge to experience a spiritual reality is the most important part of the journey.

A child has a natural urge to walk. It repeatedly falls, always picking itself up. Soon it totters, walks and runs. As it grows older, walking becomes an automatic part of its being. However, there is nothing unnatural for a young child to crawl. But if an adult is only able to crawl, we say it is unnatural, it must be the result of a disease: it is not appropriate for an adult only to crawl. An adult has the potential to walk. For an adult not to fulfil that potential is interpreted as being caused by a 'disease' and disease is the product of the individual's actions being too far removed from their potentials. When the distance between actions and attitudes is too great, disease becomes apparent.

An awareness of disease leads to an intensification of life. If focuses the attention on a need to regain balance, to concentrate on recreating harmony in life.

When a disease takes a physical form, then often the quest for health starts with physical needs. In cancer, this emphasis is often essential to restore the physical to a point where life can continue, life's experiences can continue and the quest can continue. The glorious feature of human life, the reason why we instinctively hold onto it so dearly, is that it provides the unique opportunity for physical matter and spiritual essence to become one. Meditation can give a direct experience of that spiritual essence, but it is not until that spiritual reality is combined with the physical reality of the world around us, that the end of the quest is found. Ultimately, happiness can only come through regaining whole health — health in body, emotions, mind and spirit, and for that to be expressed as an integrated whole.

If there is one key to this health, it is meditation. In its stillness, stress is discharged and personal experience of a deep, inner reality gained. With this experience, fear is overcome and personal confidence gained. For the experience in meditation is an extraordinary one that takes us beyond the normal day-to-day mundane experiences of our physical body and its environment. The experience becomes transcendental — it transcends our normal experience and we experience what is left after we leave our body and psyche behind.

That experience is inevitably a wonderful one. People with a religious background inevitably link it with their religious experience. Others express a mystical, often inexplicable joy.

As a flow-on from such an experience comes a natural urge to regain that sense of oneness in every aspect of life and the knowledge that that oneness means balance, harmony and health. Hence a natural urge to eat natural, whole foods and to prepare them well. Hence the urge to exercise and to seek help from appropriate sources to correct any physical diseases. Hence the urge to express the emotion of love fully and unconditionally. Hence the urge to be positive in attitude and radiate positive thoughts. And hence, of course, the urge to be at one with that spiritual oneness every moment and manifest it in every facet of life.

With the experience that meditation provides comes a natural self-esteem, purpose in life and a natural ease that provides the discipline necessary to achieve your life's purpose. Cancer taught me all this. Perhaps it was actually life, not cancer — no worry, it was well worthwhile. There are a lot of people currently, whom I judge to be smart, who are pursuing their own quest for real health, without the prompting of a physical disease. My hope is that many more will do the same.

It would seem natural that a person having been diagnosed as a cancer patient would seek to utilise every available resource in their quest for recovery. Curiously, for those who do not understand the attitudes of cancer patients, many patients do not want to actively participate in such efforts and prefer, passively, to pass responsibility for their treatment, even their life, to a doctor. There are many doctors who happily accept, and even expect, this responsibility. There is nothing right or wrong in this. Just different people, different needs. Many find taking responsibility for such major and complex questions as to which medical doctor, which treatment, etc., etc., very difficult and it is good that others can help. It just happens that I felt that the responsibility was mine and I wanted to retain it. Now I work with people who share this approach and urge them to develop and maintain a sense of personal responsibility.

Currently it seems it is a steadily-expanding, but still minority, of patients who want to utilise this approach. In addition to the medical systems resources, these people want to develop their own potentials to the full, in an effort to not only give themselves the best chance of recovery, but also to make some sense of their complex situation.

It also seems that most people, when they first come to our cancer support group do so with a motivation which is based on fear. Most commonly this is a fear of dying, or of pain, but it may run the whole gamut of possibilities — from simple fear of the unknown to complex fear of social rejection, from fear of losing control of their life or fear of experiencing disappointment through failing the major life test cancer presents — the fear of dying with unfinished business.

With fear as a motivation, patients and families are first drawn by their most immediate need and the focus of their life. Most who come are receiving standard medical treatment, and around half come on a doctor's recommendation. Our twelve-week programme presents a wide range of principles and techniques which patients and families can use to overcome their problems and to gain from what often is otherwise a very difficult situation.

We talk of the three foundation stones on which to rebuild health as being good food, positive thinking and meditation. My book *You Can Conquer Cancer* is used as a manual and each week we meditate for about half an hour before discussing the week's topic for about one and a half hours.

For a support group such as this to work, it must offer hope. Hope not only relies on wanting to do something, but for it to be real hope, and there must be a real prospect of actually achieving that something. Most who come to a cancer support group fear the cancer and their attendance expresses a hope for recovery. If they are to keep coming, they must not only retain their basic desire for a recovery, but they must also believe that by attending there is a better likelihood that they will. A cup of tea, a nice chat, and a pat on the back is not enough! People do not come back for more of that. While the need for support from peers going through the same experience is real and valuable, what sustains a support group is motivation backed by the opportunity to learn and to practise genuinely beneficial techniques.

Around one hundred patients and support people, family members mostly, attend our group's basic programme each week. Again, those who come do so for a multiplicity of reasons. Some seek only the support of contact with other patients and the reassurance which that brings. Others put all their energies into seeking an ideal diet, or channel their will into forceful, positive thinking. However, while the motivation remains as fear, there is a sense of panic, urgency and haste. There is so much to do, so many questions to be answered, so many techniques to utilise, even changes to be made . . . and it all needs to be done now — not even tomorrow is soon enough.

Not infrequently, as they become involved in a self-help programme, patients and families with a fear motivation can exceed their physical and psychological limits. Their quest for health and harmony is so frantic that, of itself, it generates more tension and more stress.

There is no doubt in my mind that the patient's efforts *can* make all the difference between success and failure. A patient's hopes and fears, attitudes and actions, or very level of well-being can influence the outcome of cancer dramatically. So we come back to *how*. How to channel that urge for recovery positively! How to transmit fear into confidence!

Obviously, the techniques *are* important. There does need to be good food. The emotions and thoughts do need to be positive. But more importantly, the attitude needs to be right.

With very few exceptions, I feel it unwise to ignore the basic principles, and the basic techniques on which good health can be built, but if the motivation behind the practice of those techniques is not a positive one, they will not be sustained. They will not be integrated into a happy, healthy lifestyle.

Here again we encounter the value of meditation. By discharging stress and providing experience of a greater spiritual reality, meditation dissolves fear and replaces it with a heartfelt urge, a natural and powerful motivation to recreate health in every aspect of being.

Meditation can provide anyone with this profoundly positive life motivation, so why doesn't everyone practise it? Here fear often acts as a barrier. Fear of the unknown, fear of negative reports or the bad connotations meditation has for some as being a cultish thing. Perhaps more importantly, however, is the instinctive fear of the consequences. It may be unsatisfactory, but it is safe to view yourself as a victim of life, to say to yourself 'Why me?' has no meaning and relegate yourself to the backwaters of random chance. However, you only have to pause in silence for a moment to know that the still small inner voice is real and that it knows. It knows, you know. If your actions are not in accord with your attitudes, you know.

Many people, while basically unhappy, are content to continue in their set pattern, living life as an external event. To take account of life's inner nature is challenging to say the least. It takes courage, can involve you in major life changes, but as a lure it just might end up with you finding happiness.

So, personal responsibility is there to be accepted by those who dare! And meditation offers the means to a harmonious end.

Now, traditionally, meditation was only one step in a five-step process. At present, we have a problem in semantics, the usage of words, in that 'meditation' as a word is being used commonly to describe the whole of that process which has been employed by virtually every major world culture and religion as a means of personal development. It invariably began with:

1 Concentration The act of concentration almost always included a technique for *relaxation*, as the two are synergistic. The focus for concentration was generally one of the following:

A *A sound*
Here the aim is to concentrate on rhythmically repeating the sound. This can be done aloud (as in chanting) or quietly to oneself, as with a mantra.

A mantra is a sound — usually a word or group of words, which is repeated over and over quietly to yourself. Any sound or words can be used; people have learnt to meditate using the words 'coca cola' as a mantra! However, if the words or sounds have inner meaning, they are likely to mobilise inner spiritual activity as well.

A widely used Indian mantra is 'Om Namah Shivaya'. (Pronounced 'om numaa shivaa-yuh' it means 'I honour my own inner state'.) Christians could use this too, or choose a prayer, or a phrase such as 'Be still and know that I am God' or any other inspiring words.

B *An object*
The object is stared at with the eyes open, the aim being to hold the attention on the object and to think of nothing else. You could use an object with:

obvious inner meaning, such as an icon — a religious painting, or a mandala, or an Eastern geometric design with spiritual significance.

abstract symbolic meaning, such as a candle whose light, fire, shape etc. can be interpreted as being symbolic of spiritual healing etc.

no connotations at all. For example, anything from a speck on the roof to a fly on the wall.

C *A thought*
Again any thought will do. Traditionally, the thinking was based around the subject of an ideal such as honesty, truth or love. Currently it is well appreciated that we can use this technique to dwell on a problem, to think about it in depth and find new insights, new solutions. This process is an added bonus and another good reason to practise the technique. For example, one could choose to concentrate on thinking about 'food' and aim to dwell on anything to do with that subject.

D *An action*
Finally, and perhaps surprisingly, action is a good starting point for some people's meditation. More and more long distance runners are aware of the high that comes after ten to twelve kilometres of exertion and the altered state of consciousness rhythmical exercise brings. Many are addicted to the running without realising the pleasurable effect is virtually the same as that felt by meditators. The Chinese employ Tai Chi as a meditative act, and in Karma Yoga the Indians aim to make every daily action a meditative act — a good ideal!

Whatever the focus of concentration, it usually takes some effort and practice to be able to hold the concentration on that focus and not to think of anything else. Once you can do this, you are doing what is traditionally described as meditating.

2 Meditation Traditionally defined as the ability to focus the concentration on one thing only and hold it there, it is a single-minded concentration. This is very much an act of the conscious, rational mind and if it is done for long enough, the mind will go into contemplation.

3 Contemplation This is a more abstract, intuitive way of thinking. Whereas in meditation, the rational mind is at work, analysing, comparing, inferring, deducing; in contemplation the thoughts are more abstract, intuitive, creative. In meditation, one tends to take parts of the whole and analyse them in detail; in contemplation, all the pieces of the jigsaw fall into place and you can see the whole picture.

4 Unification After contemplation, you can pass into another state of consciousness, wherein the sense of separation is lost. If a candle had been the object for concentration, then when you begin, you sit and place the lighted candle at eye height about one metre in front of you. The natural, normal experience is to feel that the candle is 'there', that you are 'here' and there is a distance between. In meditation the rational mind is controlled to avoid other thoughts and all attention is focused on the candle. If the mind does wander, then it is brought back to the focus of the candle with a gentle reminder that this is not the time for other thoughts. In contemplation the symbols of light etc. may be reflected upon and in unification the sense of being separate from the candle changes. The concentration on the candle is so complete that you come to feel as if you are part of it. You and it, and even the process of being aware of the candle, merge into one extraordinary experience.

Often this experience will extend beyond the candle to include the whole universe, making it a true mystical or transcendental experience, with the power to satisfy your quest for direct contact with a spiritual reality and to leave you with a smile in your heart and a twinkle in the eye that does not rapidly fade.

5 Illumination It is sometimes possible then for you to experience the direct knowledge of Truth. Completely new information may come to your awareness with a conviction that leaves doubting its correctness as an impossibility. If in contemplation one can gain fresh insight through hearing in the stillness a small inner voice, the voice of Illumination is loud and clear and unmistakable. Such revelations come with the authority of being straight from the source, and lead to enlightenment.

Now the problem of semantics. Traditionally meditation was defined as single-minded concentration, one step in a five-step process aimed at self-enlightenment. Currently meditation as a word is used loosely. Many people think of it as the five-step process or just have vague notions of it involving doing something funny with your head. Perhaps the state of unification is closest to what many people think of as being 'meditation'. In *You Can Conquer Cancer* I resorted to italics to differentiate the two, as most people associate meditation with something more than simple concentration. So here again we leave 'meditation' as in concentration, as is, and use italics for '*meditation* the process'. The usage of the words will be clear.

How can we best learn to *meditate*? There are three options to be aware of.

1 *Use no method*
Meditation is really a very simple state — being still in body and mind. Some people are able to literally and simply sit down, be still, and immediately *meditate*. This process is greatly facilitated by being joined or led by another person who is actually *meditating*. Traditionally, the Indian guru has been able to teach *meditation* by such example. By radiating a calm and depth of experience, the student could be guided into that same experience.

Dr Ainslie Meares applies this principle in a Western medical context. Many cancer patients and people with a wide variety of particularly stress/anxiety related illnesses have sought and gained his help. Having written many books on the subject, he now expects new people to have read them and to be prepared to enter into the experience. He has no preamble or introduction but sits his groups in large arm-chairs and then communicates his own experience of *meditation* by means of touch and simple, abstract sounds made as he moves among the patients.

For those who are prepared to surrender or let go into this new experience, it works well. However, many find their mind fights it, trying to analyse, assess and question. So often, the mind acts as a barrier to the experience.

2 *Progressive Relaxation*

This technique provides a formal focus for concentration which is in fact a part of the end point. The aim in *meditation* is to be still, or relaxed, in body and mind. By using the process of relaxing the body as the focus of concentration, there is a double benefit. If you concentrate on the *feeling* of relaxation, how your body feels as it relaxes, it further assists getting away from rational thought and into abstract feelings. In fact, by concentrating on a process of progressive body relaxation, you meditate upon relaxation and then by *feeling* the relaxation and identifying with that feeling, you move rapidly into contemplation. As the body relaxes more, there is a reflex relaxing of the mind and as you merge into the feeling of being deeply, totally relaxed, you become at one with relaxation.

The added benefit of this technique, and why I recommend it as the standard starting point, is that by just learning how to relax physically, there is the added benefit of letting go tension and with it the effects of stress. Regular periods of deep physical relaxation go a long way towards defusing stress. This is comforting to people whose minds like to wander and for whom it takes time to enter the stillness.

By using progressive relaxation as the starting point, the very first session will almost invariably bring positive benefits. It simply relies on concentrating first on the feet and the feeling in them. By then contracting the muscles in the feet, one becomes more aware of the feeling of tension. Then by relaxing the muscles, letting them go all loose like a floppy rag doll, one gets the feeling of relaxation.

As you move up through all the muscle groups of the body, calves, thighs, buttocks, etc., in progressive steps, you learn to relax thoroughly, physically.

Again, if you concentrate on the feeling of relaxation and do not wander off into other thoughts, you can move into stillness very easily. If thoughts do persist, come back to the body and feel into the relaxation even more, or perhaps repeat over and over words like 'relax', 'letting go', 'it's a good feeling' etc. — like a mantra. The aim is to keep it simple and to avoid forceful thinking.

Sitting down with the intention of '*meditation* or bust' is bound to be a flop! The attitude must be passive, the expectations nil. This is the only way to achieve a stillness of mind and anything else invariably generates more thoughts, more obstacles to the experience of simplicity itself.

3 *Concentrate on anything*

As previously explained, literally anything can be used. There are so many techniques of *meditation* taught today, but they all use the same essential process. It begins with a technique which aims to produce a result — stillness. It is the end point that is important and, as a sort of Catch 22, even the end point really should not be important. The technique is certainly of little value other than as a tool — a stepping stone to higher consciousness. So there is no need to get preoccupied with flash techniques, fancy rituals, secretive mantras or whatever. *Meditation* is a simple process, readily attainable and open to all. Its benefits stem from its simplicity and, once it has been experienced, you may well find you do not need your initial technique anymore but can bypass it and recreate the experience more readily.

Ideally, you will become so much at one with the depth of experience found in *meditation* that it will permeate from your very being into every aspect of your daily life.

In practical terms, this means a greater level of physical relaxation noticeable during your day with markedly reduced tension, better sleep patterns and more efficiency. A better emotional state will automatically follow as you feel good about yourself and more at ease with others. As a flow on you will experience greater mental clarity with an absence of anxiety and then the bonus benefit of a direct experience of a spiritual reality with the profound sense of well-being that it produces.

Cancer patients regularly comment to me that their illness was worth having as it pushed them into making these discoveries — discoveries of a new level of inner health. Growing numbers of smart people in the world today are discovering that they too can experience life as a joyous, meaningful event, without having to be sick first. Their inner health becomes obvious to all through its outer manifestation — total health.

CHAPTER 11

INTUITIVE HEALING

Mora McIntyre

PATTERNS OF THE PAST

The role of intuition,* its value and its development, is an area full of mystery, misunderstanding and a great deal of ignorance and suppression. Perhaps the greatest superstition of our times has been the myth of the supremacy of the rational mind: totalitarianism of the intellect which leaves vast areas of human experience and potential arid and uncultivated.

---

* My own experience of intuitive approaches to healing began in 1977. As a child I had always been aware of other levels of 'reality', but like many children I did not realise for quite some time that this was not shared by everyone. I was *aware* of a 'knowing' of the power of my own intuitive connection but that was accompanied by a sense of alienation through being brought up in a time when there was no validation or recognition of the intuitive.

In 1977, through a series of remarkable events and 'coincidences', I found myself attending a workshop on advanced healing with a Californian sensitive, Anne Parks. Here I found that not only were my intuitive gifts recognised, but that they could actually be put to use in the healing realm.

What was unusual about Ms Parks was that she plainly did not belong to the world of psychic operators I was familiar with, yet she was clearly a very gifted person. Nor did she fit with the alternative medical practitioners, therapists or counsellors and yet she focused on personal development.

In a subsequent interview she gave me some invaluable advice. She told me that I had very powerful psychic and intuitive abilities and that they were no use to me because I was ungrounded and emotionally out of balance.

That began a period of intensive 'training' which for me laid the foundation for an attitude to healing for which I will always be indebted.

The major part of the 'training' focused, initially, on my own development. There were weekly sessions of intuitive massage, one-to-one therapy which was a combination of transpersonal therapy and bodywork and much more; monthly energy-balancing sessions with Anne, participating in her ongoing group; plus evenings and weekends gathering a variety of skills including intuitive massage, self-nourishment, meditation and healing. To these I added other areas including basic sexuality work, past lives, psychodrama, Bach flower remedies, etc., etc.

The focal point of Ms Parks' work revolved around nourishing the Self; focusing on the self-awareness of the practitioner rather than the client and a strong input of heart-centred energy plus the need for centring and grounding. No exercises in psychic development were given prior to this work.

When Anne returned to the States, I began receiving energy-balancing from Andrew Watson, a person with a strong healing gift. Over the following 18 months I learned a lot more about the responsibilities of becoming a healing channel and about personal integrity.

(continued overleaf)

(continued from previous page)

Around this time I started attending workshops with a man called Bob Moore with whom Anne had studied. I found Bob to be one of those rare individuals who not only sees the *full* subtle body or aura, and has an extraordinary understanding of the structure and flow of subtle energy and how to work with this, but above all, dispensing with the rituals of gurudom, nevertheless demonstrates a combination of humility and heart-centredness, innocence and wisdom visible only in the highest teachers.

Apart from that period of several years' intensive learning, my own experience has been coloured by a marked lack of access to teacher or outside help which has forced me continually back on my own intuitive resources. Sometimes a lonely path and pitted with self doubts, always a challenge, I can honestly say my work has been a continual source of richness, joy and personal growth. It is a time of 'coming home'.

With a history of witch-hunting and persecution of those showing psychic talents over the last centuries in widespread areas of our so-called civilised societies, seemingly brought about by chauvinistic and power-hungry religious and political interests, all of which ultimately led to the extermination of numbers of our most intuitive people, especially females, it is hardly surprising that so much fear and unease still lingers around the areas of non-physical perception.

Nor is it surprising that when the practice of healing entered the province of the intellect, psychic extremism blossomed and the lower-levels of mediumistic activity became rampant, largely dissociated from any true spiritual significance.

In the field of healing this led to a restrictive, distorted and even counter-productive approach: a perception of the causes and remedies of disease which separated and focused upon two aspects, the mind and body, which it tended to view as a collection of disrelated components subject to malfunction. The tendency to rely on structured theories and methods perpetrated an avoidance of the more nebulous but nonetheless important areas of the subtle senses. Any consideration of the underlying significance of dis-ease, such as correlating the need to find a sense of purpose and fulfilment in life, which intuition can help us perceive, has been either ignored or relegated to the areas of religion or 'spiritual healing'.

In stressing the need for intuitive development we are looking at *redressing the balance*: and balance is a central tenet of healing as well as a primary touchstone for any kind of evolutionary development.

WHAT IS INTUITION?

Trying to describe intuition with words is rather like trying to catch a butterfly in full flight with your bare hands. Even if you succeed in capturing it you run the risk of damaging the fragile wings, distorting the subtle colours, destroying the very anatomy you seek to explain. How to describe in words, which are essentially separatist and limiting, that which is essentially inclusive and unlimited?

We can say that intuition functions beyond the limits of time and space; that it has access to the unconscious; that there is a subtle but significant distinction between pure intuition which is always aligned to cosmic balance or Universal Law and the broad areas of perception which we choose to label as 'extra' sensory or psychic (of which there are no less than 18, according to Bob Moore of the Psychic Centre in Denmark). We may connect this difference with the super-conscious or transpersonal realm but further exploration in this direction is likely to bring us up against the ineffable nature of intuitive reality.

In fact, all of us at some time or another experience flashes of intuition, whether it comes as a realisation, perhaps while looking at a painting or a cloud formation, through a dream or fantasy or during the most mundane activity. It may come in the form of a sudden insight into a person or situation, a solution to a problem, an inspiration for a poem, a mystical experience. Perhaps we may understand something about a situation which has not been explained to us: we receive clear, *immediate* information, uncoloured by emotion, often with no obvious means to arrive at this knowing, which may even appear distorted, illogical or even downright absurd at the time.

But then most of us have been brought up in a world where a child's internal communion, his world of fantasy and creative imagination, is crushed with reprimands and attitudes of derision. How many of us were told at school 'Stop that idle daydreaming and pay attention' (to this *fact*), 'Stop staring out of the window/into the fire' and, above all, 'Stop wasting time!'

We are made to feel foolish and ashamed of our innate imaginative talents, ridiculed for our simple 'understandings': we learned to disparage our own creative efforts and indeed we were told they were a distraction from the 'real task' of (men) earning a living and supporting a family and (women) housekeeping and child rearing.

For intuition to flourish we need to provide a climate where meditation, contemplation or simply spending quiet times alone with ourselves are seen as a valuable part of our daily lives.

• We need to encourage non-verbal (poetry apart) forms of expression such as music, dance and the arts and crafts; opportunities for imaginative exploration, where our power to visualise, where our total sensory spectrum, can unfold.

• We need to develop awareness of our mental control and our physical and emotional tensions and find whichever ways work best for us to relax them.

• We need to learn to *listen*, to tune in to our inner voice, to allow ourselves to experience deeper levels of our being, to follow our flow.

To navigate successfully in intuitive waters we need to learn how to recognise intuition, and then we need to trust it.

WHO NEEDS INTUITION?

There is a rather salient aspect to this treasure lurking hidden in the folds of obscurity. For not only is intuition a shining jewel to crown our competency as a full-fledged member of our species, it is also the key to our own power.

A primary feeling experienced by so many people doing various forms of therapy is one of helplessness, of powerlessness — a state of waiting to be told what to do, not do, eat, wear, read, work at, think, feel, enjoy, worship, show, hide, pretend — to respond to what is *expected of us*. But deep within there is a knowing, a sense of betrayal: that that is not who we really are. Who are we anyway? We haven't been encouraged to find out.

The underlying message remains: we believe we don't have the *power* to change; to know what we need for ourselves; to become who we truly are. The power to live our own lives seems denied us.

Intuition is potentially radical   It is even revolutionary, if you like.
It is your key to who you are.
It is your key to what you need.
It is your key to how to live your *life, perfectly.*

Without intuition we are pathetic little beings running around with our lopsided computer brains like laboratory mice in a wheel, living in blind, amputated ignorance, unaware of the magnificent dimensions of the full world outside, our birthright, our true domain.

It is nothing short of ironic, the purely irrational *faith* we put in our little computer brains: and yet, as any programmer will tell you, a computer can only produce results according to the information programmed in; and our brain areas contain such a limited collection of known and provable facts. Especially when dealing with ourselves.

I am not for one moment intending to suggest that we abandon the rational mind as redundant. Quite the contrary: we need to develop all aspects we have and learn how to balance and integrate them.

What I *am* saying is that without our intuition we are living as cripples, unable to relate harmoniously to either ourselves or our host (the Earth). That intuition is *essential* to: understanding our needs and how to take care of them; developing the empathy which can bring about positive inter-relationships; connecting with our own inner guidance; and reaching our individual and collective full human potential. And as well, it is essential to becoming an effective healing catalyst, for, to quote Assagioli: 'We cannot conceive a true and successful therapist who has not developed and uses intuition'.

So, in answer to the question 'Who needs intuition?' the answer is 'Everyone!'

A PLACE TO BEGIN

How to clean and polish this tarnished instrument till it shines crystal clear? How to remove the accumulated dross that gets in the way: the games and self-deception; the fears and desires (and especially the fear of not getting what we desire) that come from the fear of not having? The inbuilt resistances and inherited superstitions, the limiting attitudes and beliefs?

How to regain our trust in ourselves? For this is really what we are talking about. Our power to know what's best for us. How to retrieve our lost inheritance, our key to our creativity, purpose and joy through fulfilment?

Here are some suggestions with which you may choose to begin:

SUPPORTIVE ELEMENTS

1 Creating a space A useful habit to acquire is to regularly take time to be by yourself, especially at the start of the day. You will need to take whatever steps are necessary to ensure your privacy, even if this means getting a lock fitted to your door! Some elements of ritual are helpful, such as lighting candles, burning incense and surrounding yourself with whatever is most precious and beautiful to you which may take the form of flowers, photographs, a special stone, a scarf of a colour you feel particularly drawn to. Try to also include a healthy plant or two.

2 Keeping a journal Note any insights, dreams, experiences you feel contain intuitive responses. Check out your hunches, follow up your 'gut feelings'. A large ring-binder will allow you more flexibility of contents.

3 Friendly support Cultivate people with whom you can share your efforts and discoveries, people who will give you useful feedback and positive encouragement. Avoid the contemptuous, cynical or left-brain addicts and those who are likely to feel disturbed or threatened by your investigations. Watch for the heart behind heady promises of psychic scholarship, too.

4 Self awareness/self deception You may want to join a class on self-awareness, or read some books to help you develop this useful attribute to living your life, as well as developing intuition. With the best will in the world, self-honesty isn't easy when most of us have long ago learnt to hide from ourselves things we don't want to see or feel, and it often requires the help of skilled people to help us unravel ourselves.

AFFIRMATIONS

You produce your thoughts so take responsibility for what you create from them. Thinking something to yourself and stating it out loud, regularly, is a powerful way to start the change.

Some examples:

- 'I make a commitment today to developing my intuition.'
- 'My intuition is invaluable to me.'
- 'My intuition allows me to experience a greater reality.'
- 'I utterly trust my intuition.'

RELAXATION

Begin by practising whatever form you have found works best for you.

For the following exercises, sit (or lie for number one) in a comfortable position with your spine erect (this allows the energy to flow freely). Close your eyes.

Exercises For Clearing Your Channel Imagine yourself walking along a path which leads you deep into the jungle where you come to a small clearing. You notice what appears to be the entrance to a tunnel, overgrown with weeds and choked with silt and stones from which a trickle of muddy water is seeping.

Taking whatever tools you need from your rucksack, begin to clear away the weeds. Untangle them carefully, gently, only cutting where necessary until the outline of the tunnel entrance can be clearly seen. Bending to peer in, you notice a faint light within. Now squat down and begin to carefully remove the stones. You might like to place them in a pile forming a seat.

Taking a shovel, clear away the silt until the channel is quite free and notice now how the light is shining clearly through the tunnel. Scrub down the walls to remove any mould and watch as clear, sparkling water now flows freely. Reach out and dip your fingers into the water, touching your fingertips to your third eye (the point immediately above where your eyebrows would meet).

Now sit down on your stone seat and listen attentively. Sooner or later you will hear music, or a song coming from the tunnel. Know that it is your music, your song. Practise until you can hear it clearly, whenever you choose.

A Sensing Exercise: The Feather For this exercise you need to enlist a suitable person to join you. Sit opposite each other and choose to be either A or B.

A, now visualise a point in your belly, feel a tiny tug, notice a small stirring within your centre as like a frond of bracken slowly uncurling, a feather begins to emerge, reaching out, swaying slightly, damp like a newly-hatched chick.

Allow this feather to reach out towards B. See if you can get a sense of touching B. Allow your feather to convey sensations to you, perhaps heat or cold, a colour, a texture, a form. Ask for a symbol. Now, see if you can pick up a quality about that person, any deep feelings they hold, any transitory feelings they are experiencing. See if any words or images come into your mind regarding them. (Always note your first, immediate impressions; don't judge, analyse or censor.) Now, see if you can send a feeling of love and light and well-being towards them through your feather.

Finally, withdraw your feather; coil it back up and store it safely in your centre. Send it your blessings. Place your hands over your centre for a moment. Remove your hands, placing them palm downwards on the floor and become aware of your contact with the ground.

Taking your time, open your eyes and share with your partner that you have received and they have experienced. Now you can swap places.

A Non-Intuitive Checklist
When trying to distinguish intuition, it's helpful to check out your experiences against a list of *non*-intuitive responses. For example: is my perception:

Fearful? Is it subject to anxiety, doubt, etc?

Full of longing? Does it fulfil a desire I am unable to fulfil in actuality (like a wish fulfilment fantasy)?

Does it correlate with a superstition?

Is it bound by my belief systems?

Is it coloured by emotion?

Is it changeable? Can I control or direct it?

Does it bear a strong moral overtone? Does it contain a should/not?

Does it sound just like parent/teacher or other authority figure?

Is it seductive? Or does it have a nagging voice?

Is it accompanied by a sense of self-importance, of 'scoring', of ego satisfaction?

Can I explain it? Justify it? Rationalise it?

Does it involve analysis or evaluation before it can occur?

Is it a slow, lengthy, drawn-out process? Is it a struggle?

Does it only occur in limited conditions?

You may also like to ask yourself 'Where do I feel this in my body?' There are certain distinct 'feelings' we all have which have nothing to do with intuition. The caution based on fear and anxiety, which we may call a 'still, small voice', may be nothing more than that (except that it is probably stopping us from living a full and happy life). The fear of taking risks, and letting go of something which makes us feel secure, of moving away from habitual modes of behaviour, has nothing to do with intuition. Nor has the wilful 'it must be intuition' justification for something we *want* but feel we shouldn't think, feel, have or do.

Guessing is a good way to start your intuition flowing and imagining (or image-ing) is also. But neither should be mistaken for the real thing. To quote Frances Vaughan in her book Awakening Intuition,

The distinction between imagination and intuition is precisely this. Pure intuition is knowledge that comes out of experience of formlessness and silence, whereas imagination gives form to the formless and is conceptual in nature.

INTUITIVE HEALING

Working with intuition demands a holistic, all-embracing attitude to health and human capacity which cannot be contained with a technique. It requires that we re-examine the attitudes and beliefs that we bring to the dimension of healing. For it is more about our *approach* than about theories of dis-ease or formulas for treatment.

Working as an *effective* intuitive healing channel does not necessarily require any specific skills on the part of the practitioner *in terms of what we do to the client.*

(Although these may, or may not, be useful to us.) It does not require *per se*, learning theories, techniques or formulas for any kind of diagnostic or treatment procedures.

Nor does it necessitate developing amazing psychic skills or affiliating with any religious, spiritual or esoteric school or master (although, once again, this may, or may not, be useful).

What it *does* require is almost the opposite: a willingness to let go of the sense of security derived from form, to become an open channel. This involves focusing on developing awareness of our *own* state; taking responsibility for keeping our personality or ego levels out of the way (centred); for being fully present in the here-and-now (grounded); for maintaining a relaxed but alert, open, receptive non-judgemental state of consciousness (heart-centred); so we can simply let go, trust and tune-in.

Put simply, the state of consciousness of the practitioner is more important than any knowledge, skills or techniques.

The intuitive bridge   There has been a wide gap between the medical/remedial/therapeutic approaches to healing and that of the psychic and spiritual. This gap is now beginning to be bridged, for example, by some of the newer developments in rebirthing, psychosynthesis, forms of transpersonal therapy and other holistic approaches.

In talking about holistic health one cannot leave out *any* aspect of the human experience if we are to avoid the very separation we seek to avoid in using the term 'holistic'. In using the *intellect* to understand our reality, we seek to measure, control and quantify: to be scientific. A clearly definable process is sought in which the practitioner may identify in order to achieve stability, security and an assumed sense of safety of action.

However, this very framework can lead to inflexibility, limitation and even to error. It may be defined as a 'yang' (that is, 'male') approach and certainly many people do feel safer working within a prescribed context.

With the *psychic* levels, the process is different. During channelling the unconcious attitudes and emotional blocks may interfere with the operator's ability to work as a clear channel. With the trance, or *unconscious* medium, the appropriateness of information transmitted may be affected by disconnection with physical reality. Lack of self-awareness allows for distortion and projected self-delusion. Personal accountability for their actions is often forsworn when mediums place themselves at the disposal of the entity or source they channel.

This is where true intuition, which is always in the service of the heart and aligned with the Divine Loving Source, provides the key. For it both frees the practitioner from the limitation of our personal storehouse of knowledge and the need to try to understand the client, while at the same time protecting us from the very real dangers of psychic distortion.

It can also help free us from notion of being 'the healer', thus allowing the client to draw through us, as the *therapeutic channel and catalyst*, whatever form of healing is required. As the focus of accountability shifts, we become responsible for monitoring our ability to remain tuned-in without interference from our personality.

Patterns of growth — pushing your limits   People search for their limits for one of two reasons. Either we wish to find the walls of our limitations to enable us to feel safe; *or* we want to contact them to enable us to let go and move beyond these limits.

We can look at patterns of personal growth like this, as a continual process where there is no final goal as such. It repeats itself but each time goes a little further out/

in. (The inward circles parallel the outer in that each time around, *in order to expand*, one has to make a deeper inner connection.)

A question of balance   Apart from the multiferous levels of personal and societal limitations, all of which can be transcended, there are other underlying 'rules' which are not transmutable. These may be referred to as cosmic or universal laws, the laws of nature, God's laws or what you will.

There is a law which does not allow for a certain state of being to *become* until all the requisite changes have taken place: a form of limitation which is an essential factor in contributing to universal balance.

There are no bypasses. It is simply not possible to reach certain levels of advancement or states of being without this balance.

Hence various forms of short cuts to enlightenment or wherever, like the forced raising of the Kundalini energy, can only serve to exaggerate imbalances already contained within the organism. The altered states of consciousness brought about through the use of psychedelic drugs do not in themselves produce a whole, healthy, optimum-functioning being. The evidence of imbalance is all around us:

• The psychic genius who is unable to sustain a warm, loving relationship.

• The mother who has learnt to scream out her anger and frustration but still lacks the power to act and move beyond it.

• The spiritual disciple who has spent years in self-disciplined isolation, meditating, continuously, who, when returning to the world, cannot provide for himself nor relate to his children.

• The wordly businessman who has daily analysis and knows his every trauma backwards, who spends his weekends letting it all hang out in a variety of different workshops, yet who cannot bear to be alone with himself.

One of the dangers of spiritual teachings, then, is that they can be used out of context; especially when used by a different culture they may serve merely to rationalise our blocks.

Hence, to someone brought up in a puritanical society where Christian teaching has been distorted to promote sexual guilt, immersing oneself in an Eastern discipline which advocates celibacy may serve as a comfortable way to avoid the problem; unfortunately it rarely solves it.

Isolation   It seems likely that the sense of isolation we as a culture tend to suffer from is a primary cause of all forms of stress, imbalance and disease. And one of the problems of focusing on emotional release is that it can leave the person hooked into the concept of the need to 'get rid of our shit' and can fail to connect us in to our more positive feelings; it may also leave us with an even greater sense of separation from our fellows.

It therefore becomes vital to work in ways which re-connect us with our fellows, which is where working with and validating the higher feeling levels becomes urgent.

In *Despair and Empowerment in the Nuclear Age* Joanna Macy talks about the importance of recognising our transpersonal feelings (I am using the phrase 'transpersonal' to refer to the feelings which go beyond concern for ourselves or people we know; for example feeling of distress for the suffering of others and including our planet, fears for the future of our species, etc.). It is through sharing these feelings that we may come to rediscover our essential interconnectedness.

The ability to empathise,* to connect with our own and each other's inner strength, becomes especially necessary as an adjunct to opening the heart centre and developing

* The feeling of *em*pathy is closely linked with our intuitive and higher-feeling levels, whereas *sym*pathy hooks into our personal distress.

compassion in order that we do not become engulfed by the suffering of others. This may be described as making a spiritual connection and this is where developing intuition becomes profoundly necessary.

THE INTUITIVE THERAPIST:

Some useful concepts:

There are some primary concepts which underlie working as an *effective* intuitive channel. You will need to examine your motivation, receptivity, and ability to trust. You will need to develop self-awareness, together with knowledge of certain disciplines.

1 It becomes vital to learn how to *ground* your own energy in order to maintain contact with material reality: to be firmly anchored in the world helps to avoid becoming drained, for you need to be clear you are not giving of your own energy.

2 To know how to *centre* or move beyond the personality level where ego needs (such as the need to prove oneself a 'great healer') do not interfere: to move into a calm, quiet space or altered state of consciousness.

3 To bring a really strong healing dimension it becomes important to be reasonably *in balance* yourself and open on the heart centre (unconditional love). This means the giver becomes able to transmit a stronger 'voltage' without risk to himself or the receiver.

Using intuition in this context implies acceptance of the principle of a Divine Loving Intelligence underlying all and into which the channel can tune, thereby serving as a vehicle for healing. Indeed, this connection needs to be strong and will become stronger with us as the channel/therapist is continually faced with nowhere else to turn.

It can be a scarey space to be in for, once you move out onto this path there is no book of rules, no method, or technique to cling to. Your mental catalogue of stored information is no use to you, your individual talents and skills may come in handy but they cannot serve to guide you. There is only one door and either it is open or it is closed. Trust is the key, although it's a good idea to keep the hinges oiled.

Trust *With awareness of one's own state of clarity and heart-connectedness and the means to help achieve them, we can simply let go and allow.*

• We can trust whatever comes out of our mouths to be appropriate in content and context.

• We can trust that we will be able to act appropriately whatever the need.

• We can trust *ourselves* which means that we can be fully *there*. For it is the quality; the integrity, depth and lovingness which the practitioner brings to the work which is all-important in the result.

We live in a time where we are having to realise the truth of the ancient maxim 'the only constant is change'. It is a time where we vitally need to find ways to let go of our striving to make the world safe by clinging to concepts of rigid order, control and holding on (to people and possessions, attitudes and beliefs).

This is a time for letting go, in the safety of our own inner-connectedness, to the whole: to let go and enjoy the ride. And this urgent need applies very much in the field of healing where many symptoms of stress and disease are caused by our difficulty in adapting to change, by our subconscious fears of chaos.

There is really only one choice open to us: to continue to be consumed by fear and anxiety, or to re-gain our connectedness so we can let go into love. And the experience of trusting is an important one in learning to let go and love.

Most of us, however, live in a world where at every turn our trust is betrayed: by advertisers and politicians' promises which don't fulfil the fantasies they inspire; by our colleagues or school mates deserting us in the face of threats to their own survival in a hostile environment; by parents who say they love us but don't accept us as we are.

As a result of this early elimination of trust we continually make statements and then deny their truth, make promises to each other (like a phone call, a date) and then break them. We smile at people we feel nothing for: in fact we have come to expect betrayal to the extent that we are often not even aware of it.

A part of my work takes me into the classroom with children of varying ages where I teach intuitive massage and relaxation, using guided imagery and self-awareness, and it is here that I have witnessed the strongest confirmation of the need for trust. Children have such a beautiful, inate ability to tune in and heal that it is tragic that none of these areas are generally included in the school curriculum. But the sad fact is that, in many cases, these talents have been thoroughly exterminated well before the child leaves school.

To provide people with a safe place to experience trust, so they can really let go and explore whatever is there for them, is to create a profoundly healing experience.

In order to be able to do this we need to trust ourselves and intuition can help us do that. It provides us with a sense of 'rightness' and connectedness which we can feel without having to justify. We can learn to let go of our safety devices and be open in a spontaneous, giving way.

The Feeling Levels Being open on the feeling level is a part of the process. The term 'objectivity' serves no purpose here unless it can be interpreted in terms of avoiding *reacting* to the client whilst allowing *response*. What there can be is a suspension of judgment of the client, and of investment in the outcome of the session.

Compassion is a feeling and one could say that the term charlatan could best be applied to those people who operate in the healing realm with no sense of compassion.

In the areas of feelings there can still be found a strong 'yang' element amongst many professionals, including those on the 'alternative' fields, which demands that feeling be avoided in favour of 'clinical detachment'. The practitioner is expected to disconnect from his own feelings whilst in many cases actively encouraging the client to get into theirs.

This attitude can be understood if one recognises that many practitioners fail to distinguish between different levels of feeling. It is helpful to recognise the difference as follows:

1 The emotions attached to and motivated by our sense of self-preservation and allrightness contain responses to perceived threat (which may come from the client) and expectations absorbed about 'proper' behaviour for a practitioner. They include a wide range of emotional responses such as fear, resentment, envy and lust which may manifest themselves as non-acceptance of clients or the need to manipulate them (in order to feel safe, etc.) and do not serve us in our role as therapist. In terms of the subtle energy, these feelings emanate from the area of the solar plexus.

2 Then there are other forms of feeling response which one can say operate from a 'higher' level and which emanate from the heart centre. These are feelings unconnected with our own needs such as compassion, empathy, reverence, wonder, etc. (All these feelings do in fact serve us for, on a much deeper level than that of ego survival, they *re-connect* us, which gives us a real sense of safety in belonging.)

These feelings can occur when the practitioner is open to some extent in the heart centre. They serve an important function as they can be directly transmitted to the client, especially through the energy of the hands. Not only will these feelings help forge a bond of trust and openness, *they carry in themselves a healing vibration* which may be felt and absorbed by the clients and may enable them to get in touch with their own higher feelings.

It is precisely the inclusion of this level of feelings which can bring a very powerful dimension of healing to the session. As the world gradually seeks to redress the 'yin' balance of feminine energy, so these kinds of concepts will become more readily accepted and understood.

INTUITIVE CHANNELLING

We are looking at two distinct forms of channelling.

One is where the practitioner or channel *receives information* which is then communicated to the client. This information may include pictures, flashes, colours, sounds, sensations, words, etc.

The other is where the practitioner receives and transmits pure energy. On this level the practitioner interacts with the client's subtle energy. This can be done from a distance when it is sometimes called absent healing.

Tuning-in Tuning-in is rather like changing gear. For some people it comes naturally whereas for others it is a learned process. This state becomes more clearly recognisable with frequent practice.

The experience for me is one of letting go of my thinking mind and my subjective emotional (not-feeling) state: of entering a state where I am neither attached nor detached but, to quote Vimilar Thaker in her talks on relationship, 'in a state of alert, perceptive awareness'.

My awareness of myself changes, my breathing may slow as my body becomes relaxed but alive and responsive to signals for action (*including* response on the feeling levels). Outside noises and distractions fall away. It is a state of stillness, of openness and, above all, of trust.

Similar to a meditative state, it differs in that my consciousness is focused on my client rather than 'the still point within', whilst maintaining open receptiveness to my channel. If I am working with my hands, the 'energy' begins to flow into them.

As I move into this state of consciousness, I have no need for my defences. My perception of my client becomes one of acceptance. My being becomes charged with a peaceful energy where love and compassion are simply there.

One of the most moving experiences which occurs in my daily work is to realise how I can feel love towards anyone, anyone at all, once our defences are down.

This illustrates how, to the extent that we learn to defend ourselves from one another in order to avoid hurt and rejection, so do we cut ourselves off from love, warmth and the sense of belonging.

Candles and incense Apart from offering a point of light as a reminder of the precious spirit we carry within each of us, together with the cleansing properties and pleasant smell, rituals with candles and incense can help us slip into the receptive state of consciousness. Music and certain colours may help us too.

INTUITIVE COUNSELLING

One of the big differences between intuitive counselling and most psychic readings (sometimes called 'spiritual' readings) is that whereas the latter may focus on giving clients information about their character, past, present and/or future events, and may even extend to include giving them rituals and exercises to work with themselves, they are not usually interactive in therapeutic sense. Counselling involves some special considerations.

Taking responsibility   This is an important part of therapeutic integrity. If you are going to use your gifts of perception responsibly, you will need to be able to allow your clients to 'work through' the effects of the session as deeply and in as free a manner as possible. You will need to develop experience, depth and balance within yourself to the extent that you can be there *appropriately* during someone's expression of grief, terror, rage, or whatever they may experience.

It is also important to remember that words can act as powerful triggers so be aware that sharing your perceptions may have devastating effects.

A client came along to me one day complaining of a pain in her right foot. I 'saw' her foot trapped under a beam of wood which was preventing her from escaping a fire. As I described this to her, she screamed, curled up in a ball making clawing movements with her hands, her eyes dilated with terror.

We worked through her experience and it turned out to be a powerful session. She was able to let go of fearfulness which had lain dormant, manifesting as nervous tension and a bodily holding pattern, which had been preventing her from leading a relaxed, enjoyable life.

Whether or not this was a 'real' past-life memory is not important here. The point is that it serves to illustrate the need for being prepared to handle whatever comes up there and then.

Appropriateness   It may be that your client is neither ready nor willing to hear your insights or may be busy reaching insights of his or her own. In my experience, developing an intuitive channel seems to bring about a certain safety factor where inappropriate information simply doesn't appear.

All this depends on your ability to remain a clear channel. In terms of sharing negative impressions, it's a good idea to check it out with your channel first: if in doubt; don't share it.

It is by being connected through your intuition to the loving source that you can know the appropriateness and timing of what you say to your clients.

Receiving guidance   Most psychic operators believe that they are working through guides which they may classify as being deceased relatives, healers who have 'passed over', entities from other worlds, advanced souls, angels, beings from the Devic kingdoms or spiritual masters, etc. Whether or not one accepts these connections as 'real' depends on your individual perspective. They often provide the practitioner with a sense of security and in some instances a valuable partnership develops.

However, one needs to apply caution in seeking such intermediaries for several reasons.

• The 'guide' can operate from many levels, which include the mischievous, frivolous and even quite stupid. They may also seek to disguise their true nature.

• They can become a distraction from making a connection with the direct source, which is a delicate process.

• Their presence can lead to an avoidance of personal accountability. There is a vast difference between abandoning one's conscious awareness to allow oneself to be used as a medium, and becoming a *conscious* channel.

It seems to me that at this time it is the latter which is most appropriate. For it is in maintaining the link with the flow of your own heart energy whilst channelling, that you are able to monitor the quality and become aware of distortion as it occurs.

Discrimination   When opening to the psychic areas, we need to use discrimination. We need to ask ourselves questions like:
'Is this information useful?'
'Does this information or experience serve to bring me closer to my heart centre? Does it have the ring of an unconditional loving source?'
'Does it help me or my client to evolve in a balanced way?'
'Does this unground me and take me into areas of gamesyness, ego scoring, compensation for feelings of lack of self-worth?'
'Does it bring feelings of fear, paranoia, distrust into my life?'

   Alone, the psychic senses can wreak a nice variety of havoc in one's life: upsetting relationships, bringing imbalance, even paranoia and a sense of out-of-touchness with life. All of this can affect the lives of those people who come to you as clients. You will therefore need to be willing to be completely honest with yourself.

Psychic versus Spiritual   There are many levels of non-physical reality which the psychic senses may apprehend. However, none of these are necessarily any higher or more spiritual — if by spiritual we mean seeking accord with the Divine Harmony, Universal Love, God, etc. — than any other.

   The wisdom of the spirit seems to lie firmly anchored in the heart which brings us ever into contact with life, not away from it; into contact with ourselves and our surroundings, and with others, thereby creating an opportunity for loving expression.

   I met a weary traveller one day, resting on his 'path'. He made the remark: 'It's so much easier to love God than people!'

The Channel in Action In acting as an intuitive channel one is essentially reflecting back to clients what they already know for themselves but cannot get access to or see clearly, for this knowing is often buried beneath layers of acquired distrust, doubt, confusion or simply not paying attention to that level of one's being.

If your words are intuitively accurate, the client will recognise this and respond in various ways.

Working intuitively means following *patterns*. So, as you allow your relaxed but conscious awareness to fill, as you empty it to your client, inter-action takes place. You 'feel' or 'sense' the responses and follow the pattern.

You will begin to know when you are 'getting warm', closer to something important to your client. At these times you may feel the need to input more energy to the client. This is done by a process of intensifying and focusing energy and channelling it to the client. I often do this by eye-contact or by touch, perhaps a hand on the knee or whatever feels appropriate.

When the client starts to release feelings, you can discover intuitively the appropriate response, which might be to hold the client firmly in your arms, or to keep a distance and remain quiet, or something else again.

Variety of input Suggestions for using other processes, or specific exercises including all kinds of input, can come through on your intuitive channel. No book, course or form of rational knowledge can guide you as to appropriateness. There are so many factors involved with each individual and even, if you knew them all, how are you equipped to weigh them?

• You may become aware, for example, that the clients' choice of *colour* for clothing is not helping them. You may then be able to feed them information about what they do need: the appropriate colour/s, which shade, in what relation to themselves (that is, clothing, jewellery, where to wear it, bed-linen, decor, a card on the wall, etc.) and for how long they need to use these colours.

• Or there may be certain kinds of *music* from which they could derive benefit. It may soothe them and slow them down, stimulate them, or even aggravate a condition to bring it into focus.

• There are some very powerful ways of using *nature* to re-balance ourselves on many levels. Your intuition can suggest them to you so you can share them. For example, connecting with rocks can help us to slow down; water helps to cleanse and release emotions; trees, especially visualising their roots, can help us to ground ourselves; looking at the sky can help awaken intuition.

• One client may need to *dance* his or her way through pain to joy, another to *sing*, another to jump into life vigorously or tentatively begin to open up to relating, whilst yet another may need to withdraw into a period of silence. Your intuitive channel can indicate which.

I always tell my clients that if what comes up on the channel for them 'feels right' do it; but if it doesn't, let it go.

In working with people intuitively it is important to help them develop their own intuitive process in order that they do not become dependent on your insights. Even more important is that it helps them to regain their own sense of power and integrity.

Expectations One situation which I encounter, using the intuitive channel, is a series of demands and expectations on the part of the client (or one's own conditioning) that they must be supplied with a diagnosis, a framework to interpret their 'problem' and regular 'progress' reports.

It takes both courage and clarity of intent to refuse. It sometimes helps to point out to the client how this kind of information (even supposing you had it all intellectually mapped out) can actually get in the way. It can lead to rigid self concepts as the client's mind starts to work on the 'problem'.

Here, you need to help your client do individually what you yourself are attempting: to let go and trust.

If you are sincerely coming from a place in yourself of loving intuitive attention, some part of your client will sense this, even though he or she may not be prepared to acknowledge it. This is where the function of the channel becomes educational.

INTUITIVE TOUCH

I find that a very grounded way to start learning intuitive channelling is through the vehicle of touch. It brings us into direct contact with any resistance we may have towards accepting another person in an unconditional way. For if we can't bring ourselves to touch someone's body there is no way we can bring a truly open, loving dimension to a session and any healing effects will be limited.

Touch is a good place to begin because it brings us into contact with our own bodily (physical) reality. One of the interesting things I notice about many psychically developed people is that they are neither comfortable with the body level nor with their sexuality. Obviously this is a generalisation, but it draws attention to the need to work with the physical, emotional and sexual levels of our being. Working through the 'lower' energy centres rather than the 'higher' ones becomes a necessary preliminary if we are to make a strong connection into the heart centre and become a balanced channel.

The hands are a very good medium through which to tune-in to the client. They avoid many of the mind-traps we lay for one another. They also give us something to *do*, and within the touching is a clear opportunity to express the love with which we may create the conditions of trust and openness needed for a meaningful session of healing.

Touch also provides a good focus to help us reconcile the physical, psychic, sensual and sacred aspects of ourselves which can lead to a sense of *completeness*.

As distinct from the many different techniques of massage which teach a *method* of touching the body, the intuitive approach seeks to free the form and allow for the touch to flow and be guided solely by the tuning-in of the giver to the needs of the receiver. If this connection is total, then the touch can only be appropriate and healing.

The hands can function as the perfect co-ordinator when guided by the intuition, which bypasses the constraints of a limited mind. For it is not *what* you do, but the *way* that you do it. Anyone with a reasonable amount of imagination can discover an infinite variety of ways to connect their hands with another body. It is the quality of touch which is all important. There can be no 'right' and 'wrong' strokes with this approach, only a lack of sensitivity or tuning-in to the needs of the receiver.

Patterns of appropriateness In giving a massage in this way certain tendencies do become apparent, but in observing them, it's important not to turn them into fixed rules.

• Keeping the hands still allows for the build-up of energy awareness and connectedness.

• With most Western adults it is appropriate to *draw the energy down* and not up the

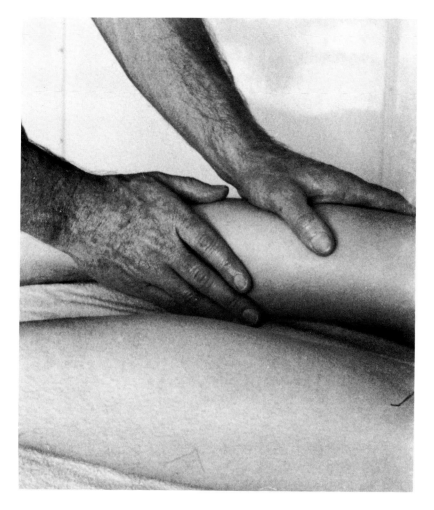

body. This means to emphasise the downward strokes and perhaps conclude with some long strokes from the top of the body down and off the hands or feet. (*Note*: this is quite opposite to many techniques which teach that the strokes should go *towards* the heart, a place I often start *from*. This is because they are concerned with the blood circulation rather than energy. This is a good example of where you can trust your hands to know best, once you are fully tuned-in.)

• Working *slowly* often seems to allow a deeper connection and release than faster movement. However, it may not be appropriate to release too much too soon. Again, this is something you will know if you are fully tuned-in through your hands. Moving slowly also allows the receiver to relax and slow down too.

• Using a fairly *firm touch* forms a stronger bond (again, not always). It also implies acceptance.

• *Rhythm and flow*. Massage can be a form of dance: tactile poetry, shared meditation in movement. A celebration of the body, it needs its own continuum, its own rhythm.

• *Tenderness* brings a much deeper response than pain. This may be because it seems so rarely available outside of specifically sexual or parental relationships. (In my personal view, any use of force or pain is a violation of the trust placed in us and produces tension and resistance while fixing in more fear than any release can justify.)

Communion   Touch is a vital form of communication. It can often get through where words get in the way. The directness of a caring touch can say so much: 'You are okay just as you are', 'You are unique and beautiful', 'I totally accept you', 'You belong'. (This last statement is vital in view of the tremendous isolation so many of us feel.)

Intuitive massage allows both giver and receiver to experience a deep sense of communion: beings capable of infinite expansion and love. For, in giving a massage whether professionally or to a friend, comes the opportunity to experience oneself as a truly loving, giving person. Hence the giver also receives.

CHANNELLING ENERGY

Protection   In channelling energy, if the practitioner wishes to lead a long and healthy life, it is essential that we learn to channel in such a way that we will not drain our own energy.

Working in these areas it is *motivation* which offers the best protection. The need to develop the heart centre so the motive does not attach to personal gain becomes of paramount importance. Getting our approval, prestige or self-esteem from psychic activities is a dangerous game.

Energy fields   Implicit in working intuitively is developing a heightened awareness of energy fields. The nature and degree of awareness (that is, clairvoyance, or the ability to *see* energy, clairaudience, to *hear*, and clairsentience, to *sense*) naturally varies.

Energy is a popular term at present. The term 'energy balancing' is applied to many diverse forms, from quite dense levels of physical energy, such as that worked with in bio-energetic exercises, to the ultra-fine quality of energy used in the construction of the subtle body. In this section I am referring to the latter, which many people believe reveals itself visibly through Kirlian photography.

Laying on of Hands   Some people prefer to transmit healing energy by keeping their hands in a fixed position. In the classical stance, the practitioner stands behind the client with his hands on his shoulders with the client sitting on a chair.

Or they may place their hands for specific periods of time in particular patterns over the body (as in Reiki channelling).

Working intuitively, one may find the hands wish to remain in one spot. In my own work, however, I rarely find that they do so for more than a few minutes at a time.

This may have to do with my intention, which is not so much directed towards alleviating specific conditions as towards bringing the clients' awareness to themselves and how they can utilise the numerous benefits of healing, cleansing and re-balancing to create their lives around learning to balance and heal themselves. That way they will no longer need to become sick but are enabled to fulfil their unique potential.

Energy Balancing   During this process I simply let go and let my hands, and sometimes even my whole body, 'do it' for me. This is like giving oneself over to the dance. An onlooker might observe my hands making an infinite variety of movements, smoothing, stroking, circling, pulling, pressing, shaping, pausing to hover over a certain spot somewhere above (and sometimes in connection with) the physical body.

I am aware of magnetic currents which draw and repel the hands. Many clients feel varying sensations during this process such as heat, cold, draughty sensations, tingling or pricking. They may actually see lights, colours or even pictures.

What is happening is a profound re-balancing of the deeper levels of the clients' being and the result will provide them with a powerful basis for achieving health and well-being.

A TYPICAL SESSION:

To keep notes or attempt to diagnose the client and his or her problem is not my practice because I prefer each session to occur with freshness, spontaneity and a sense of immediacy. It also avoids the risk of the client feeling categorised.

Although each session is different and has its own dynamic, there is a general pattern. A first session will almost always involve the client sitting quietly at first with eyes closed, letting go of outer distractions in order to focus inwardly.

During this period I am allowing impressions to form which may include patterns of light, shade and colour around the client's energy field. I simply *observe* these. I do not bring in my rational mind to try to organise this information or to categorise the client, or make deductions.

This is usually followed by a period of verbal interaction. I frequently seek to focus clients' awareness of their innermost sense of themselves and may ask them what is most precious to them in their lives rather than the standard approach of focusing on what they feel is wrong with them.

At this time flashes of information often appear. They are often visual, in the form of pictures or more abstract patterns of light and colour which need interpreting. They may come as words or phrases like bubbles rising to the surface of a pond. Sharing this information serves to focus the clients' attention on an era or event in this, or another, life. They act as triggers, reminders which may help the clients gain understanding about certain things they are experiencing.

During one session, the image of a china teapot with blue violets on it came up. The client then remembered the time when she had been given the teapot and her mother had broken it. This event symbolised a cutting off of her mother's affection which had been traumatic for her and which she had locked away in her memory until that moment.

When the client talks, I am 'sensing' him or her and watching for patterns, observing their body language and breathing rhythm.

I may suggest some 'homework' which has suggested itself to me intuitively. Usually this includes ways of nurturing the self, which might be something as apparently simple as buying themselves a small present and giving it to themselves each day for a week. It is surprising how difficult some people find it to do that, especially women who are accustomed to forsaking their own needs to take care of those of others.

Or perhaps I will ask clients to record their dreams, a phrase to repeat, or situation to visualise. (It is often valuable to visualise oneself having or doing something you haven't thought was possible or allowable for you.)

Or I may ask the client to make a series of sounds or movements, wear a specific colour, do some painting or clay modelling, etc. Anything at all may conceivably present itself here.

I had one client who found great difficulty in moving out of his intellect and contacting his feelings. He had had a horrific childhood where he spent several months shut in a wardrobe to avoid persecution during the war. He subsequently spent a great part of his free time attending lectures and groups on esoteric and healing subjects, but none of them touched his real need: to escape out of his head.

I asked him to do a series of drawings of the energy centres allowing whatever shapes, colours and forms presented themselves. He came back with several positive drawings, in which he had intuitively expressed the bright, beautiful, loving aspects of himself he had been unable to get access to previously. By pinning them up on his wall he was daily confronted with this reality in a way which he could not deny. This marked the beginning of a definite growth in his ability to acknowledge his feelings.

I use a lot of non-verbal exercises and find they provide a powerful way to help us work with our feelings intuitively.

Because I work with most of my clients for a series of sessions, I am able to include at a later date a selection of self-balancing exercises. The client can then begin to build a personal daily programme and take responsibility for his or her own process of growth and healing.

I encourage clients to do these exercises from an attitude of giving something good to themselves. Once they become a 'duty', the purpose is defeated.

The exercises include breathing, visualisation, usually very slow movements, sounds and colour. They help with the release of physical tension, creatively expressing feelings, sexuality, grounding and the balance of yin and yang (female and male energy).

When the client is ready, I suggest they participate in class situations with small groups. There, they can validate and extend their trust boundaries and learn nurturing skills which will enable them not only to exchange with others but, in doing so, to experience themselves in a giving capacity.

Next, the clients will usually lie on the bench for a session of massage and energy balancing. They will have on as few clothes as feels comfortable. It may take a few sessions before some clients feel *safe* enough to move into complete nakedness. For many people, this in itself can be a healing experience. Once again, it concerns trust.

I begin with nurturing, to the degree that the client is able to receive. It is vital at this stage that a deep level of safety be established because only then can the client really let go.

For many people this degree of safety and acceptance has not been available to them since early childhood (and, tragically, not always then). I cannot stress strongly enough this need for safety for this allows clients to receive a deep input of healing energy they will otherwise resist and close off from.

I am aware during energy balancing of a continually fluctuating magnetic field which draws or repels my hands. During this process the clients may find that, even though their eyes are closed and I am not touching their physical body, they can sense the exact position of my hands above their body.

The massage and re-balancing may last just over an hour, occasionally longer. It is a process which, once begun, proceeds until I sense completion. Much like making love, it is important not to hurry the process or to leave the client incomplete.

After this part of the session I deliberately *do not* fill the clients' heads with information about where they are at. Nor do I encourage them to talk. Rather, I ask them to let go into sensing the movements within themselves, trusting their own healing process. The whole session usually lasts for two hours.

Then I stress the importance of allowing themselves at least an hour before getting involved in the pressure of daily life again, to be quiet with themselves: preferably to find a green space where, sitting with their back propped against a tree, they can fully integrate the experience.

INTUITION — OUR HIDDEN TREASURE

One of the wonderful aspects about intuition is that it can encourage you to *play*. To play with words, concepts, ideas, visions. Suddenly the blinkers are off, the limits are lifted and you are free to romp and explore. There are no win/lose games, no 'right' or 'wrong', only an endless opening up to discovery.

It can be like a treasure hunt, blindfold, with only your 'nose' to guide you: dancing from one 'clue' to the next you are free to pause and look deeper, or just have fun, or, like the ardent sleuth, you can shoot higher and higher and what comes back on your intuitional boomerang is always tinged with the joy and excitement of doing it for yourself!

No books, no teachers, no need for outer authority; suddenly you are free! Inside, you know everything anyway. Somewhere in the collective unconscious or the universal knowingness lie all the wonderful treasures you could ever wish to find, and all you need is your channel.

CHAPTER 12

PAST LIVES THERAPY

Zoë & Malcom Hagon

Like much that happens in our world, past lives therapy began by chance; the right person at the right place at the right time.

The pioneer of this revolutionary approach to healing was English psychiatrist, Dr Denys Kelsey. In 1948, while practising medicine in an English military hospital, he became aware of the potential of hypnosis in the treatment of psychological conditions. This led him into the field of psychiatry and extensive work with patients using hypnotic regression in the treatment of neuroses. In the beginning the possibility of reincarnation and regression into past lives could not have been further from his mind.

His early work was confined to regression into the present life early years of his patients. Through this technique he witnessed the recall of memories from adolescence, childhood and, on occasions, the birth experience and even conception. During these sessions he uncovered causes for many psychological problems which, hitherto, had defied resolution.

Ten years of such work paved the way for his meeting, work with and subsequent marriage to author and clairvoyant, Joan Grant. Famous for her historic novels, actually autobiographies of past lives she had led and which she had the capacity to recall from memory, their coming together brought a new dimension to their lives. For Dr Kelsey, the theory of reincarnation seemed now totally believable. It supplied a logical answer to why some patients responded so positively to regression while others, excellent subjects though they were, were unable to uncover the causes of their neuroses and resolve them simply by recalling past memories of their present life.

Working together, it was a natural progression for Dr Kelsey to start regressing patients beyond this life if the source of their problem could not be found within their present life memory. When regression proved difficult, Joan would often step in and relate the relevant experience to the patient, providing another means of their integrating it into present consciousness. In this way the work of Dr Kelsey and Joan Grant combined and so emerged a whole new approach to psychological healing.

Inspired by the work of Dr Kelsey and Joan Grant, other therapists entered the field of past life regression, or past lives therapy as it has become commonly known. Through the introduction of other techniques, practitioners like Drs Helen Wambach, Maurice Netherton and Nancy Shiffrin have greatly extended its potential as a healing tool and helped foster awareness within western culture of the philosophy of reincarnation, a belief which is part of the lives of almost a billion people.

No professional of whom I have read, or with whom I have discussed past lives therapy, entered this field on a purely professional basis. Dr Wambach voiced the ques-

Dr Helen Wambach — researching past lives

tions that have rung in my ears for as long as I can remember: 'What are we here for? What is the purpose of all the emotions, struggles and anxieties of our time?'

Working in the same manner as my husband, through hypnosis, Dr Wambach not only used past life regression as a tool for therapy, but also undertook an extensive research programme which she wrote of in depth in her book *Life Before Life*. In group sessions across America she worked with over 1,000 subjects, leading them gently back across the years to their birth experience and before. Her findings make fascinating reading and add substantial weight to the theory of reincarnation. The majority of her subjects experienced comparatively ordinary lives and from both class and sex standpoints the data gained compared closely with actual population statistics. Of the 1,000 plus life experiences recorded in her research programme, Dr Wambach found only eleven cases where she could positively disprove that which had been recalled and reported as an actual past experience.

Like many of Dr Wambach's case histories, those recorded by Dr Maurice Netherton and Nancy Shiffrin are not particularly pretty — trauma, the root cause of many present-day problems that stem from past life experiences, is caused by ugly and often almost unendurable situations. Though both practitioners work toward the same end, the significance of Dr Netherton's work is that it embraces yet another technique for releasing from the subconscious the keys to a patient's problems.

Zoë Hagon and her husband Malcom

Best described as 'the trigger method', Dr Netherton's technique involves analysing the speech patterns of his patients for recurring phrases that seem in some way to relate to the problem. The patient is then asked to lie down and, with eyes closed, concentrate on the phrase, repeating it over and over until a mental image is 'triggered' into consciousness. Once begun, the impressions so released often flow with a rush and the patient finds him/herself reliving the experience directly related to the problem.

Like all therapists who work in this field, Dr Netherton writes that though past lives therapy treats reincarnation as a proven fact, it is, of course, nothing of the kind. We all treat reincarnation as a reality, for this is essential if the therapy is to be effective. Each patient will recreate or remember experiences from the past which will bring new understanding and therefore a defusing of the intensity of their present problem. Whether that which they encounter is a past reality or the product of a highly creative imagination is, for some people, a very difficult question to answer. In my view, it is pointless to question the veracity of that which the subconscious releases and the patient experiences. Though one may have a deep and yearning desire to establish the 'truth' of reincarnation, the task at hand is not a search for proof but understanding for the patient of the problem to be overcome.

Of the two techniques covered for bringing past life memories into waking consciousness — neither of which should be attempted unless under the guidance of a highly-experienced therapist — the commonest is still hypnosis. Though limited by the fact that not all people can readily be hypnotised, I feel it is preferable to the 'trigger method' in that it allows the therapist to shepherd patients gently through their experiences. Under the trigger method the therapist appears not to have the same degree of control and therefore finds it more difficult to remove patients from the reality they are experiencing should the need arise.

There is yet a third method, that which I use and which has evolved purely through my personal experience. This, coupled with the work I have done with my husband over the past ten years, has reinforced my belief that reincarnation is a reality. Of all the possible answers, only reincarnation most logically explains that which I have witnessed and experienced.

Initially working with my husband in the same way as Joan Grant worked with Dr Kelsey, I was his eyes on the reality our patients were experiencing. Though highly

We had to look very carefully at the nature and origin of dis-ease in humans . . .

effective in treating a wide range of problems, it was sometimes rather laborious. This was due to the need by some patients for lengthy inductions to achieve the desired depth of trance needed to bypass the barriers of their subconscious.

During consultations we often found that patients could be helped simply by my tuning in to the relevant experience stored within their subconscious and relating it to them. From this evolved a type of spiritual counselling I term a 'life reading'. In this, I become one with my patients on a mind-to-mind basis and, whether of present or past life origin, I am able to picture the experience clearly in my mind and narrate it.

The majority of patients relate to what I perceive in one of three ways. They either visualise clearly what is being described, experience the emotions of the event, or actually find themselves triggered into and thus reliving the experience itself. Whichever be the case, by leading them gently through the experience, a release of the associated emotions is achieved and the person is able to resolve his or her problem.

Over the years we realised that it was not necessary that patients believe in past lives. Whatever one's philosophy, if a chord is struck, a positive response results. In addition I have found that anyone who has either practised meditation or had some experience in personal development or emotional release work finds it relatively simple to regress into the relevant past with my assistance.

Initially our work seemed to point to past life regression being confined to the treatment of phobias and compulsions — in broad terms, psychological conditions or neuroses. As time progressed however, it became increasingly apparent that if this be the case, we would have to totally re-think what such terms encompassed. This required looking very carefully at the nature and origins of dis-ease in human beings, be they structural, organic or psychological.

Two interesting cases come to mind to illustrate this. The first is that of Peter D, who had a long history of back pain and numbness in his right leg which stemmed from a riding accident some 22 years previously. The condition slowly worsened to the point where he was forced to give up the business he loved — raising horses — and indeed almost all other strenuous work. After exploring many therapies to no avail, he finally visited an orthopaedic surgeon. X-rays showed two ruptured intervertebral discs pressing on the sciatic nerve. Here lay the cause of the pain and numbness; logical medical solution, surgery.

It was after this last diagnosis that Peter came to me. Not so much in desperation, but in the hope that possibly there might be an alternative to such radical treatment.

The session that was to be the turning point for Peter began, like so many, on a seemingly totally unrelated topic. My strongest initial impression was that here was a man with a tremendous capacity as a natural healer. When I mentioned this, he seemed to shrink from me although, as he said, there was no logical reason for his sudden feelings of apprehension. Aware that I had struck a subconscious nerve, I probed further and soon became aware of describing a life in which he had worked as a travelling healer prior to the time of Christ.

Experienced in meditation through his studies in this life of Buddhism in Japan, he soon found himself in tune with me as together we began the journey through his life of long ago. Initially gentle and quiet in his ways, he avoided public acclaim. However, as his reputation grew, so did his ego. He began to make much of his own personal power with the inevitable consequence of upsetting the local priesthood. After many warnings to curb his tongue and admit that that which he was doing was the work of the Gods and not of his making, they threatened him with crucifixion, a common solution then for disposing of trouble makers.

He refused to give in to their demands and the priests made good their threat and bound him to a cross beside a public road. After an interminable time of agony which Peter experienced as frighteningly real, the man that he was then could tolerate it no longer and begged to be cut down. Enduring humiliation, shame and a massively dislocated back, he dragged himself away to die.

After experiencing the death and releasing the emotional pain and anguish associated with this incident, Peter felt the physical pain in his back slowly diminish. Over the following week he put it to the test by doing intense physical work. Surprisingly, nothing seemed to affect it and thus, two weeks later, he returned to his specialist. The surgeon admitted to being amazed at the apparent change in Peter's condition. Wanting to verify his preliminary check, he carried out a full examination of Peter's back and took another series of X-rays to assess for himself the true nature of the condition. There was no evidence of any damage, the back appearing to be completely healed. Peter spent the next hour describing to the surgeon the strange experience he had gone through!

To explain the connection between current conditions and those incidents which seem to belong to another life is not simple. It necessitates, in the absence of proof, acceptance of reincarnation — acceptance that a part of ones non-physical self survives death and continues to form part of our totality life after life. Variously referred to as the spirit or soul, this aspect either forms part of or has a deep and profound effect on our subconscious mind.

In Peter D's case, almost 2,000 years elapsed between one back injury and the next. Within the subconscious of the healer as a result of the crucifixion and subsequent death, the belief was either born or compounded that severe back injury/pain resulted in greatly diminished mobility and eventually death. Because of this attitude, that continuing aspect of being responded to Peter's present life injury by reviving the subconscious belief and filing the problem in the 'impossible to recover from' basket.

Researchers today lean heavily toward the belief that we both create and perpetuate physical and psychological conditions to fulfil one or more subconscious needs. Illustrations of this often come to light in the guise of an illness that is prolonged as a means of gaining love, attention, sympathy, etc. Impressed upon the subconscious either by oneself or others, and often quite inadvertently, this 'programme' is usually so deep that it will neither be recognised nor accepted if pointed out by another.

If such an attitude can be impressed on the subconscious within the current life and have effects lasting years as is the currently held belief, then, in accepting reincarnation, it is also acceptable to suspect such a programme could stem from another life. Mindful of this, Peter was able to integrate the long-past memory, at which time the subconscious, perceiving the different circumstances, conditions and emotions surrounding the incident, simply let go of the original belief. This allowed the natural healing processes to commence and led to complete recovery.

As extraordinary as Peter's case was in that the condition was structural, normally the result of an accident or age deterioration, and therefore beyond total remission, Cathy H's problem was physiological, again difficult to accept as stemming from a past life let alone curable by regression.

Diagnosed as suffering from endometriosis, a condition where pieces of the uterine lining form small cysts in either the muscle of the womb and so enlarge it, or in the ovaries or other parts of the pelvic area, she had not been free of pain since beginning menstruation at age nine. During the following nine years she saw countless doctors and was told, among other things, that it was a woman's lot to suffer and the only way to alleviate such suffering was to be perpetually pregnant. Great advice for an 18 year old girl!

'I was spending more and more time away from work, and had run out of sick-leave and holiday-leave,' she told me at our first meeting. 'My employer didn't believe that periods could cause so much time off and was looking for a replacement.'

Confined to bed because of the pain and desperate because of her imminent dismissal, she sought out yet another doctor. 'To my surprise he was sympathetic, believed he knew what the problem was and, wanting to examine me during a period, booked me into a Sydney hospital that same day for a laparoscopy.' This operation was performed by a well-known Sydney specialist and the GP was in attendance too to verify his diagnosis.

Confirmed as having endometriosis, Cathy was placed on a course of Danocrine, a synthetic hormone which, it was anticipated, would stop her periods and allow the body to re-absorb the cysts. Costing $130.00 for three weeks supply, permission had to be obtained from the Health Department before any chemist could dispense the drug. Within eight weeks of commencing treatment, Cathy had put on two stone in weight, developed unsightly body hair and was contemplating suicide. The condition remained unchanged. In desperation, she found her way to our door.

Working with my husband at the time, we used hypnosis for Cathy's regression. An excellent subject, she relaxed quickly and, on being directed to travel back in her memory to the origin of her problem, found herself experiencing a life as a dancer in a saloon in the American west. 'It was strange,' she told us later. She felt herself and yet was aware of being someone else. 'I felt my being change. It was not imagination or a memory, I was there.'

The relevant experience of this life began when a brawl broke out in the bar. Feeling ill, she had gone to her room upstairs when the commotion started. Leaving her bed, she went to the stairs to see what was happening. The scene she described before her was one of chaos. Then her body suddenly jerked. Calming the agitation that was now apparent in her, we discovered that shooting had broken out and that she had been struck in the stomach by a bullet and collapsed. She began calling for help, but no one heard. Then she became aware of the smell of smoke — a lamp had been smashed and the building was burning. Her voice quivering with fear, she told how she tried to crawl away but couldn't. She then passed out.

At this point Cathy told us later that she became aware of being an onlooker to all that was happening. People were rushing everywhere and the old wooden building burned to the ground. The girl who she had been in that life died that night in the fire.

She then experienced a different life in early America, this time as a simple country girl in her mid-teenage years. Her mother had died when she was about ten years old leaving her to look after her younger brother and sister and contend with a sadistic and alcoholic father.

As the years passed and she grew toward womanhood, her father became bitter and more sadistic. One day he forced himself upon her and brutally raped her. The result of this was a traumatic pregnancy. As she became less able to work, his cruelty increased until one day she ran away. Seeking refuge in a small hut, she lived out the remaining weeks of her pregnancy alone and grew very weak. When labour commenced she was panic stricken. She had no one to turn to and was too weak to help herself. Finally, in utter despair, she took a knife and killed herself and her unborn child by stabbing herself in the stomach.

As relevant and traumatic as these two experiences were, they formed only part of the problem. At her next session, Cathy journeyed back still further into her memory to recount yet another traumatic life. This time she found herself as a young nun — Gabriella — during the inquisition of Loudun. An orphan, she had been raised by the nuns and trained to join their order. She related her childhood and teenage years, spoke affectionately of Sister Teresa who tutored her, and bitterly of the hardship of scrubbing out the cells and the corridors on her hands and knees.

When the inquisitors from Rome arrived, she told how all those who could, bought themselves off. Justice needed to appear to be done, however, and hence she and other hapless expendables were tortured and purged of the devil. She finally and painfully died, having hot coals placed upon her stomach and thrust up inside her.

This life experience was so traumatic that it took a further session before Cathy could integrate it into her consciousness. Once this was achieved, however, she was able to adjust to the idea that all she had experienced were lives or chapters of her past. At this point her condition began to change. She not only gave up all the pills, but also began having regular, pain-free periods for the first time in her life.

Interested, like Peter D, to ascertain the results of her experiences from a conventional medical standpoint, Cathy returned to her doctor. He examined her and declared that, as far as he could tell, she was completely free of the condition. He inferred validation of her regression treatment by stating that it would have been impossible for the drugs to have been so effective in the short space of time since he'd seen her; approximately four months.

As with Peter, Cathy's problem came about because the subconscious built up a misguided belief. In this case it was that pain in the pelvic area was normal, the trigger being when she began menstruating. Once this attitude was corrected, the way was open for the problem to be overcome.

One of the commonest problems we've encountered over the years is being overweight. Pam O was such a person. She didn't overeat, and though trying a wide variety of diets and therapies, seemed incapable of shedding even a few kilos. Under hypnosis she recounted a life when she lived with her daughter, her son-in-law and their three children in a cabin on the edge of a forest. Their life was a frugal one, conditions hard and food often scarce.

One winter their lack of food became desperate and, rather than see those she loved suffer and slowly starve, she left them in order that they might have a better chance of surviving. She slipped away one night and walked into the forest. Shortly after she died from starvation and exposure.

Within the week following this experience and the release of the pain associated with it, Pam discovered she had lost weight without even changing her diet. This continued until she reached her desired weight, and there she stayed!

A possible explanation for the results achieved in cases like Pam's is that part of the work of the subconscious mind is to maintain correct bodily function/s. However, what it deems correct is, by virtue of its frame of reference, very subjective and based solely on its assessment of experiences gained during this and previous existences. If the strongest significant memory was, as in Pam's case, starving to death, then the subconscious will do everything in its power to avert a similar situation, thus causing the body to literally 'hang on' to fat as a protection mechanism.

Though all the cases discussed thus far have been different, they have been essentially physical in nature. The subconscious mind seems to know no bounds, however, when it comes to influencing our attitudes and ways of coping with life. One fairly common problem I encounter is claustrophobia. Usually someone suffering from this, or one of the many other phobias one could name and who has sought help through psychology or emotional release therapy, has been offered a number of highly plausible explanations for their condition. More often than not, however, the cause seems to remain firmly buried in their subconscious and so the problem persists.

Mary A was a case in point. On the surface, her claustrophobia seemed to stem from an episode in her childhood when her mother locked her in a cupboard as a form of punishment. Knowing and accepting this didn't seem to be of any help however, until we realised that it was a trigger for something that took place much further back in her past. The next step for Mary was the reliving of a life in a convent in Europe during the Middle Ages.

Given to the nuns by her parents to get rid of her, she grew up very unhappy. The order was very strict and punishments were severe even for the slightest misdemeanour. One day, with the help of a local youth who delivered goods to the convent, she made her escape. Before she was able to leave the district, however, she was caught and brought back to the convent. As a punishment, the Mother Superior had her walled up in a tiny cell. There, deprived of food, light and air, the terrified girl finally died.

Bringing this experience into consciousness and integrating it allowed Mary to let go of her fear of suffocation — what claustrophobia is all about. It also helped her to understand why she had been so terrified when her mother locked her in the cupboard as a punishment. Such an action had brought back the emotions of the death by suffocation all those long years ago.

There have been cases which, in hindsight, patients have laughed about. At the time, however, the experiences are all very real. Yvonne J was an intelligent, rational woman in her late twenties. Rational, that is, until she saw a spider. Regardless of the size, they terrified her. The incident that brought her to the realisation that she must do something to overcome her fear was when she was confronted by a tiny spider on her shower curtain. Reacting in panic, she rushed naked from her ground floor flat into the street.

Under regression she recounted a life as a medicine woman in a small African village. One of her tasks was the education of the chief's children. When two died in quick succession, she was blamed and sentenced to death. Her end was a particularly gruesome one — being thrown into a pit of spiders. It took eight days for her to die, and what she suffered made my flesh crawl.

Once Yvonne recognised and accepted the fact that her fear was the result of a long-past experience, the emotional reaction to spiders slowly ceased. I've since seen her handle a spider, a small one admittedly, while I stayed a discreet and cowardly distance!

Phobias take many forms and can have their origins in long-past experiences or relatively recent ones. Whilst spending some time with Dr Kelsey in the UK a few years ago, he told me of a patient, Elizabeth, who came to him with an intense fear of flying. She travelled much in the course of her work and the incident which finally convinced her to seek help occurred on a plane flight from Malta to London. Responding to her fear, she had taken the hand of a complete stranger sitting next to her. When he finally managed to extricate his hand from her grasp, she was horrified to find that she had punctured his palm with her nails and drawn blood. Realising the seriousness of the situation, she approached Dr Kelsey for help.

After exhausting all the usual avenues to no avail, he decided her problem was most likely a hangover from some past life experience. Under hypnosis, he asked her to go

Phobias take many forms . . .

back to the incident that was the cause of her fear. She was silent for a time and then began to describe in great detail the life of a young soldier during World War II who had been trained in demolition and sabotage.

Through his eyes, she began by describing the base where he was stationed and the preparation for a night mission over France. She told of the issuing of parachutes, the blessing of the mission by the chaplain, and then began to recount the mission itself. The plane took off and climbed out over the channel. The night was dark, and the early stage of the mission uneventful.

Suddenly, from a calm, relaxed person whose voice betrayed no hint of fear or anxiety, Elizabeth's attitude changed to one of severe agitation. The plane in which she, as the young man, was flying, was detected and fired upon. One shell exploded against the fuselage ripping it open. The torn metal twisted inward, pinning her (the soldier) about the throat.

The plane was hit several times and spun out of control. Gripped by the horrifying realisation of imminent death, the soldier struggled to free himself. All efforts were futile, however, and the intensity of those last moments was vividly illustrated by his dying plea; 'Oh God, get me out and put me safely on the ground.'

According to Dr Kelsey, dying with this desire and the intense fear of the moment, the emotional energy so generated was more than sufficient to leave a lasting impression on that aspect of her non-physical which formed part of her totality in the subsequent life. As a result, every plane flight triggered the emotional impact of this memory, thus causing an intense, though seemingly irrational, fear. Once the young soldier's experience was brought into Elizabeth's consciousness and faced, however, the fear subsided. When I saw Dr Kelsey last I asked about Elizabeth and learned she's still in her travel job and has had no further problems.

Though past lives therapy must not be regarded as a blanket answer when all conventional forms of treatment fail, it should not be dismissed either. It is, for want of a better term, 'causal therapy', in that it has the potential to go beyond the accepted symptomatic treatment modes and get to the root cause of a problem. Though every person is different and every case must be assessed with this foremost in mind, I have, over recent years, been able to place our cases into four broad categories. These are physical, Peter D's back for example; mental, the phobias and compulsions; emotional, those concerning personal relationships, self worth, etc.; and spiritual, when traumas seem to stem from lives devoted to religious, spiritual or similar callings.

A recent example of an emotional problem stemming from a past life was the case of Chris P. He came to me because he felt very blocked emotionally and, as he put it, had never been able to love.

I took him back to a life when he was a young Red Indian who was in love with a girl from another tribe. Though this was considered an insult by her people and punishable by death, the time finally came when he could bear the situation no longer. Throwing caution to the wind, he went to the girl and they made love. This proved disastrous as he was discovered by members of her tribe and publicly humiliated. He was put to death by having rocks placed upon his chest until the weight crushed him to death. The worst aspect for him was the pain of loving the girl and seeing her forced to watch him die.

As Chris released the intensity of the experience, it was as if a great burden was freed from his heart and being, allowing him to be able to feel love again. After reliving this experience he was able to understand why he had been unable to love in the past, and looked forward to the future with a newfound joy.

Though last, the problems of spiritual origin are by no means the least common. Eleanor J came to me and explained that she was terrified of anything to do with spirituality. She had recently completed a meditation course which had brought to the surface a stream of seemingly groundless and illogical fears. When, after discussing the problem in some detail, I mentioned that I felt she had a strong capacity to heal, she visibly paled.

The life we looked at was one when she was a young girl who had a reputation for helping people with problems. She felt she was channelling 'goodness' into them, or what today would probably be termed healing or spiritual energy.

One day the local priest sought her out. He was suffering from what we would term epilepsy, though he looked upon it as devils being in him. She knew she was powerless to help him, and felt that the problem actually stemmed from him doing something 'un-holy'. She still tried to help him however, and needless to say he grew steadily worse and it became so noticeable that he laid the blame on her shoulders, accusing her of putting the devils in him.

Hearing of this, the priest's followers came for her and threw her into the local pond. She floated to the surface and this, as custom dictated, proved her to be a witch. She was then dragged from the water, stripped of her clothing, tied to a pole near her home and burned to death.

Once this session was over, Eleanor was able to understand her irrational fear of spiritual growth and so was able to begin developing in the field of healing quite naturally.

As can be seen in most cases of a therapeutic nature, the cause of the problem for which help has been sought has been a death experience which had a traumatic impact on the very essence of the person's being. After the death, however, there always comes a sense of peace and tranquillity. This is actually a bonus with this form of therapy in that, once experienced, the realisation is born within the patient that life is not finite. Because of this, the fear of death is greatly diminished.

In all the cases I have encountered, I have never come across more than the very occasional person whose name I recognise from the history books, and certainly neither my husband nor myself have ever met a Cleopatra or a Leonardo da Vinci. Most people were very normal beings facing the same problems and frustrations we encounter today. Only their endings may be said to be more traumatic than the present-day norm — if there be such a thing.

There is still no concrete proof of reincarnation. What is important however is that the therapy embracing it does offer hope for those with seemingly insoluble problems. As I say to those who come, belief is not the issue. The proof of the pudding is in the eating.

Patients experience elements of their past lives for the purpose of gaining under-standing of problems encountered in the now. For my part, because of the way I now work, I do not question the reality of past life experiences. For those who work through hypnosis or the trigger method, however, the question of fantasy may never be far from view. Yet where lies the dividing line between fantasy and reality? And should a fantasy fulfil all the requirements for laying a problem to rest? Is it indeed a fantasy?

Past lives therapy is but one of many tools for exploring human totality and helping in the quest to understand the nature of disease. If only a fraction of the population can be helped, then it must be worth considering.

ACKNOWLEDGEMENTS

The editor would like to acknowledge the assistance of the Australian holistic journal *Nature & Health* in which shorter versions of the chapters on Guided Imagery, Creative Self-expression, Autogenic Relaxation Training, Neuro-Linguistic Programming and Intuitive Healing were originally published.

PHOTOGRAPHY CREDITS

Irene Lorbergs: 11, 14, 15, 21, 25, 41, 57, 61, 65, 68, 70, 71, 124, 135, 163, 167; Mikla: 19, 47, 160, 169; Michael Ney: 29, 31, 33, 36, 38, 79, 82, 83, 84, 86, 87, 89, 91, 93, 95, 96, 97; Psychosynthesis Training Centre of New South Wales: 43, 51; Jo Whittaker: 55; Bill Anagrius: 74, 75; Cinetel Productions: 119, 120, 121; TM Centre: 123 (left); Wind Sung Sounds/Lotus Music Centre: 126; Polygram Records: 127; Japetus: 129; News Ltd.: 141; SYDA Foundation: 144 (upper), 145; Laurence McManus: 144 (lower); Ian Gawler: 147, 148, 149; Ralph Hadden: 176; Harper & Row: 182; Malcom and Zoë Hagon: 184

BLACK & WHITE AND LINE ILLUSTRATIONS

Psychosynthesis Training Centre of New South Wales: 42, 44, 45, 46; Satty: 49, 115, 183, 185, 193; Fai Chivell Hast: 108; Nevill Drury: 191

THE CONTRIBUTORS

CHRISTOPHER COLLINGWOOD is a psychotherapist currently in private practice at the Sydney Healing Centre, Balmain. He uses a unique blend of neuro-linguistic programming, Ericksonian hypnosis and provocative therapy in working with problem resolution, phobia reduction, psychosomatic disorders and life-skills enhancement. Christopher is also involved with training in the field of personal growth and business communications through the organisation New Learning Pathways.
Contact Address: Sydney Healing Centre, 236 Darling Street, Balmain, Sydney, Australia 2041. Ph: (02) 810 6100

NEVILL DRURY was born in England in 1947 but has lived most of his life in Australia. Especially interested in the sources of creativity and imagination in the subconscious mind, he has explored occult meditation techniques since 1968. In 1980 he was a keynote lecturer at the International Transpersonal Conference and presented workshops utilising inner-space music and guided imagery. Nevill holds a Masters degree in anthropology and is the author or editor of 20 books, most of them in the field of consciousness studies, occult mythology and alternative medicine. His most recent book, which has been published internationally, is *Music for Inner Space: Techniques for Meditation and Visualisation.*
Contact Address: C/- *Nature & Health* magazine, 176 South Creek Road, Dee Why, Sydney, Australia 2099. Ph: (02) 981 0465

JANNA FINEBERG, PhD, is a clinical psychologist who earned her doctorate from the University of California, Los Angeles. She has been aiding people with their personal growth since 1972. In addition to her traditional therapeutic training, Janna has studied and taught a wide range of alternative approaches to healing, and has been involved in the area of holistic health since 1975. Janna uses imagery extensively in her current work and her exploration of the creative arts and health marks the newest direction in her work — one which she feels touches upon the ideal possibility of activities that are both enjoyable and produce true well-being. She is currently presenting classes and workshops using the arts for personal growth and has also produced a relaxation cassette tape which can be used prior to imagery exercises, and for stress reduction. She is also offering a workshop series titled 'Rites of Passage: Rituals for Life Transitions in the New Culture' both in Australia and overseas, upon invitation.
Contact Address: The Natural Healing Centre, 149 Keen Street, Lismore, New South

Wales, Australia 2480. Ph: (066) 21 3441. After December 1985, c/- *Nature & Health* magazine, 176 South Creek Road, Dee Why, Sydney Australia 2099

KYM FORRESTAL is the founder and director of the Psychosynthesis Training Centre of New South Wales. An Australian, Kym lived overseas for eleven years, where he studied numerous psychological and spiritual approaches to personal and transpersonal growth. He has taught at the University of California, was on the training staff of the Psychosynthesis Training Center of High Point Foundation, Pasadena, California, and is an educational consultant. In addition to teaching psychosynthesis, Kym conducts professional training seminars in the applications of guided imagery in psychotherapy. *Contact Address:* Psychosynthesis Training Centre of New South Wales, 127 Old South Head Road, Bondi Junction, Sydney, Australia 2022. Ph: (02) 389 0193

IAN GAWLER is a veterinary surgeon who had a leg amputated due to bone cancer in January 1975. By March 1976, the cancer had returned and his condition was such that he was expected to live for only a few months. Yet now he is living a full, healthy life. The transformation has been largely due to the good effects of meditation, positive thinking, good food and healing in its many forms.

In 1983 Ian and his wife Gayle founded the Australian Cancer Patients' Foundation. The aim of the Foundation is to provide a full and active range of support services for cancer patients. The Melbourne Cancer Support Group is now conducted by the Foundation and a bookshop, resource lists, tapes, seminars, personal support and contact point are provided. The aim is to help patients and their families help themselves as a natural addition to what can be done medically for them.

Ian has given numerous seminars and, with his family, has appeared widely on radio, television and in the press. He has recently released *You Can Conquer Cancer*, which fully explains his approach. This book, which is being published internationally, is not only a self-help manual for patients and their families but also an excellent guide to disease prevention and, better still, to a truly healthy lifestyle. *Contact Address:* PO Box 77, Yarra Junction, Victoria, Australia 3797. Ph: (03) 830 5577

DAVID GOROVIC is a Russian-born psychologist and graduate of the University of New South Wales. For the past few years he has specialised in stress management training for individuals and groups, employing a wide variety of methods including biofeedback, relaxation and meditation as well as providing individual counselling and psychotherapy.

David has conducted a number of courses, workshops and seminars on stress management, biofeedback, communication skills and personal development methods for various organisations and groups, including the Australian Broadcasting Corporation, the N.S.W. Education and Health Departments and the Workers' Education Association. He has been a frequent contributor to *Nature & Health*, *Australian Wellbeing* and other publications and has been interviewed on radio and television on the above topics.

David is the founder of Biofeedback and Stress Management Centre in Sydney, where he is currently practising. *Contact Address:* GPO Box 4993, Sydney, Australia 2001. Ph: (02) 30 3005 or (02) 29 4140

ZOE and MALCOM HAGON are both healers and therapists, each holding a diploma in psychology. They are the founders of the Iona Foundation for Appropriate Industry,

Technology and Healing in the mountains of New South Wales near Oberon. Here they are establishing a healing centre and community where people can come as patients for therapy, or just as those interested in growth, and learn to live in harmony with others and the land.

Zoe was born in England and graduated from the Middlesex Hospital, London in 1969, as a physiotherapist. A spiritual healer for ten years, she has gradually progressed into the field of spiritual counselling and past lives therapy. She now specialises in working with people who have not been able to find a solution to their problems through the current medical and paramedical fields.

Malcom is an author, psychologist and medical hypnotherapist and has been involved in the field of human relations for over 20 years. The early part of his business career was in public relations and journalism, during which time he studied various aspects of paranormal healing. In 1980 he wrote and published *Journey Within*, an introduction to psychic development and healing.
Contact Address: Iona, PO Box 81, Oberon, New South Wales, Australia 2787. Ph: (063) 35 6246/35 6220

FAI CHIVELL HAST studied fine art at an early age after escaping the confines of secondary school mathematics. She later worked in theatre and television, both on stage and behind the scenes. She has also studied psychology and interior decorating. Widely read in the arts of meditation, alchemy and mythology, she has also studied natural healing and at one time ran a successful colour therapy clinic while lecturing and holding classes in colour and related therapies. Fai was co-founder and publisher of the lifestyles magazine *Ziriuz* and actively researched and reported her chosen fields. She has also written for *Nature & Health*, *New Idea* and *Home Beautiful* and is a frequent radio guest. She is currently writing and researching a documentary and runs a colour correspondence course. She is married with three teenage children.
Contact Address: Colour Correspondence Course, 76 Burwood Road, Hawthorn, Victoria, Australia 3122

CHRISTOPHER MAGAREY is an Associate Professor of Surgery at the University of New South Wales and a visiting surgeon at the St George Hospital, Sydney. His main research has been into the natural defences of patients against their own cancers. He has also studied psychological factors in patients with cancer and, more recently, the effects of meditation. He has published numerous articles on these subjects in international journals and has given lectures in Australia, Britain and the United States. He has also spent many months in India studying and practising Siddha Yoga meditation under the guidance of Swami Muktananda and his successors, Swami Nityananda and Swami Chidvilasanda. He teaches meditation in weekly classes at the St George Hospital.

Major Siddha Yoga Foundation ashrams will give information about the hundreds of smaller centres throughout the world where anyone can attend, free, to learn about and to experience meditation. These include:

Siddha Yoga Foundation, 50 Garnet Street, Dulwich Hill, Sydney, NSW 2203, Australia

Siddha Yoga Foundation, 202 Gore Street, Fitzroy, Melbourne, Victoria 3065, Australia

Siddha Yoga Dham, 15 Fitzroy Square, London W1P 5HQ, England

SYDA Foundation, PO Box 600, South Fallsburg, New York 12779, United States of America

Gurudev Siddha Peeth, PO Ganeshpuri, PIN 401206, District Thana, Maharashtra, India

MORA McINTYRE was born in Oxford, England. She trained in the arts, experienced a great variety of work situations, travelled, and had two children before undergoing a major life-transition in 1977. She then began exploring various aspects of psychotherapy, healing and self-development. Seeking to connect the psychic, psychological and spiritual dimensions, she focused particularly on sensitive and intuitive approaches with American healer Ann Parks, and on practical ways of working with the auric field with Bob Moore of the Psychic Centre in Denmark. She is currently extending her programme of classes and workshops, which emphasise intuition and creative, non-verbal forms of development. She is also engaged in teaching intuitive massage in schools while running a private practice and writing.
Contact Address: 6/56 Hewlett Street, Bronte, Sydney, Australia 2024. Ph: (02) 387 6351

ALEX NICOLSON qualified as a Master Practitioner of neuro-linguistic programming in 1983 and has worked closely with Christopher Collingwood since that time in the application and development of therapeutic techniques. He is interested in a wide variety of alternative therapies relating to effective communication and the development of human potential.
Contact Address: PO Box 479, Milsons Point, Sydney, Australia 2061

ANDREW and JACQUELINE STAITE are currently practising as autogenic relaxation therapists. Andrew was born in 1951 in Birmingham, England. Educated in Birmingham and in New South Wales, he worked as an editor and counsellor for the National Association for the Childless. He commenced private practice as a relaxation trainer in 1981 and produced his current series of video programmes in 1983. As a writer he has had various articles published in health journals and magazines.

Jacqueline was born in 1949, also in Birmingham. Educated there, she qualified in biology in 1970 and worked for four years at Birmingham University before taking up teaching. She has now joined her husband in experimental work with relaxation training.
Contact Address: 6 Milton Road, Bentley Heath, Solihull, West Midlands, England B938AA. Ph: (05645) 5069
In Australia: Jo Whittaker, A.R.T. Centre, 206/83 Longueville Road, Lane Cove, Sydney 2066. Ph: (02) 427 0770.
or, Michael Nelson, 40 Cavendish Avenue, Wantirua, Victoria 3152. Ph: (03) 222 1113

BIBLIOGRAPHY

1: Managing Stress

GOLDWAG, E. M. (ed.), *Inner Balance*, Englewood Cliffs, New Jersey 1979, Prentice-Hall

PELLETIER, K., *Mind as Healer, Mind as Slayer*, New York 1977, Delta

SCHULLER, R. H., *Turning Your Stress Into Strength*, Irvine, California 1978, Harvest House

SELYE, H., *Stress in Health and Disease*, Reading, Massachusetts 1976

SELYE, H., 'Stress! The Basis of Illness' in E. M. Goldwag, 1979

SELYE, H., *The Stress of Life*, New York 1956, McGraw-Hill

2: Imagery and Self-Healing

BRY, A., *Directing the Movies of your Mind*, New York 1978, Harper & Row

GAWAIN, S., *Creative Visualization*, Mill Valley, California 1978, Whatever Publishing

SAMUELS, M. & S., *Seeing with the Mind's Eye*, New York 1975, Random House

SHORR, J. E. *et al.* (ed.), *Imagery: Its Many Dimensions and Applications*, New York 1980, Plenum

SIMONTON, C., *Getting Well Again*, Los Angeles 1978, Tarcher

WHITE, J., & FADIMAN, J., *Relax*, New York 1976, Dell

3: Controlling Pain Through Imagery

ASSAGIOLI, R., *Psychosynthesis*, London 1975, Turnstone

ASSAGIOLI, R., *The Act of Will*, Harmondsworth 1973, Penguin

BRESLER, D. E., *Free Yourself From Pain*, New York 1979, Simon and Schuster

BRY, A., *Directing the Movies of your Mind*, New York 1978, Harper & Row

CRAMPTON, M., *The Use of Mental Imagery in Psychosynthesis*, New York 1970, Psychosynthesis Research Foundation

FERRUCCI, P., *What We May Be*, Los Angeles, 1982, Tarcher

GERARD, R., *Psychosynthesis: A Psychotherapy for the Whole Man*, New York 1964, Psychosynthesis Research Foundation

PECK, C., *Controlling Chronic Pain*, Sydney 1982, Fontana

SAMUELS, M. & N., *Seeing with the Mind's Eye*, New York 1975, Random House

SIMONTON, C., *Getting Well Again*, Los Angeles 1978, Tarcher; New York 1980, Bantam

4: Relaxation Training and Behaviour Modification

ARIETI, S., *Creativity: the Magical Synthesis*, New York 1976, Basic Books

BENSON, H., *The Relaxation Response*, New York 1975, Morrow

GAWAIN, S., *Creative Visualisation*, Mill Valley, California 1978, Whatever Publishing

MORRIS, D., *The Human Zoo*, New York 1969, McGraw-Hill

PEARCE, J. C., *Magical Child*, New York 1977, Dutton

SELYE, H., *Stress*, Montreal 1956, Acta

5: Neuro-Linguistic Programming

BANDLER, R., & GRINDER, J., *Frogs into Princes*, Moab, Utah 1979, Real People Press

BANDLER, R., & GRINDER, J., *Reframing*, Moab, Utah 1982, Real People Press

DILTS, R., *et al.*, *Neuro-Linguistic Programming Volume One: The Study of Subjective Experience*, Cupertino, California 1980, Meta Publications

GRINDER, J., & BANDLER, R., *The Structure of Magic* (Vol. 1), Palo Alto, California 1976, Science and Behaviour Books

GRINDER, J., & BANDLER, R., *Trance-formations*, Moab, Utah 1981, Real People Press

JACOBSON, S., *Meta-Cation*, Cupertino, California 1983, Meta Publications

6: Creative Self-Expression

LINDEMANN, H., *Relieve Tension the Autogenic Way*, New York 1974, Wydon

LUTHE, W., *A Training Workshop for Professionals*, Denver 1977, Biofeedback Society of America

LUTHE, W., & SCHULTZ, J. H., *Autogenic Therapy* (Vols 1–6), New York 1969, Grune and Stratton

ROSA, K. R., *You and A.T.*, New York 1976, Saturday Review Press, Dutton

7: Colour Healing and Colour Therapy

AMBER, R. B., *Color Therapy*, Calcutta 1964, Firma KLM Private

BABBITT, E. D., *The Principles of Light and Color*, Malaga, New Jersey 1925, Spectrochrome Institute

BIRREN, F., *Color Psychology and Color Therapy*, Secaucus, New Jersey 1961, University Books

BIRREN, F., *Color and Human Response*, New York 1978, Van Nostrand Reinhold

CLARKE, L., & MARTINE, Y., *Health, Youth and Beauty through Color Breathing*, Millbrae, California 1976, Celestial Arts

DAVID, W., *The Harmonics of Sound, Color and Vibration*, Marina del Rey, California 1980, De Vorss

GALLERT, M. L., *New Light on Therapeutic Energies*, London 1966, James Clarke

HELINE, C., *Color and Music in the New Age*, La Canada, California 1964, New Age Press

KARGERE, A., *Color and Personality*, New York n.d., Occult Research Press

LUSCHER, M., *The 4-Color Person*, New York 1977, Pocket Books

MAYER, G., *Colour and Healing*, Sussex 1960, New Knowledge Books

SANDBACH, J., *The Mysteries of Color*, Chicago 1977, Aries Press

STEINER, R., *Colour*, London 1971, Rudolf Steiner Press

VON GOETHE, JOHANN WOLFGANG, *Theory of Colors*, Cambridge, Massachusetts 1970, M.I.T.

8: Music and Self-Transformation

ASSAGIOLI, R., *Psychosynthesis*, London 1975, Turnstone
CARLSON, R. J., *Frontiers of Science and Medicine*, Chicago 1976, Regnery
CLYNES, M. (ed.), *Music, Mind and Brain*, New York 1982, Plenum
DESOILLE, R., *The Directed Daydream*, New York, 1966, Psychosynthesis Research Foundation
DRURY, N., *Music for Inner Space*, Dorchester 1985, Prism Press and Sydney 1985, Unity Press/Harper & Row
DRURY, N., *Vision Quest*, Dorchester 1984, Prism Press
DRURY, N., *Inner Visions*, London 1979, Routledge & Kegan Paul
GOLEMAN, D., *The Varieties of Meditative Experience*, New York 1977, Dutton
HAMEL, P., *Through Music to the Self*, Salisbury 1976, Element
HARNER, M., *The Way of the Shaman*, San Francisco 1980, Harper & Row
JAFFE, D. T., & BRESLER, D. E., 'Guided Imagery: Healing Through the Mind's Eye', in J. E. Shorr *et al.* (ed.) *Imagery: Its Many Dimensions and Applications*, New York 1980, Plenum
MEARES, A., *The Wealth Within*, Melbourne 1981, Hill of Content, and Bath, England (forthcoming 1985) Ashgrove Press
RADHA, S. S., *Kundalini Yoga for the West*, Boulder, Colorado 1978, Shambhala
SIMONTON, C. and S., 'The Role of the Mind in Cancer Therapy', in R. J. Carlson, *Frontiers of Science and Medicine*, Chicago 1976, Regnery
TART, C. (ed.), *Altered States of Consciousness*, New York 1969, Wiley
WATKINS, M., *Waking Dreams*, New York 1976, Gordon & Breach
ZUCKERKANDL, V., *Man the Musician* (Vol. 2), Princeton, New Jersey 1973, Princeton University Press

9: Meditation — The Essence of Health

CADE, C. M., & COXHEAD, N., *The Awakened Mind*, New York 1979, Delacorte Press
CAPRA, F., *The Tao of Physics*, London 1975, Fontana/Collins
MAGAREY, C., 'Healing and Meditation in Medical Practice', *Medical Journal of Australia*, Vol. 1, 1981, pp. 338–341
MAGAREY, C., 'Holistic Cancer Therapy', *Journal of Psychosomatic Research*, Vol. 27, 1983, pp. 181–184
MEARES, A., 'Atavistic Communication by Touch in the Psychological Treatment of Cancer by Intensive Meditation', in *The Journal of Holistic Health*, Vol., IV, pp. 120–124
MUKTANANDA, S., *Meditate*, New York 1980, State University Press of New York
MUKTANANDA, S., *Where Are You Going? A Guide to the Spiritual Journey*, New York 1981, SYDA Foundation
MUKTANANDA, S., *Play of Consciousness*, San Francisco 1978, Harper & Row
PELLETIER, K., *Mind as Healer, Mind as Slayer*, London 1977, Allen & Unwin
TROPP, J., *Cancer — A Healing Crisis*, Smithtown, New York 1981, Exposition Press

10: Cancer as a Path to Enlightenment

GAWLER, I., *You Can Conquer Cancer*, Melbourne 1984, Hill of Content; Wellingborough 1985, Thorsons
MEARES, A., *Cancer — Another Way?*, Melbourne 1980, Hill of Content
MEARES, A., *Dialogue on Meditation*, Melbourne 1979, Hill of Content
MEARES, A., *The Wealth Within*, Melbourne 1979, Hill of Content; Bath, England (forthcoming 1985) Ashgrove Press

11: Intuitive Healing

MILLER, R., *Psychic Massage*, New York 1975, Harper & Row
VAUGHAN, F., *Awakening Intuition*, New York 1979, Doubleday
WALSH, R. N., & VAUGHAN, F., *Beyond Ego*, Los Angeles 1980, Tarcher

12: Past Lives Therapy

GRANT, J., and KELSEY, D., *Many Lifetimes*, London 1976, Corgi
NETHERTON M., & SHIFFRIN, N., *Past Lives Therapy*, Melbourne 1978, Compendium
MOSS, P., & KEETON, K., *Encounters with the Past*, London 1979, Sidgwick & Jackson
RAMSTER, P., *The Truth About Reincarnation*, Adelaide 1980, Rigby
STEVENSON, I., *Twenty Cases Suggestive of Reincarnation*, Charlottesville, Virginia 1974, University of Virginia Press
WAMBACH, H., *Reliving Past Lives*, New York 1978, Harper & Row
WAMBACH, H., *Life Before Life*, New York 1981, Bantam